ALSO BY J. VANESSA LYON

*Lush Lives*

*The Groves*

*Figuring Faith and Female Power in the Art of Rubens*

# BLACKNESS THIRTEEN WAYS

PANTHEON BOOKS ◆ NEW YORK

# BLACKNESS THIRTEEN WAYS

## ART, LIFE, & THE REVISIONS *of a* MULATTA LESBIAN

J. VANESSA LYON

FIRST HARDCOVER EDITION PUBLISHED BY PANTHEON BOOKS 2026



Published by Pantheon Books, a division of Penguin Random House LLC, 1745 Broadway, New York, NY 10019.

Pantheon Books and the colophon are registered trademarks of Penguin Random House LLC.

This memoir is a work of personal recollection.
Some names and identifying characteristics have been changed to protect the privacy of the individuals involved.

Library of Congress Cataloging-in-Publication Data
Names: Lyon, J. Vanessa author
Title: Blackness thirteen ways : art, life, & the revisions of a mulatta lesbian / J. Vanessa Lyon.
Identifiers: LCCN 2025050759 (print) | LCCN 2025050760 (ebook) | ISBN 9780593701942 hardcover | ISBN 9780593701959 ebook
Subjects: LCSH: Lyon, J. Vanessa | African American women authors | Authors, American – 21st century | Lesbian authors – United States | African American lesbians | Women art historians – United States | Art historians – United States | Black race | LCGFT: Autobiographies
Classification: LCC PS3612.Y568 Z46 2026 (print) | LCC PS3612.Y568 (ebook)
LC record available at https://lccn.loc.gov/2025050759
LC ebook record available at https://lccn.loc.gov/2025050760

penguinrandomhouse.com | pantheonbooks.com

Printed in China
10 9 8 7 6 5 4 3 2 1

The authorized representative in the EU for product safety and compliance is Penguin Random House Ireland, Morrison Chambers, 32 Nassau Street, Dublin D02 YH68, Ireland, https://eu-contact.penguin.ie.

*To Jane,*
*my mother,*
*with love, respect, and gratitude*

Why so, the Genius alone knows – that companion who rules our star of birth, the god of human nature, though mortal for each single life, and changing in countenance, white or black.

— HORACE, *Epistles II*

# CONTENTS

# AUTHOR'S NOTE

Toward a less arbitrary and asymmetrical style, where race is concerned, I have opted to capitalize both White and Black, as well as Mulatta, in this book. Along with the epigraphs, the far from comprehensive Further Reading appended to some but not all chapters is, most often, intended to draw the reader's attention to key authors whose work has shaped my approach to writing about (or to how not to write about) racial identity and the representation of women of color in general and Black women, including Mulattas, in particular.

# BLACKNESS THIRTEEN WAYS

PROLOGUE

# PASSING OUT

Aha! Been "passing," have you? Well, I've queered that.

—NELLA LARSEN, *Passing*, 1929

I WAS TRYING to think when I first had a sense of myself as a Black woman; a Black girl. Not when it was first explained to me, the thing in need of explanation being my brown skin and black curly hair and dark, dark eyes in relation to my mother's pinky-pale skin and blue ones.

There was a sofa in the apartment. More of a daybed, really. It was a solid, minimalist DIY carpentry project my grandfather on my mother's side, a frustrated mid-century modernist, had made, probably originally for his "apartment" in the basement of their modest Park Hill ranch in Denver, Colorado. This was when my grandparents were in the process of divorcing (she claimed it was over Nixon). When the two of them were sharing the same house with my teenage mother and her daughter (me) in the pre-K years before we, too, moved out.

I see it as a glossy-white, twin-size platform whose protruding edge always left a band of red on the backs of my thighs.

The explanation took place on this homemade couch. It felt (the explanation) appropriately creative to me, whereas the daybed filled me with ire. Even as a child of eight or nine I was keenly aware of the look of things, of whether their appearance and histories were proper to the settings I might someday be seen to have lived my life in. In a way that must have had a lot to do with books (my mother was finishing her BA in English Lit) and especially with glossy shelter magazines like *House & Garden,* I formulated a Whartonian worldview while living in a second-floor 1.5-bedroom apartment with an unplanted square of dirt off the downstairs neighbor's back porch.

On one of our thrift store trips, when I was probably in second or third grade, my mother scored a bunch of *New Yorker*s from the 1940s and '50s, which, being a good reader, I subsequently pored over as if they were ancient texts. Through osmosis, I became persnickety and old-fashioned, a time traveler dropped into a foreign present. Little Lady Fauntleroy in the age of the Bee Gees and *Logan's Run.*

I was an enemy of impropriety. But—and yes, yes, maybe because—I sensed there might be something deeply improper about me. Not having a tastefully upholstered department-store sofa to sit on as I digested my origin story struck me as indecorous.

It didn't bother me that the story came as a drawing. My mother, still in her very early twenties, was an artist. I knew this because sometimes we drew together. Before I let the pen touch my own blank page, I would sneak a look at what she was doing, set up in the part of the living room where light streamed in from double-hung windows, a giant clipboard balanced on her knees. I learned to copy the way she glanced up every few seconds, even as she was making the next confident mark. The square of brown composite board on her lap had rounded corners and a long slot along one edge for the artist's fingers, both palette and easel. At the time, my mother preferred fine-tipped German Rapidographs. Their thick, reservoired barrels were refillable. You had to learn to manually siphon India ink into them from a small plastic bottle. With the acuity of an architect, my mother made detailed and accurate yet totally personal drawings of, say, the deco wicker lounge chair that was, to my mind, elegant, our standout piece.

The chair was a heavy, substantial article of furniture with a wide, canted back made for sunning, possibly on the deck of a steamship. Like the daybed, it was white. Painted most recently with thick, surely oil-based, shiny paint. It had a swoopy, wave-like profile. I admired its original vanilla-colored Naugahyde upholstery, box welted and dotted along the sides with small round metal vents for the air to escape through when someone sat down. (As I would later learn, our downstairs neighbor, now an entomologist, had stolen the thing off someone's porch, leaving it to us when she moved back to Manhattan.) I was proud of that chair. In life and in the drawing, which my mother signed and dated. After, she sandwiched the ruffled sketchbook sheet between some mat board and a raw-edged plate of glass fastened with metal clips and a cord. This drawing would later hang on a wall in our first house too.

One night we'd been sitting on the ersatz sofa watching our small black-and-white television. The aluminum foil balls on the antennae weren't doing much, so I'd had to jump up to swivel the rabbit ears around for better reception. It was definitely a Shakespeare play — *As You Like It,* maybe — performed by grainy bearded men in capes and words I didn't think were English. It scared me a little. Not unlike Albinoni's unbearably sad "Adagio," which, along with the chipper fluting of Jean-Pierre Rampal, forms part of the soundtrack of those years. But watching was a way to be closer to my mother, who I knew liked classical things. When at last the imperious strains of the *Masterpiece Theatre* theme began to play, it was bedtime.

My mother wanted to talk to me about something first.

That was when I really got to know the deco chair.

While she spoke in simple terms of complicated matters, I mentally deconstructed the scaffold of painted reeds twisted and bundled in various thicknesses like so many fasces.

The previous Christmas I'd been given a tastefully illustrated book entitled *Where Do Babies Come From?* and it had definitely given me pause. I'd like to see that book again because in my mind it's all slender White hippies in bell-bottoms, painted in the style of Rossetti.

The author didn't mince words, but inasmuch as I looked nothing like the lithesome Pre-Raphaelite children who emerged from their mother's WOMB as a result of SPERM and EGGS and LOVE, I must have felt the need for additional details.

My mother got one of her smaller spiral sketchbooks and sat back down beside me. She unscrewed the cap of her Rapidograph and opened to a fresh page. Gradually, three small, near-perfect circles appeared in a horizontal line. I watched intently as she left the first circle blank and skipped the middle one. She colored in the third one until the paper warped from the ink. Next, she filled the middle circle with parallel lines. The pen moved from edge to edge, first in one direction, then perpendicularly. This was the beginning of a densely hatched grid. The more lines she made, the grayer the circle became until its tone was somewhere roughly between the empty white circle and the dark, black, saturated one.

If there was a verbal accompaniment to this visual aid – and I'm sure there was since my mother was, in those years, what she always said I was to her, my sunshine — I don't remember a word of it. I remember that chair, in whose complex design and mysterious advent I took comfort. And I can picture the diagram with its three circles, in which I found none.

At the same time, the diagram feels like something I would make — have made, in fact — to explain Renaissance intaglio printmaking techniques to students. It was a perfect illustration that might have provided answers to a child who already wondered why she stood out and if she would ever belong.

But it didn't. My mother's drawing did not help me understand myself. On the contrary, it seemed to raise previously unconscious concerns about my being (in some way) Black. The drawing may have made me aware, however dimly, that there was more to the story. A blacked-out, redacted more, about which I knew absolutely nothing.

Because we didn't talk about my father. I might as well state, right now, that I wasn't conceived in violence or without consent — except that of my parents' parents. That we didn't talk about my Black biological father in my White family when *Loving v. Virginia* had been decided just two years before I was born, is, I suppose, not all that surprising. In 2000, when I was thirty-one, Alabama became the last state in the US to abolish anti-miscegenation laws. I grew up in the West, in Colorado, where Black communities tend to be much smaller than on either coast or in the Midwest or South. For now, just know that my father didn't come up. Ever. As a result, I had no rehearsed response when strangers asked what I was — which they did almost daily until sometime in my forties, when my age, or possibly the antagonistic roadblocks I vibe when I can see a stranger heading in that direction, largely seem to have put a stop to the unwelcome inquiries.

Back in my thirties, before I dropped myself into the legendarily diverse stewpot that is UC Berkeley, I had already vowed that my reply to "What are you?" no matter who asked – and BIPOC people rarely do – would be "Oh, I never answer that question." Although I've always made an effort to toss off the phrase in a firm yet playful manner, as if being pressed to reveal a secret recipe, my rebuff generally dissatisfies the inquirers. Their typical response is defensive, dismissive, or scolding: "Oh, come on. It's not a big deal. I'm just curious."

I, too, am curious.

About a lot of things – why those jeans, why this husband, or that third glass of wine – but self-control prevents me from asking questions others might deem rude and invasive. If you're ever about to ask someone potentially not-White (which is probably why you're asking) that question or a variation thereof, just don't. If they want you to know, it will come out organically. If it doesn't, consider why it feels so important; what will that information get you?

Writers of color keep explaining how offensive and unsettling it is to be asked to disclose or document our ethnic or racial makeup in the course of a casual conversation. Diversity trainings discouraged such questions. But still they persist.

More annoying than the race question, to me anyway, is the display of surprise, if not indignant irritation, that has greeted my refusal to answer. I had to stop responding after one too many: "Oh, really, I would never have known. I thought maybe Polynesian. Or, I dunno, Indian. South Indian not American Indian. So Black. Really? Wow. Huh."

Like the truth meant they'd lost the guessing game.

Because that's it too. Women like me are a conundrum. Apparently, we either look just like someone else, usually from a totally different racial group. Or we are terra incognita ("You're so exotic!") in need of discovering. In more generous moments, I might point out the multitude of phenotypes and bodily variations among women of African descent. Which is to say, we may recognize ourselves as members of the same club as we pass each other on the street. But we are not a monolith. These very variations — shape of the nose, hair tone and texture, eye color, melanation, abundance (or not) of hips and ass and belly and breasts — can and do make the difference between being read as, to invoke the usual epithets: Mulatta, mixed, light-skinned Black, Black biracial, or White-passing. But parentage, too, is part of the equation. A person can have two parents who identify as racially Black and fall under some of these headings as easily as a person with one Black and one White (or non-Black) parent.

For my part, I realize that to some people I am patently not Black. Not Black enough. Culturally and pigmentationally out of the running. If an Oreo, the profligate, white-chocolate-dipped kind. A Zebra, perhaps. But never a *sista.* Which makes me the representative of an ambivalently racialized species intentionally misrecognized by Whites to our advantage and adamantly unrecognized by "real" Blacks as a result.

There's nothing I can do to change those hearts and minds.

But I am officially done taking shit from both sides simply for being born. For looking like I look and being who and how I am. These essays explore what it has meant for me and to me to be routinely categorized and mis/understood as "Mulatta" and/or "White-passing" in my everyday life as a woman who is legally Black and unequivocally a lesbian. I am, in addition, an art historian who is fascinated by the politics and aesthetic forms of representation. In these pages I'm here to intervene in (really, to fuck with) conventional art historical methodologies, by demonstrating what happens when, working against the grain of my academic training, I allow my subjecthood and positionality – my identity – to shape the way I read gender, race, and sexuality in works of visual art. I interrogate re-presentations of race and racism broadly in this account. But on the matter of being Black, I speak only from personal history and experience, telling a story that only I can tell with the suspicion that it is not, in the end, unique to me.

# 1

# MAKE ONE UP

TO SOME, declaring oneself as White with a Black father is passing. To others, declaring oneself Black with a White mother is disingenuous. A half-truth, even. A not-making-it-clear that you aren't the real deal – except, it bears saying, according to the one-drop rule by which American demography and, in many ways, American culture and politics continue to operate.

White people may not think of you "like that." While often among Blacks it's beware the nefarious "light-skinned," implicitly bougie, deviously shape-shifting, passable woman unaware of, or willfully trading on, our cultural valorization vis-à-vis darker-skinned women. Light-skin privilege and colorism are insidious and soul killing, all the more for their ubiquity across cultures. I am sensible of this truth, having unwittingly benefited from and having studied histories of colorism. I do not equate my experiences, or the intersectional racism and homophobia I have experienced, with those of (straight) Black-identified people with darker complexions and stereotypically – but not essentially – "negroid" features. Even Black lesbian lambswool butches of a certain age are likely to be treated differently than me if they are more "readably" Black.

But treated by whom? In my experience, those of us who are supposedly racially unreadable are frequently received by both White people and other Black people as unacceptably and culpably so because we fail to "own" our privilege or place in the hierarchy. (I disavow the phrase "racially ambiguous," which, as I see it, transforms the of-color subject, who is inevitably possessed of a particular, even if undisclosed, identity, into an object whose identity is acceptably confounded by an outside observer purporting to be confused about it. We are not, in other words, ambiguous to ourselves. Nor in many cases is ambiguity meant as a neutral term.) While it often goes unacknowledged, colorism is a relative and contextual form of bias that operates differently, like all cultural biases, across class, gender, sexuality, etc. To pass or be seen to pass in one setting is to be perceived as "diverse" or merely ethnic in another. Same you, different read. Light-skin privilege grossly and unjustly affords me certain social, educational, and economic benefits regardless of my disgust that it is doing so; regardless of my historical knowledge of how discrimination based on appearance has articulated racial alterity in this country.

But colorism is not the same as White privilege or White supremacy. There is a limit to how much Mulatta mileage supposedly passable women, especially trans, nonbinary, gender-nonconforming, working-class, and/or queer ones, can get from our racially indeterminate, lighter-than skin. Still more maddeningly – again, I will speak only for myself – the underexamined though routinely deployed forms of bias solely reserved for someone Black like me are disbelieved and dismissed or downgraded in a hierarchy of oppressions by White people who have never needed to pass or Black people who would not likely be accused of trying to. I recently found myself unfollowing a Black lesbian performer whose art/posts I have long supported after watching a sexy video in which she claimed the "best" Black queer couples were dark skinned whereas light-skinned couples being (insert euphemism for fucked up and not in a good way) should basically just disappear so the real Black people can do their thing. I was surprised by how much this stung, how betrayed I felt hearing it from a queer woman of color with whom I had felt aligned but who clearly had nothing but disrespect for me and mine merely for existing in her Blacker world, let alone trying to find women-loving-women love in it. Who are cis Black men who have never been accused of betraying the race with their appearance to give Instagram tutorials on the evils of White-presenting vs. White-passing?

When the actress Rashida Jones (Kenya Barris's "mixed" wife on the Netflix show *#blackAF*) was characterized as having passed for White by her browner-skinned sister IRL, she spoke my mind exactly:

"'Passed'? I had no control over how I looked," Jones said. "This is my natural hair, these are my natural eyes! I've never tried to be anything that I'm not."

Passing is not now nor has it ever been as uncomplicated as some would like. In the first place, who decides whether someone is passing or passable, and by what standards? Although Whites were first to employ foot-long rulers (to judge hair texture) and paper bags (to grade complexion) in an attempt to ferret out the subtlest tells of non-White otherness, Blacks soon used these methods too. In the early twentieth century, Black-hosted paper-bag parties were not unusual in cities like Washington, DC, and New Orleans. Whites examined women's nail beds for purple crescents indicative of "Black blood," just as Black spotters were paid to keep those suspected of passing from entering White establishments and social clubs. Despite the typical arbitrariness of this bigoted kind of close looking, discourse around the phenomenon of passing tends to have tacit expectations that universal, transferable, transhistorical — and self-evident — criteria exist for "visible" Blackness. The irony here, of course, is that claims from Black observers, no less than White, to be able to "see" someone's race have deep and demonic origins in the falsehoods of "race science." The Enlightenment embrace of phrenology (the hypothesis that the shape and size of the skull indicates intelligence and mental capacity), along with other pseudoscientific pronouncements on genetics based on appearance, is how "we" got here in the first place. It's a kind of profiling, the proverbial judging of the book by its cover, and it always leads to trouble.

Perhaps unavoidably, most writers on passing, Black and White in particular, find it difficult to gauge Blackness without referring to their own lived experience as racialized or deracinated persons in the world. Race is real, but race is also a construct. That one drop of Black blood isn't going to show up at the DNA level. In what follows, I put phrases like "mixed race" and "biracial" in scare quotes in order to underscore their constructedness; when members of different races have a child, that child is not technically the fruit of a "mixture" of distinct, readily distinguishable, red plasma proper to each parent's racial identity. Outdated semantics have only exacerbated cultural notions of what it means to have parents who identify, respectively, as Black and White. The notion of "mixedness" has, I believe, encouraged Blacks and Whites in particular to think of people like me as innately "mixed up," disloyal to our race/s, unable to declare a "side," and/or irrevocably "tainted" by the wrong kind of blood.

Yet paper-bag brownness, Black or "African" features, and even "woolly" hair are relative, subjective, and changeable qualities. They are meant to oppose the superior control that is Whiteness, itself rarely parsed beyond the vague catchall of "European" features. The fact is, presentation and representation have a lot to do with who is perceiving and receiving. As Nella Larsen's *Passing* character Clare assures her friend Irene: "You'd be surprised, 'Rene, how much easier it is with white people than with us."

Black people can be very hard on other Black people, even and especially when they can "tell." Yet White people are notoriously bad at discerning the subtleties of race and ethnicity. Historically in the US, when seeing wasn't believing, parentage assigned identity. If your mother was Black and enslaved, so were you.

As a child, I found out very quickly that people writ large feel most at ease when they can put labels on each other. By design, labels are abbreviated and classificatory; supposed to tell the truth about whatever they're stuck to.

When I realized I could write my own labels, the world opened up for me. But when I was starting grade school in a middle-to-upper-middle-class neighborhood in the 1970s as the brown child of a White single mother, nothing seemed less possible.

Miss Davis was our first-grade teacher. She was Black, but she was not nice, and she routinely ordered the Mexican American kids to stand facing the wall for what, even to their enemies, seemed like petty offenses unworthy of such humiliation. A black-haired little boy named Hector was always being told to "go to the corner." He was branded as a bad kid that year, and I don't think he recovered his reputation among the teachers in the five grades that followed.

Hector and a girl named Christina Mendoza were "bus kids," as my classmates referred to students who arrived and departed each day on a yellow fleet. The rest of us walked from no more than eight or ten blocks away to the landmark that was the red-stone, late aesthetic movement elementary school formerly attended by Mamie Eisenhower and Douglas Fairbanks Jr., whoever they were. "We" lived in Capitol Hill. The bus kids hailed from a seeming war zone referred to as "the projects" by the eventual debutantes and bar- and bat-mitzvahed golden children who were my peers. I don't think those of us who didn't live there knew the phrase was an abbreviation for "housing projects." We just knew you got treated differently for being a "bus kid." It might mean you were poor. Or it might mean you didn't do well on tests and had to leave class to work with the White moms who were volunteer tutors. The office ladies always assumed I was a bus kid, and I didn't like them assuming that just from looking at me. "Apartment number?" they would ask in a condescending tone, as if only bad people lived in multiunit buildings. I never visited Denver's housing projects as a child; I was never friends with the bus kids.

I know now that brown, pigtailed Christina, whom I picture in a fancy frilly pink dress with cap sleeves even as she threatened to beat me up at lunchtime, was Mexican or Mexican American, "Chicana" she might have answered had anyone asked.

I wore dresses too. Dresses only. No Toughskins. No Garanimals. Two Annie Hall–style, menswear-derived shirtdresses from a store called The Denver – I had them on constant rotation, vastly preferred to whatever was available from Target. While I, too, had a party dress – mine was floral peach – I liked to think I wore it only on appropriate occasions. Like the day the class went to the symphony, when I added white gloves, which I had scrubbed to immaculacy in the bathroom sink. Plus an orange vinyl, oddly Gilded Age–type accessory that looked like a huge change purse on a chain. My mother braided my long black hair and pinned it on my head, Frida Kahlo – or Rosa Parks – style. White socks. Fake patent-leather Mary Janes (definitely from Target).

Self-imposed respectability. It's mortifying to think about.

I had been to the symphony before. My grandmother brought me once in a while. We'd take a cab (neither of my grandparents drove after their divorce, but we didn't talk about that either) to a restaurant a block from the concert hall. It wasn't a fancy place, but going out somewhere with tablecloths seemed to me like just the thing one should do before the symphony. Although I would have preferred the more traditional repertoire from my mother's albums, my grandmother, who listened almost exclusively to the classical station on her radio at home, thought I'd enjoy the poppier stuff. Once, we saw a funny and very French Michel Legrand, mesmerizing in a blue velvet blazer as he played "The Windmills of Your Mind" in a way that made me know I would remember that song sung by him for the rest of my life. The windmills of my heart. My grandmother meant everything to me.

So I would wear one of my outfits, and my grandmother, a steel-haired Wyoming feminist who had sworn off skirts and dresses just as I refused to wear anything but, would take us out on the town. After, we'd taxi back to her small house on a quiet street, where I spent the night, as I did most weekends. The next day I was in charge of popping a tube of Pillsbury rolls on the sharp corner of the counter. When they came out of the oven, I iced them (orange, not cinnamon) to go with our cheesy scrambled eggs. At night we lay side by side wrapped in blankets on lawn chairs, and she talked about the Tetons and pointed out the constellations when the sky was clear.

My grand elementary school, that turret-towered behemoth, occupied a full city block in the heart of the Mile-High City, not too far from the former mansion of Molly Brown, a woman who was apparently unsinkable. The building had an unlikely four entrances. At each corner a broad flight of flagstone steps ascended to a vine-filled triumphal arch whose double doors faced one of the cardinal directions, not unlike Palladio's Villa Rotonda.

Meanwhile, in the carceral state that was Miss Davis's classroom, a tough, White, inveterate Garanimals fan whom I'll call Mindy Barnstable was commanded to kneel at the old oak supply closets lining the back of the classroom. The charge: "sassing."

To kneel for an extended time on rough Victorian hardwoods with only a thin layer of tangerine polyester between them and your bony seven-year-old knees was for sure corporal punishment. Mindy was a bully, and I never felt sorry for her back then, though what I remember of her kickball skills and proficient use of cuss words tells me she might be an estimable butch today.

Now that I am a teacher, I recall with utter astonishment some of the things we did in school growing up in the 1970s and '80s. The whole first grade was made to perform "the Hustle" in celebration of the bicentennial, for one. And my sixth-grade teacher, an aberrantly strident Episcopalian, smuggled into a vehemently public school a curriculum of reading workbooks surely designed for a parochial – Evangelical – one. Summoned by reading level, my classmates and I took our places in a half circle of plastic chairs at one end of the room as she quizzed us, each according to their gifts, on the wondrous workings of "Yahweh." Later, when I learned about these things at seminary, I wondered whether Miss Dumont had made the Jewish kids pronounce the unpronounceable name of the God of Israel when it was their turn to read aloud.

Although Miss Davis assigned us first graders an art project from time to time, one in particular stands out. The class was given a mimeographed, horizontally oriented sheet of paper divided into three zones: two side by side, like a diptych, at the top, with a smaller window beneath it.

There were no instructions on the page, but once everyone had passed one to his/her/their neighbor, Miss Davis told us what to do.

"Draw your mother and your father and you," she said. "And children. Do not play!"

For all the obvious reasons, drawing my father was a bridge too far. I had never seen the man. Not in human form or mechanically reproduced. I had nothing to base his portrait on. My mother, I could draw. That was not an issue. I'd been allocated my own notebook and markers long before first grade.

I'd give my kingdom for that worksheet. Sadly (though not for Miss Davis), it was handed in, never to be returned. I definitely drew my mother. Maybe I gave her the sharp brown bob she rocked with her enviably straight hair; maybe I gave her the glasses she has always worn, giant roundish ones at the time. Maybe I implied her Whiteness with the peach-colored crayon that everyone of every color seemed to be using for skin even if it was no longer labeled "flesh."

I raised my hand.

"What if I don't have a father?" I distinctly remember asking.

"Make one up," Miss Davis said without a moment's hesitation.

Now there was an idea.

Orphans and people who haven't met their parents tell stories about dreaming up identities for these people – imagining them as Daddy Warbucks, a foreign prince, or some sports superstar. Or as Meredith Baxter Birney or Jane Wyatt. But while I figured mine was out there somewhere, I never tried to imagine him. It seemed a waste of time. Likewise, I think I was already pretty clear that in my White world there wasn't a place for what was missing.

I returned to the task at hand.

"Who is that?" Miss Davis asked when I was done.

"That's Mr. Becker," I said.

Mr. Becker was the portly, genial, positively pasty White father of a girl named Sarah who became the platonic form of girlhood to me. Her dad was a corporate attorney for a sportswear chain, and he and his stay-at-home wife, also my Brownie leader, had six children, of whom I was assuredly not one.

2

# ALL THE BETTER TO SEE YOU WITH

A WOMAN FACES left, her arms and lower body blocked from view by a stretch of parapet or possibly a table. She turns her head incrementally toward the picture plane, just enough to reveal the eye farthest from view. The woman's face is long, and her bare, prominent forehead with its receding hairline takes up nearly as much of her countenance as the rest of her features combined. Her chins are round and jowly. The brilliant, raking light pouring in from the upper left corner has blanched away the details of her scalloped shift and bodice, but one can easily make out the elaborate lace of her plumed head-covering in shadow.

The woman's small eyes are peculiarly unfocused.

The solid black dot of her right pupil points improbably at the viewer. Though closer, her left eye is scarcely visible under a heavy but browless brow. Her nose is what? Most art historians would call it "flat" and be done with it. Likewise, what else could her lips be but "full"? Lightly coded adjectives for "Black" or "African" features are frequently used to describe the enigmatic figure who is the subject of this print by the Dutch artist Rembrandt van Rijn.

Around 1630, when he was twenty-four, Rembrandt made the etching while living in the town of Leiden. The print and its sit-

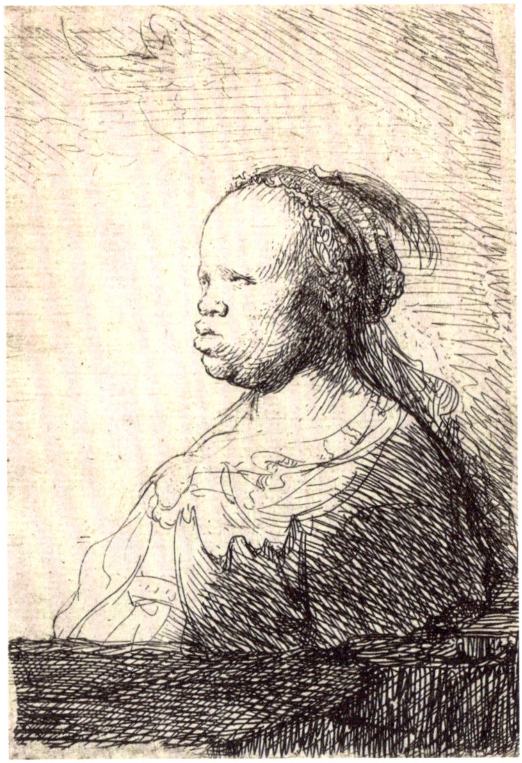

Rembrandt, *The White Negress,* ca. 1630

ter have long intrigued scholars, who have wondered what the artist was playing at. Did the young Rembrandt mean to suggest the arbitrary nature of race by conveying imperceptible Blackness through the unmarked portions of a white page?

At the very least, the etching is an attempt to show off what he knew of Italian art. In his sparing, almost notational, bust-length portrait, one is struck by the Northern artist's self-conscious employment of the very Southern concept of *chiaroscuro* – literally the light/dark, high-contrast effect that had made its way to the

Netherlands via the works of the proto-realist Lombard, Caravaggio, and his followers.

Like many of Rembrandt's works, the print is widely praised for its naturalism. Despite being executed almost four hundred years ago, it looks accurate to many viewers today. People are tricked by attention to detail and supposed imperfections; to some, the woman is believable precisely because of her perceptible flaws. Her unidealized appearance. Her unsightliness. (A devotee of staging in service of seeming candidness, the artist – best known for his truthful likenesses – was something like the Annie Leibovitz of his day.)

As a printmaker, Rembrandt had a penchant for the (exaggeratedly?) wrinkled, unkempt, and wild-haired. It's worth remembering, however, that caricature was just getting started in the Baroque age. Moreover, except in the realms of the mythological or figure study, it is relatively rare to encounter seventeenth-century depictions of non-White women, especially by famous artists. The White women Rembrandt went on to paint sometimes defy Greco-Roman ideals, but they are generally presented as respect-worthy or at least sexually desirable. The racialized woman in Rembrandt's etching was an unusual subject for any early modern artist. So unusual, in fact, that some scholars contend she cannot have existed. Art historian Martha Gyllenhaal believes that instead of basing the figure on a live woman, Rembrandt must have used a plaster cast as a model. During and after the Renaissance, bust-length portraits were often intended to evoke ancient Roman statues of highborn or virtuous people. The woman in Rembrandt's etching does indeed have a somewhat sculptural, almost veristic, or excessively true-to-life, look, as if she, too, might be a specific individual of some importance.

But regardless of whether she had a name — and many of Rembrandt's sitters are given them — his subject has been known as *The White Negress* for more than a century. Only recently has the moniker been challenged by art historians. Should the title be replaced with something less offensive and more PC? Is such an unflattering depiction degrading or was that just how the person looked and good for him for showing it? What does this tell us about Rembrandt's feelings about Black people?

If you look up Rembrandt's etching in print catalogues or museum collections or online, its unrevised title is sometimes explained as "ironic," even "humorous." It has lately been introduced as the "so-called" *White Negress.* Clearly, some people find the notion of a white Black woman incommensurable with race, or history, or Rembrandt as they know him. Others evidently find the image funny; an oxymoron. Historicity aside (and I am of two minds on revisionist language), it shouldn't need to be said that "Negress" is an ugly and troublesome term. A dangerous reduction of Blackness and womanness to something essential and base and inescapably universal, always the same everywhere and in every incarnation throughout time. Emptied of intersecting identities — or any sense of subjectivity — the Negress is nobody. But she is also killingly all.

There was a bus stop about two blocks from the second-story rowhouse apartment my mother and I lived in. From there I could take the number 10 to within about three streets of my grandmother's house. After the divorce, my grandmother bought her own house. (My grandfather had moved into an apartment to recapture his errant youth with other World War II veterans on the lam.) Her new neighborhood, still in the city of Denver, was made of wide streets, tall trees, and brick houses built in the 1950s and '60s. Whenever I came that way, she met me at the cute bus shelter and we walked home together.

One afternoon I packed a small bag and walked through my neighborhood of Queen Anne houses, 1920s apartment buildings, and eccentric Denver duplexes until I arrived at the bus sign, near an alley on a two-way street.

I would have been nine or ten. If I wasn't wearing the peach party dress, it was something like it, something with a bow that tied in the back and puffy sleeves. I guess I thought riding the bus, where I would be seen and judged by strangers, warranted respectable attire.

It was broad daylight. And the street was busy enough. But nobody else was waiting at the stop that day. Just me in my dress with my small bag. At the time it was a perfectly typical, perfectly safe-seeming thing to do. Kids went places alone back then. Walked, rode our bikes. I had checked with my mother; I had told my grandmother when to expect me (she taught me to read a bus schedule), and I had done exactly this several times before.

The voice came from behind. In the alley.

What was my name, it asked.

Officially, my name is Jamie, after James, my grandfather. But I've used my middle name, Vanessa, since I was in second grade. I answered to Jamie only from my grandparents, who called me by that name until their dying days, when I was well into adulthood.

Vanessa, I responded, to a man beside the large metal dumpster.

He was Black, wearing a T-shirt, and not very old, as I would later tell the policewoman and the lady bus driver, though I'm not sure what counted as not very old to me at that age. And I don't have an image of the man now. Just the rewind of the smooth sound of his very adult voice.

Come over here, he said. I want to talk to you.

I edged nearer even though I realized getting too close would mean entering the alley. I was enough of a city girl to beware of alleys, which you should never go down by yourself, even to take out the trash. So I stood at the edge of the asphalt while he beckoned me from his camouflaged blind near someone's garage.

I took a step toward the man. He said, Let me fuck you, Vanessa. Come over here and let me fuck you.

He motioned, then lunged, toward me.

But I leapt back. Back to the strip of lawn with the red RTD sign. Cars went by. Cars full of people looking out their windows, seeing me but not knowing what was happening. And me not knowing how to make them stop. Who to call for help. I remember him coming into the light then. I remember him tall, coming at me, and me, off the curb, straining to glimpse the bus. Begging for it to get there.

And then, miraculously, it came, barreling toward me through the intersection. The bus wasn't slowing down. But when I frantically waved my hands, the driver pulled over. The doors whooshed open and I ran up the steps and inside.

---

My PhD advisor, cochairing a conference session in Amsterdam, asked me to consider giving a paper on gender if I had anything that would fit (I work more on Flemish art of the Southern Netherlands than Dutch art of the North). Here is (basically) what I sent:

This paper pursues the possibility that Rembrandt's *White Negress* should be understood as a rather sensitive portrait of an African woman with hypopigmentation, often referred to as albinism. This interpretation solves three of the etching's most puzzling problems. First, it explains both the unusual appearance of the woman's eyes, which might be read as crossed or wandering (people with albinism are often born with eye issues, including vision impairment, light sensitivity, and nystagmus, a rapid back-and-forth eye movement). Second, it admits the *White Negress*'s ambiguous—and ambivalent—racial and religious iconography. There are at least two possible interpretations of her appearance. Viewed negatively, she is visually impaired, that is, blind. Blindness was a typically ableist Renaissance metaphor for the inability to see what is true or, in an orthodox sense, right—which, from a Dutch colonial perspective, makes the depiction of an African woman as an unseeing heretic, appropriate. Viewed positively, even a sightless Black African woman can be en-lightened, which is to say "illuminated" by God's dazzling grace.

Moreover, classifications by previous art historians of Rembrandt's etching as the portrait of an actual African woman with "unnaturally" pale or "white" skin suggest the technical challenge he may have set himself, namely to use mere black marks on a white page to delineate the appearance of unmelanated "black" skin in an individual racially marked as dark. For these reasons, it seems to me the woman's represented "whiteness" is willfully misrecognized in common readings of her skin as incompletely rendered or abandoned before completion.

The remaining advantages of acknowledging the sitter's hypopigmentation are primarily historiographical. Scholars have largely failed to critically or theoretically address the presence or absence of race in Rembrandt's etchings — and here I would foreground the later "Reclining Negress" of 1658. For example, in the recently revised series *The Image of the Black in Western Art,* one writer laments that even Rembrandt, otherwise known for his eclectic and tolerant social circles, unstinting representation, and general humaneness, submits to the unpleasant racist assumptions that pervaded European culture. My paper exhorts art historians to seek nuanced alternatives to the usual approaches — where Black figures in the age of transatlantic slavery are either wished into what, to the usually white author, is a more palatable state of representation OR written off as "exaggerated" caricatures or monstrosities simply because they display what some viewers imagine to be nonnormative, e.g., non-able, non-Greco-Roman, bodies and features.

---

A Broadway musical review of Fats Waller's hits called *Ain't Misbehavin'* came to Denver, and my mother took me to a matinee. I wore the French Vanilla Annie Hall shirtdress with the grosgrain ribbon tie and the reversible vest, which I loved because it doubled the times I could wear the dress. The cast was all Black. Two men and three women. Two very flamboyant men.

*One never knows. Do one?*

Three kinds of women. I was entranced, and my entrancement terrified me. I learned that Black women could be (a) skinny and loud and a homewrecker, (b) voluptuous and silly, or (c) fat and nasty. And a little sad. I was already being called fat by the White sons of bankers at my school and couldn't figure out why they picked on me when there were other girls, mostly brown, who fit the bill. But those girls were nicer. I was already mean. Already sad. I didn't want to be cute and didn't think myself pretty. Before I was even in school, I had played doctor with other girls in the shadowy gap between the wall and the sides of the tall blond bed frame. I never cared about boys.

A kid in my grade named Jackie did a made-up dance to a tape recording of that song "Brick House" on "performance day" in the auditorium. I didn't want to shake my ass or the breasts I was trying to hide. I didn't want to be Nell Carter. Or get the kind of laughs Armelia McQueen got. And I would never be the skinny boy-crazy dingbat.

*I'm White inside. But that don't help my case.*

---

A naked woman lies on her side, back to the viewer, legs pressed together and slightly bent, one arm partially visible along her rib cage. Her wrapped head pushes into the darkness. In histories of Western painting we call this trope the reclining female nude, and it goes back at least to the early sixteenth-century Venuses

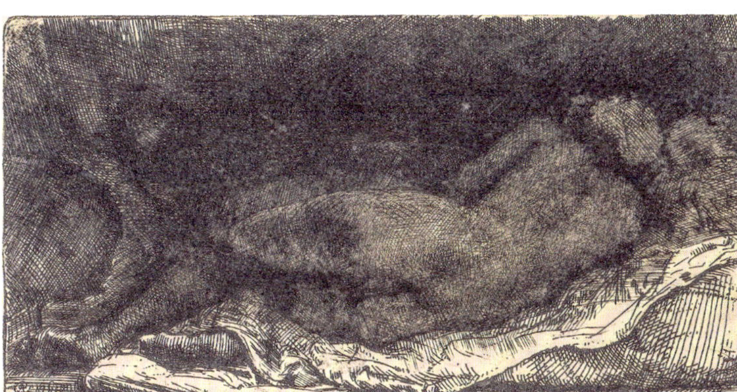

Rembrandt, *Negress Lying Down*, etching, 1658

of Giorgione and Titian. Back to those mythically soft-fleshed White women sprawled across luxurious beds or languishing in verdant landscapes that make their hills and valleys analogous to uncharted territory. But this partially obscured woman is not them.

While shown from behind, she doesn't much resemble Velázquez's opaquely mirrored *Rokeby Venus,* painted about a decade prior, probably when the Spaniard was in Italy. In Rembrandt's etching of 1658, no cupids, no musicians, no pastoral setting accompany the naked woman.

Lately, museums have removed the racial epithet. At the turn of the eighteenth century, however, while the transatlantic slave trade was still active across Europe and the US, cataloguers usually called the print *Negress Lying Down.* Sometimes *Lying Negress.*

Scholars continue to debate her race, but they generally assume she was real.

Sumptuously tactile and printed on warm, sepia-colored Japanese paper, Rembrandt's image surely urges the eye to roam. To explore. To know the woman by her skin. Here again, the Dutchman throws down the gauntlet to his peers (I see you, Peter Paul Rubens), who build flesh from layers of colored oil pigment—something he can do too, if he chooses. Here, though, porous textures, smooth sheens, and inky hollows required no paintbrush. Here the language is the incised line and the bitten plate; the syntax is the crosshatch.

Plump thighs, the V of her waist and hips, and the figure's rounded shoulders imply femaleness according to the conventions of the time.

*My, what a fine ass you have.*

So what color is she?

It would be easiest if she were White. If she were the artist's mistress. A local from the neighborhood. Even before Black Lives Matter, curators wanted to get rid of the "Negress." If White, another Venus. If Black, a slave. If White, a nameless sleeping girl candidly sketched. If Black, a "servant" exploited and sexualized—her own darkness can't hide her. To me, she is indubitably Black. But also a little blue.

---

FURTHER READING

Fowler, Caroline. *Slavery and the Invention of Dutch Art.* Duke University Press, 2025.

3

# TYPECASTING

> Still, the centuries have not dulled
> the sullenness of the child's expression.
>
> —NATASHA TRETHEWEY,
> "De Español y Negra Produce Mulata"

IN ONE OF my favorite settler colonial paintings—if I can say this of so disturbing a genre—a woman wears a dress the old me would have killed for in 1763. Strewn with delicate blooms and buds and feathery leaves in shades of coral, olive green, and blue, this flowering hillock of a garment extends beyond the picture plane and into the beholder's world. Within the painting, the woman's snowy bodice and colorful skirts emerge from the surface of an otherwise earthy and monochromatic scene. If the meticulously painted printed flowers on her skirts aren't enough to catch the eye, a stomacher of tightly gathered red fabric rosettes resembling carnations delineates the V shape of her torso. As is often the case in eighteenth-century portraits, clothes are meant to silently supply the viewer with information about the character

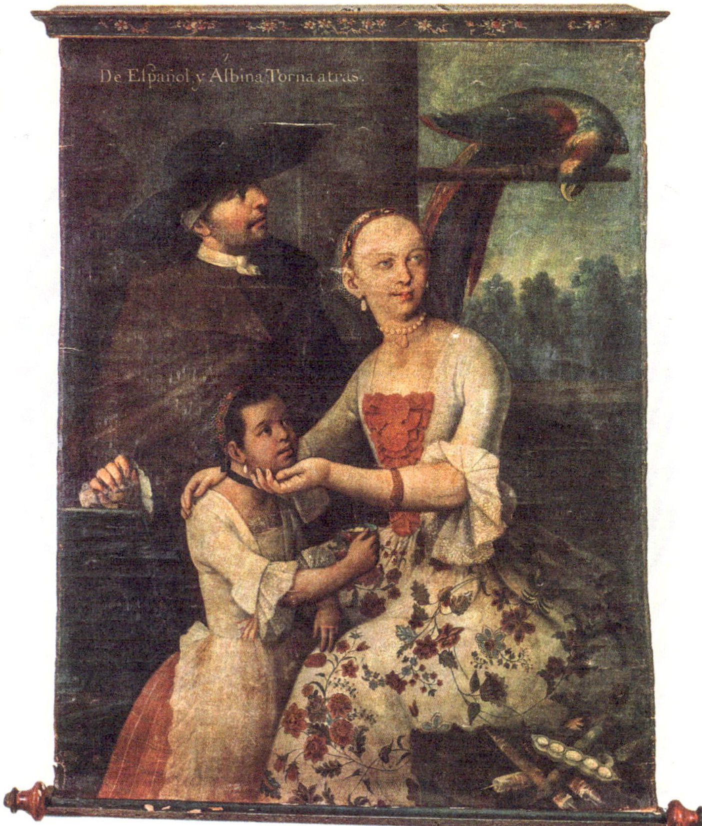


Miguel Mateo Maldonado y Cabrera, *De Español y Albina, Torna Atrás*, 1763

and class of their wearer. If, for example, this wealthy lady has been reflowered after being deflowered, as the painting's theme would suggest, the outcome of that experience is positioned between her legs, where, in fact, we find a brown-skinned child whose dress is a more understated version of her mother's over-the-top ensemble. Both figures wear chokers – the mother's, of pearls; the daughter's, of black ribbon — allusions perhaps to their correct place in the hierarchy of a Mexican society where even nice clothes and good looks can be deceiving.

Our fashionable lady is one of the trio of personages — two parents and their child — whose presence defines a *casta* painting. In a colonial "New World" context, the word "*casta*" refers to lineage or breed and, more precisely, to the racialized bloodlines associated with genetics and genealogy. A complete series of *casta* paintings typically consists of sixteen to twenty individual images, each of which purports to show what happens when a specific combination of races mixes.

Prior to the colonization of Mexico and Peru by the Spanish, *casta* paintings did not exist. Few developments in the history of art attest so creatively to contemporary anxieties in Europe and the Americas about racial purity — and the need to detect it in order to protect it.

*Casta* paintings flourished exclusively in the eighteenth century. Across an ocean from the Spanish metropole, with its courtly collection of Italian and Flemish Old Masters, a novel art form was born in the colonized periphery of the Americas. This new pictorial varietal emerged from the mixed-up uncultured culture where, try as one might, the old categories of rank and breeding were no longer so easily defined. As an artistic genre, *casta* paintings are at once a product and a producer of the corresponding historical period baptized in history books as "the Enlightenment" or "the Age of Reason." Their creation invites some reasonable questions: What forms of humanistic learning and Enlightenment can be so designated when just beneath their pseudoscientific skin lurks the bloody and brutal heart of chattel slavery? Capitalism makes good economic sense for sellers. If a being is a thing, she must also be a commodity (etymological synonyms for which are "obligingness" and "utility"). But where living goods are bought and sold, how does one judge their quality, that is, their suitability, that is, their value?

With just these questions in mind, the canvas I'm describing was created by Miguel Mateo Maldonado y Cabrera at the height of the transatlantic European slave trade. Cabrera was a constantly in-demand and, luckily for him, highly prolific painter who worked in viceregal Spain, as the colonies were known. Of Spanish and Indigenous descent, the Mexican painter was most celebrated for his Catholic stories and saints. Yet today, the most famous single *casta* series from the period was a one-off for Cabrera, seemingly his first and last foray into the genre. We do not know whether, as a "mixed-race" artist himself, he decided not to return to the subject matter because he was uncomfortable depicting the dangers of race mixing. It is nonetheless clear that he approached the task in a subtler and more artistically ambitious manner than his peers had. Scene for scene, his series is dense with visual information yet no less enigmatic for the racist ideological punch it packs. A confident and stylish painter of real people, he is a solid technician whose rendering of seemingly superfluous details – the blue shadow of stubble on a Spaniard's chin or the near-botanical accuracy of a floral textile – distinguishes his series from those of his many, often less gifted, anonymous contemporaries.

Not displayed in fine arts museums until very recently, *casta* paintings trade in pseudoempiricism, providing teaching tools for a new kind of natural history. Intriguingly, however, the reality effects of Cabrera's settings and the natural, if somewhat theatrical, behavior of the figures who inhabit them belie the genre's purpose.

It all looks so truthful – as if you could pick these people out of a colonial crowd.

Which is a taxonomical problem. Because *casta* paintings are not meant to be portraits, whose mimetic intent is to reproduce or memorialize actual, historical individuals. According to the requirements of the *casta* genre, Cabrera's people should rightly come off as generic. As stereotypes. Difficult though the artist makes it, his eighteenth-century viewers were supposed to remember that his figures are imaginary; not raced persons but personifications of race.

Because they have no individual identities, his subjects have no names. Instead, they are given capacious labels such as: *Español* (Spanish man), *Negra* (Black woman), or *Indio* (Amerindian man). Labels transform individuals into allegories – perceptible bodies that stand for intangible abstractions – in this case, abstractions not only of race but of gender and what would soon be called "class."

For the genre's intended audience, the colonizers back "home" in the Spanish capital, a *casta* series had an educational, propagandistic, and proudly cautionary purpose. If these paintings from the age of Voltaire were an Enlightenment play, their moralizing theme would be the costs and dangers of miscegenation in New Spain. The denouement of a *casta* series is thus the tragic decline of racial purity and, ultimately, of civilization, that results if distinctions between castes are not properly policed by the ruling elites.

But back to that lady in the pretty floral dress.

In the painting titled *De Español y Albina, Torna Atrás* (From Spanish Man and Albino Woman, Return Backwards) a disarmingly pallid woman dominates the scene. The mild-looking peach-faced man to her right is her Spanish husband, or perhaps simply the father of her child. The girl on whose shoulders the pale woman rests her arm is, of course, their daughter. Or rather, the girl represents the category of subject labeled by the Mexico-born Spanish Creoles in power as a racial *throwback.*

What we see is not necessarily what we get. Of all Cabrera's sixteen reproductive scenarios, this one is the most visually confusing because the looks of the offspring of this racial combination seem to defy reason. It's something of a visual riddle. Explicitly the painting asks: How do a Spaniard (Español) who is White by lineage and a woman (Albina) who is (quite literally) White by appearance produce a brown-skinned daughter (torna atrás)? Implicitly it asks: What the hell went wrong here?

The answer is found in the annals of eighteenth-century science. As LACMA curator and art historian Ilona Katzew and others have been careful to note, throughout this period explanations for the skin condition of albinism were closely linked with biological notions of race and its historical origins. Surprisingly, in Cabrera's day albinism was widely believed by Europeans to affect Black Africans exclusively. In other words, while very few Blacks were albinos, all albinos were Black.

"White Negritude" was therefore viewed by some colonizers as a rare if hopeful reversion of some Black individuals "back" to a primordial state of White goodness and moral purity. As such, the figure of the albino was cited as proof for monogenesis, the theory that all humans are descended from one, in this case White, race.

Absent the woman's classification as *Albina,* the viewer—and especially the twenty-first-century museumgoer—might be misled by this genetically Black female's appearance. Indeed, without the presence of a child whose skin color attests to the darkness of her ancestors—four generations back by the common arithmetic—"we" might never have known to recognize the deception in our midst.

Cabrera's is surely one of the earliest artistic depictions of racial passing as trompe l'oeil. In fact, the painting is a kind of training manual for White supremacists. By rehearsing the process of real-world racial discernment for the viewer; by engendering the power and process of registering someone's heredity through informed observation, the image undermines the attempts of this "woman" and other women like her to be seen as other than we/they "truly" are. This *casta* painting draws the viewer's attention to the Black Albina passing before her eyes.

Look again! it warns. Don't be fooled.

The irony is, of course, that the albina is outed as Black by her preternaturally pale skin; she is *too* White to be true. But there are other clues to the white woman's potentially mistaken identity, and the dress is first among them.

Cabrera's series is notable, though not unique, for the absence of one seemingly crucial racial category among its cast of characters. Of the sixteen possible mothers portrayed in his groupings, the pure and untainted Española, the desirable White Spanish woman with *limpieza de sangre,* or pure blood, is nowhere to be seen. Of all the combinations represented, the brown or Black "mixed-blood" child is never the product of a White mother and a male *other.* One obvious explanation for the omission is the real-life model of colonization and enslavement perpetrated and perpetuated by male conquistadors who raped and, in some cases, intermarried with (or kept as concubines) the women they encountered and exploited in New Spain.

But in addition to massive numbers of nuns, lay Spanish noblewomen were no less critical actors in Spain's colonization of the Americas. Isabel of Castile had ordered Catholic women as well as Catholic men to intermarry with highborn Indians in Mexico as early as the first decade of the sixteenth century. Throughout the eighteenth century (White) Spanish women frequently appear, for example, in colonial legal archives as litigants in court cases—even filing for divorce. It becomes doubly interesting not to find elite Spanish women as maternal types in Cabrera's series if only because they were everywhere in New Spain. What the artist gives us instead, as if to underscore an almost ontological difference from others of their sex, is women who only appear to be Spanish purebloods; women who pretend. And surely the most pretentious of all Cabrera's female subjects is this albina in the splendid calico dress.

Calico, also known as chintz, may conjure up bolts of patterned pioneer stuff purveyed by the likes of Harriet Oleson in Laura Ingalls Wilder's Walnut Grove, Minnesota, or the lavish floral upholstery in a Mario Buatta great room from the Reagan years. As with so many things that have come to define Anglo-American good taste, however, the fabrics we see in Cabrera's images are, in fact, second- or third-order European appropriations of Asian inventions. There is nothing innately English about chintz, and there is certainly nothing originally American about calico. As the name suggests, Calicoes (from "Calicut," i.e., Calcutta) were originally Indian printed cottons of varying complexity, quality, and cost. In the late seventeenth century, British and Dutch encounters with Asia resulted in a feverish thirst at home for such stylish, multipurpose (and washable) stuffs. Within a century, the French, English, Spanish, and Dutch had learned the Asian printing techniques well enough to set up their own factories in an effort to supply the demand domestically—an economic imperative, given the burgeoning export trade.

Historian Marta Vicente describes a heady late eighteenth-century "craze" for calico in viceregal Spain—where Spanish ladies, newly arrived in their colorful chintz dresses, set off a furor among local women of all classes to get ahold of the same look from a local, Mexican source. Women begged, borrowed, stole, even sold sexual favors, for chintz. Worse yet, according to the wags, the Mexican fashionistas had no sense of propriety; they wanted to wear their fancy dresses not only on special occasions but every day.

Cabrera's albina is one such indecorous Mexican.

There she sits in her sober surroundings with her soberly attired Spanish husband, a flamboyant bird in all her finery. Cabrera's images have been compellingly explained as tools of empire building and identity construction – not only reflecting society but creating it. Where the contemporary implications of privilege and prejudice are concerned, the scholar Magali Carrera approaches the genre with both sense and sensitivity. Other authors seem to have forgotten that however (pseudo)scientific or instrumental its foundations, the racial hierarchies Cabrera and others brought to life have had a lasting and devastating effect on non-White peoples throughout the Americas. I think of the late Gloria Anzaldúa's self-identification as *prieta,* "so dark and different," inspected at birth for "the dark blotch, the sign of indio, or worse, of mulatto blood," regardless of the European appearance of her blue-eyed grandmother.

Cabrera's White Negress is surely in pictorial conversation with the same tropes seen in Rembrandt's images and embraced by Dutch colonizers of Africa in the previous century. Yet, to my knowledge, despite the oddly detached cupping gesture she makes and her unfixed, if not sightless, gaze, the Mexican painter's version of the albina has not been understood as visually impaired.

There are signs she should be. For much in the way Rembrandt presented the bust-length portrait in his print, Cabrera offers the albina woman as a meditation, no less ambivalent, on vision, recognition, and revelation. While the viewer is taught to read this

Mexican White Negress for what she is, she herself may be incapable of seeing things – literally or metaphorically – as they are.

And yet, in the play of looks Cabrera constructs, it is the bird we must be wary of. Even as the dominant male in this would-be family portrait, the Spaniard's only purpose seems to be directing the viewer to the large, colorful, and quite aggressive parrot poised at the threshold of the outside world. The parrot, in turn, telegraphs the viewer's gaze across the mother's bosom to the uplifted brown face. The little girl might be attempting to placate the angry bird with a dish of seed – even as her clueless mother holds, or holds on to, the child she cannot, or does not, regard. The mother seems completely unaware that the girl may be in imminent danger (parrots have a bite strength of several hundred pounds). Likewise, the girl's soft Spanish father, gloves off, is so transfixed by the "exotic" bird, it's hard to imagine his intervention on anyone's behalf.

Viewed carefully, it's a strange scene full of unlikely gestures and odd exchanges that make it difficult to surmise what Cabrera was "really" saying about race mixing. Ostensibly, his was the same difficulty faced by centuries of moralizing artists before him: how to represent a dangerously beautiful woman in such a way that the viewer doesn't fall into the same seductive trap the painting's instructional purpose would have "him" avoid. Is it coincidental that in European devotional iconography the parrot is often a Christian, specifically Marian, symbol? Some say this is because the Virgin received an avian "Ave" from the winged messenger sent to announce that she, the future mother of God, was with child. The inconceivable child of an immaculate mother. If this albina has been permitted to parrot Whiteness so shamelessly, it is the bird's job to draw our attention to women like her; women who seek to undermine true feminine modesty and racial purity.

Understanding life through art can be a form of therapy. But first, you have to know how to find yourself in what you see.

---

My grandmother had an early and promising career as a newspaper reporter. A proud Tri Delt with good grades and a mischievous past involving firecrackers and dormitory laundry chutes, she went on from Laramie to enroll at the Medill School of Journalism at Northwestern. During the war she was said to be the only woman on the city desk of *The Rocky Mountain News,* Denver's now defunct daily paper established in 1859. In the lobby of the Brown Palace Hotel, she interviewed Annie Sullivan. Patricia Neal. And Babe Didrikson, about whom she spoke with a reverence that always made me wonder.

I have a photograph of my grandmother, glamorously femme in a way I never knew her, from long before I was born. It's a black-and-white 5 × 7 of a slender woman in thick black cat's-eye glasses, taken on Christmas Day, sometime in the mid-forties. This was prior to her era of pants, and unbelievably to me, she wears a velvety full skirt and fitted leopard-print vest. We see the corner of a room with patterned carpet where she kneels beside a camera-mounted tripod, skirt tucked beneath her in the manner of a Flemish *priant.* The lens she fiddles with only obliquely addresses the viewer, which is a little unnerving. Especially once you realize she might have been facing someone with another camera (a mirror is possible but unlikely); namely, the invisible person who took the picture – a *Las Meninas* moment.

The emerald-cut onyx ring she would someday give her only granddaughter (me) is clearly visible on her ring finger. I want to

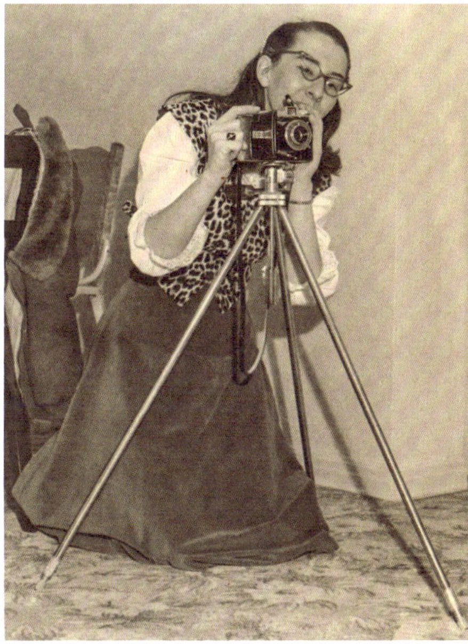

Dorothy Elizabeth (Betty) Caldwell Lyon, ca. 1943

wear it, but the little diamond in the middle keeps popping out – I've lost and replaced it more than once. You can practically smell the temporarily abandoned unfiltered cigarette smoldering in an ashtray just beyond the frame. She loved to smoke – I don't think she was entirely sorry that particular vice was to blame for her emphysema. And possibly the devastating late-in-life blindness caused by her macular degeneration. The picture affirms what I knew from her self-deprecating but evocative stories, that my grandmother was one of those wartime ballbusters who tossed back martinis in a place that served blue-plate specials – a Rosalind Russell, or a young Hepburn type. You'd never guess from this photograph – did my grandfather take it? – that she would give it all up for her husband as soon as he wanted her to.

Yet even after she left the workforce, my grandmother was a reporter. She still had a journalist's sense of narrative. It was she who would tell me the story of my life, which goes like this:

A few hours after you were born, your grandfather and I went to see you at the hospital. In those days you could look at the newborns through a big glass picture window. Sometimes people who were in the hospital for other reasons would visit the nursery to see the new babies just to get cheered up. Well, it was the cocktail hour (she always mentioned this), and we were standing there trying to find you among the forest of bassinets and we couldn't help listening to all the other parents and grandparents and everybody else. And someone would point to you and say: "Oh, look at that little Mexican baby with all the hair." And then someone else would point to you and say: "Oh, look at that little Hawaiian baby with the big brown eyes." Or still another person would point to you and say: "Look at the little Indian baby with the fat cheeks."

For the first couple of years after my grandfather moved to his bachelor pad in a '40s courtyard building near downtown Denver, I spent some weekends with him. This astounds me. Here was a guy in his late fifties living in a one-bedroom apartment (with twin beds of all things) who wanted his granddaughter to come hang out with him on a Friday or Saturday night. It's also astounding because I can't remember him actually trying to entertain me in any way while we were in that apartment. There were no toys. It was the seventies, so there was no internet. He had a turntable, but I don't remember watching TV. I didn't bring books or games. I think I can see – even feel – details like the cold, rough surface of the large, curved tiles that made up the wide sills of the casement windows I loved to look out of. The smoothness of the cove ceilings. The thick brown shag of the wall-to-wall carpet. I'm sure I studied those things for lack of anything else to do.

My grandfather had a distinctively nostalgic personal style that was at that point part Tijuana Brass swinger and part failed architect. He was neither, but could have been either in a former life. A White Anglo-Saxon Protestant through and through, he harbored a not-uncommon WASP fascination with an idea he had of Catholicism. After the war, he chose to attend college at a Catholic university courtesy of the GI Bill. I think in a slightly parallel universe with no sexy secretaries to distract him, he could have become a priest. Father Jim, a handsome Jesuit in pastel argyle socks and wide-strapped leather sandals. It all might have been different if only, after the unspeakable, never spoken of, events he experienced in the war, my grandfather had believed in God more than philandering. Be that as it may, instead of becoming a man of the cloth, he became a reporter who spent much of his life doing PR for a sugar company (newspaper articles refer to him as their "spokesman"). Even so, he was put out to pasture less than a decade before retirement—about the worst thing a man his age could imagine at the height of the recession of the early 1970s.

All his life, my grandfather had a thick mahogany crew cut and a lean, almost youthful build. Still, I think he was born a grandpa. Well before I knew him, he had achieved an aftershavey, Patrick McGoohan, striped-turtlenecks-with-sweater-vests kind of look. Along with Pall Malls (red armorial soft pack, no filters, pronounced the British way), he smoked burled-wood pipes, which he kept in a stand with concave rests for the ones he wasn't using. There was always a zip pouch of fragrant tobacco in his back pocket. His ashtrays were made of thick orange plastic, and he had a metal lighter with the kind of top that flipped closed with a satisfying clink. He kept a margarine tub of quarters on a bookshelf and let me "count" them for fun, no doubt fully aware that, even at so tender an age, I could be an unabashed thief where interesting or valuable objects were concerned.

Like my grandmother and so many White Americans of their generation, he was a staunch Anglophile, less Lawrence Durrell, as she was, and more *Master and Commander,* as if, would-be royalist in the wake of revolution, he still owed something to the empire. His people had come over later than the eighteenth century, though I don't know when. The Queen Mother was a Bowes-Lyon. But only Henry Louis Gates Jr. would know if there's a line of descent from Clarence House to my grandfather's roots in Monrovia, California, and, as I've recently learned, Tulsa, Oklahoma, prior to that.

The rows of short teak bookcases lining my grandfather's fiendishly tidy apartment were populated almost exclusively with British literature, save for the odd Ogden Nash or Robert Frost paperback. There was lowish – Patrick O'Brian and G. K. Chesterton – as well as highish – Evelyn Waugh, Forster. Trollope. Dickens. Certainly, no Austen or Brontë. Few if any women writers at all, in fact.

After my "granpob" died, I was responsible for dealing with his library, which I believe my mother expected me to keep and cart around with me for the rest of my life, even if she would likely have burned the lot rather than admit his books to her own house. I was a thirty-one-year-old grad studying historical theology at the time and, living on loans as a result, was more interested in the value of the books and how they could be converted to cash, or at least traded for books I actually wanted or needed. For weeks, I hauled the boxes around to various used-book stores until I had traded or sold or just plain off-loaded every title. Half out of guilt and half owing to the interests I shared with my grandfather, I mostly traded for things like the complete works of St. Teresa or a Sacheverell Sitwell book about books about birds.

I love book sales, libraries, and used-book stores, and now have a hundred more volumes than he did, including a growing assemblage of lesbian pulp fiction that I buy for the salacious covers, mainly. Books are objects infused with power, and their very presence can have an effect on a person. So much of the way forward for me has come in the form of the subtle messages I've gleaned not only from images, but from words and texts. My grandfather's collection felt saturated with narrowness, regret, and failure in a way that made me not want to keep it around. He lived alone and he died alone and he never had another job that was worthy of him.

Whenever I stayed over, he would sit on his twin bed on the other side of the nightstand and read me a chapter of *Treasure Island* before I went to sleep. Turns out, he read the same book chapter by chapter to my mother and her younger brother when they were growing up.

I never especially liked *Treasure Island.* Or even knew what was going on or who the characters were. But I liked that he read to me. And I liked that he liked it.

You'd think I would have been scared, being away from my mother and sleeping in a relatively unfamiliar room at six or seven. But since my grandfather was only a few feet away in his piped cotton pajamas, I guess I felt safe in his care, despite the visions of swordfights and plank-walking that must have danced in my head as I fought to stay awake.

In the mornings we ate halved pink grapefruits with a thick layer of sugar sprinkled on top. I enjoyed watching the granules melt on contact like snow on a hot sidewalk. Before serving me, my grandfather ran a steak knife along the membranes of each section. This made it easy to remove the little wedges with a spoon. In our tiny family, we laughed that whenever he found himself downtown and outside the Sugar Company, as we called it, my less-than-emotive grandfather liked to kick the building for summarily letting him go after years of faithful service.

After breakfast, there was always a plan. Typically this involved unfolding paper maps, reviewing bus schedules, assembling coupons assiduously snipped from the newspaper — his only loyalty was to the best price, which required exploring the retail frontier. He made up assignments for himself: tracking down the best record-cleaning apparatus, the cheapest salad spinner. The thickest bone-in porkchops to go with his apple sauce. We were always going somewhere.

That we had to go on foot or by public transportation limited our possibilities. Perhaps not as much as it should have. There were many interminable rides on RTD (Regional Transportation District) involving less than smooth transfers and waiting outside in unpleasant weather.

We sometimes went to the sprawling old Fairmount Cemetery, where, learner's permit in hand, I would later practice driving. Occasionally, we trekked all the way to a suburban shopping mall called Buckingham Square. Eventually, we traveled to Southern California every summer to visit his toothless, nonagenarian mother and my middle-middle cousins with the goat named Harriet and the Thoroughbred named Guinevere whom I never got to really ride, though they did let me milk Harriet once or twice.

When the weather was absolutely prohibitive of crosstown travel in metro Denver, my grandfather usually took me to the art museum, which was only a few blocks away from his apartment near the state capitol at the edge of the city center.

The museum's now-iconic jagged profile would have been a recent addition to the skyline at the time; it was only a couple of years younger than me. The quirky Italian industrial designer Gio Ponti was the principal architect. (A few years ago, a student's impossibly chic French mother, who grew up in a Ponti villa outside Paris, informed me that Denver's museum is his only building in North America.) I can imagine that the conflicted modernist in my grandfather admired the museum's Orwellian severity and maybe even the promise of its newness. I, by contrast, was afraid of it.

Beneath a crenelated roofline, the building's seven stories are entirely veneered with more than a million specially manufactured gray glass tiles, each about the size of a checkbook. To me, the stingy scatter of asymmetrical window slits and Lego-esque projections across the museum's gleaming if colorless surfaces bore an uncanny resemblance to the Death Star – which I had recently encountered at Sarah Becker's birthday party, when her mother drove us to the movies in the Beckers' white hearse of a Country Squire station wagon with the jump seat in the back, which I always requested.

It's difficult to determine the age of the figure in the painting. She is young. But whether a girl or a young woman in her teens or twenties, one can't be sure. The artist, likely Manuel de Arellano of the talented family of painters by that name, shows a face in three-quarter view. The subject has dark eyes and her stiff brown curls project enough to cast a shadow on the undefined space behind her. Her nose is unexpectedly long and her flat, unblemished cheek sits on a slightly lower plane than her equally expan-

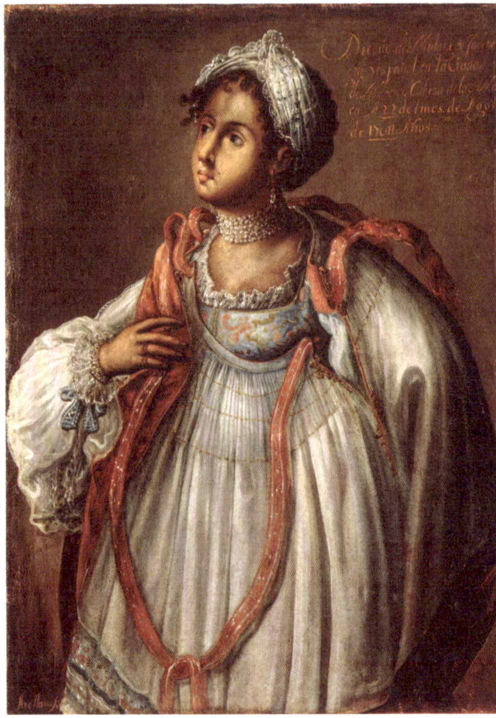

Manuel de Arellano, *Rendering of a Mulatta,* 1711

sive forehead. Near the tip of this heart-shaped arrangement, Arellano has placed a small, formulaic mouth.

If the head is an egg, the face is a mask. So much so that the considerable skull beneath her pleated headscarf feels weirdly appended to the oval of spotlighted features that is its facade. The overall effect, accentuated by the crescent of shadow beneath an uncontoured jaw, is that of a waning moon.

The figure, in other words, is neither girl nor woman. She is a mannequin. An idea, perhaps an ideal, whose painted "body" merely serves as a vessel for the notion of her race, which we are told by the inscription in the upper right is "Mulata." The female of the species *mulatto.*

This Mulatta, like most aping *castas,* is a clotheshorse. What she wears is part of the self/construction of her identity, even her race, in relation to the White, Black, and Indigenous types used by later artists to illustrate the effects of *mestizaje,* or mixing. That "her" neck is disproportionately thick is not an issue; its purpose is to draw the viewer's attention to the multiple strands – I count six – of on-trend pearls adorning her brown skin. From there the eye takes in elaborate attire, rendered with great care by the artist – more illusionistically, more "realistically," in fact, than the physique of the Mulatta herself.

The painting's pale-red inscription reads in full: "Drawing of a Mulata, daughter of a Black [woman] and a Spaniard in Mexico City, Capitol of America, on the 22nd of the Month of August, 1711." Because it includes this categorizing rubric, the work is considered by many to be the first *casta* painting. For while it does not show the two parents responsible for the appearance of this "mixed" figure, the description points to the impetus behind its creation. Arellano's painting is a portrait of a race. Its purpose, at least in part, is to describe – and prescribe – a class of persons for easy recognition by the colonial gaze.

Much has been written about this painting, chosen for the cover of more than one book about viceregal art, as if the image of the Mulatta in tastelessly lavish *poco de todo* garments speaks for empire itself. The canvas was loaned to the Denver Art Museum in 2014 by the philanthropic urbanists and oil barons Jan and Frederick Mayer. The Mayers' collection, claimed by the DAM as, outside of Mexico, "the most comprehensive representation of Spanish Colonial art in North America," now forms the core of the museum's Spanish and pre-Columbian holdings. It might be just as well that the Mulatta painting wasn't there when my grandfather led me through the dark, blood-spattered works of Spanish colonial religious art for which my hometown museum is famous. The figure of the Mulatta in question is pretty, if overdressed. The pearls, the chintzy calico dress, the finely ruched white overgarment (a skirtlike shawl that was associated with the women of her racial group) all speak to a love of luxury, of adornment. To a refined and desirable level of taste, if not respectability. Showing off to show out, she is only an idea, but I feel close to her just the same.

---

FURTHER READING

Anzaldúa, Gloria. *Borderlands/La Frontera: The New Mestiza.* 1987. Reprint, Aunt Lute Books, 2012.

Carrera, Magali M. *Imagining Identity in New Spain: Race, Lineage, and the Colonial Body in Portraiture and Casta Paintings.* University of Texas Press, 2003.

Katzew, Ilona. *Casta Paintings: Images of Race in Eighteenth-Century Mexico.* Yale University Press, 2004.

Trethewey, Natasha. *Thrall.* Houghton Mifflin Harcourt, 2012.

Vicente, Marta V. *Clothing the Spanish Empire.* Palgrave Macmillan, 2006.

# 4

# STRIPES

> Being someone who is raised to think of themselves as Black but appears to be white is a quintessentially Black experience.
>
> —DANZY SENNA

MY ELEMENTARY SCHOOL playground was a lawless site of freedom, with all that freedom entails. Under the right, or wrong, conditions, anything could go down in those spaces. We were free to violently reenact interstellar war games using tetherballs and foursquare grids (I was Darth Vader). Or scheme birthday-party exclusions with the cabal who daily formed a daunting barricade on the entrance stairs to the "big building." Or recklessly race across the ice in our treadless sneakers and, subsequently in my case, on our crutches.

We were free to openly bully each other and call each other names. Free to get "ugly," as Miss Rawls, my Black, turban-wearing, Texas-born third-grade teacher used to call it. Noses were bloodied on that blacktop. There were fights between (those who at the time identified as) boys and boys. And boys and girls. And sometimes, as my childhood best friend reminds me, girls and girls. From third to sixth grade, I lived in fear of Christina's vow to beat me up for being, basically, a snobby girl who kind of looked like her but wasn't even a Mexican. If she hadn't had to get the school bus right after school, I have no doubt she would have tuned me up good. Instead, if I didn't get the timing right, she merely taunted me through a half-lowered window as I slunk past the bus on my way home.

But neither was I innocent. Once, unable to take his incessant teasing about my weight – I had become Vanessa Fat Lyon by then – I shook a freckle-faced redhead named Freddie by the collar of his wide-striped polo shirt and told him to leave me alone. Then I shoved the punk backward onto the ground. I must have seen someone – maybe Jimmy Cagney – do this in a movie. Freddie was bigger than me, but I was working the good-girl persona pretty hard in those preteen years, so I caught him off guard.

It's amazing how fast you can establish yourself, or get established, as this or that kind of girl when you're young. Almost from inception, it seems, I was not the kind of girl who went to amusement parks (afraid of heights) or scary-movie slumber parties (nightmares for days). I was the kind of girl who did well in reading comprehension and phonics (drew a mean schwa) and had my papier-mâché sun face displayed in the cabinet outside the principal's office. These were my natural inclinations and skills, but they were also self-engineered to keep me above the fray. And it worked. Right up until the humiliation of being called the one thing or things against which I so carefully styled myself was too much to endure. Then, as now, if pushed too far, I blew. In that case, however, my uncharacteristically brutish physical response to Freddie, like the incessant bullying that brought it on, went unnoticed by the adults. Things only got worse for me with my male classmates after that, though. Despite the bravado, I was no gangster.

Before and after school, there were throwdowns between sexes and genders and races and ethnicities and socioeconomic backgrounds. As soon as a fight started, a protective circle of onlookers would form. Kids chanted encouraging slurs, some of which still pop into my mind under the most surprising circumstances. Across all demographics, there was feverish delight in crime, but I think what really got us going was the prospect of punishment—so long as it wasn't our own. There was always a tale to be tattled. For which, as we all knew, you needed Mr. Potter. Officially, he and his female accomplice, Miss Radke, were the "gym teachers." In reality, these two adults had an almost inconceivable degree of warden-like authority over every student as long as we were on the school's premises.

As is the case with dictators, the most frightening thing about Mr. Potter and Miss Radke was not the absoluteness of their power but the random and unpredictable ways in which they exercised it. That, and they were lazy. Who knows what the qualifications were back then to be a grade school gym teacher. I wouldn't be surprised if jocular, doughy Mr. Potter had a football background, while Miss Radke, with her spotless sneaker collection, seemed more like a frustrated tennis pro. I never saw either of them shoot a basket or score a goal. Rarely did the two do anything but amble and saunter and accost us with their giant whistles, as if expending the energy to grab a ball before it went out of bounds or give a fallen nerd a hand would, over time, be the death of them. Their indolence was not a form of self-preservation, it was a show of sovereignty.

Any time there were kids on the grounds, Mr. Potter and Miss

Radke stood side by side in the approximate middle of the schoolyard scanning the goings-on like lifeguards. Lifeguards you suspected would think twice before going in the water. These two White people of uncertain – but not old – age, he in creased soft-denim jeans and what I remember as a thick blue polyester sport coat, she in a plethora of matching cotton sweater and skort ensembles, surveilled us each and every school day for six years of our lives.

Preloaded with what was probably classified intelligence from the social worker, they monitored all things recess. And during the hour or so each day we were entrusted exclusively to them, they taught us gym. The enshrined phys ed rota included everything from marathons of ball-hurling "Bombardment" to squealing our heels around a room on "scooters," as those weird little four-wheeled, panty-revealing, squares of wood were known. Outside, when Mr. Potter had placidly drawn lines in the sand with a canister of powdered chalk, there was kickball and a more undemocratic version of Red Rover, where you shouted in unison at a kid across the field: "Uncle Sam, Uncle Sam, may we cross your bridge?" To which the presider screamed back: "If you have on [for example] red," until the only people whose colors hadn't been called tried to sprint to the other side before the previously captured tagged them. Woe unto the monochromatically dressed on the wrong side of that field.

In bad weather, an entire gym period might be consumed by a Howdy Doody–era square dance called "Duck for the oyster, dive for the clam." (Not to mix metaphors, but it's a chicken-and-egg thing: Did I love that song because I'm a lesbian or did it turn me into one?) Maybe I just loved square dancing in bad weather because the alternative – "rope day" – was fifty minutes of every fat kid's worst nightmare, centered on "skin the cat," a superhuman challenge every inch as tear-inducing as its name.

Again. Good underwear a must.

I grew to distrust and dislike my gym teachers mainly for what, even to a child, were their obvious racial and gender and class biases. They also did a great job instilling us with body dysphoria.

I am an Aries.

So were two beautiful and small-boned and perhaps comparably rich White girls who I would know until we went our separate ways for college. Emma and Emily. Emily's birthday was the late-March day before mine; Emma's the day after.

Emily was a close friend way past fourth grade, and I often went to her palatial house after school. In those early years, she had a beautiful kitchen where short, tightly gathered floral curtains topped the room's wall-to-wall lattice-mullioned windows, like something out of a Washington Irving tale. There was a round butcher-block table where we'd gossip through whole sleeves of Carr's Water Crackers wastefully dipped into a dwindling supply of ice-cold Marie's Ranch Dressing. Emily's mother couldn't believe we'd demolish most of a jar of that stuff in one sitting, a dubious achievement I think she blamed on me. Though delicious, the combo wasn't my idea. Mom and I were more of a homemade tortilla-chips-and-salsa family. After our snack, Emily and I would generally head outside to enact richly imagined melodramas involving stagecoaches and murder solving. There was a glider at one end of her vast green yard for the one, and a McMansion under construction on the corner for the other. After the site closed down for the day, we liked to sneak into the shell of the house and write on the pristine drywall with big flat pencils the workers left lying around. When I go home to Denver to visit, I think of our illegal trespassing every time I drive by that house. I hope somewhere beneath the skim coats our initials linger on. JVL and EKD. Emily's family had monograms on everything. As an adult, I have spent hours online designing my custom L.L.Bean totes.

I never truly hit it off with Emma, the other blond girl. Emily was funny, smart, and nice. We made each other laugh and loved hanging out together. But it was humorless and unreadable Emma who was, or would soon become, my type. And by type I mean not only the flavor of girl to whom I was (and still am) attracted, but the kind I wanted to be. It's a lesbian cliché, but good luck finding a lesbian who hasn't succumbed to it. The girl in my rearview mirror was Emma the Hitchcock blonde. Emma in a thousand cities. Emma as proto–Cate B. It would happen again in a couple of years when *Grease* came out and, pathetically, Olivia Newton-John became my role model, as would, come to think of it, Blanche DuBois in my sophomore year of high school. It's a bit like Black girls choosing White dolls. In fact, it's exactly the same thing.

In those days, Emma and her brother lived in the neighborhood simply referred to as "Country Club," and they were clearly cut from a higher thread count than even the Becker kids, who wore the base model of Nikes (white with red swoosh) and made after-school quesadillas they called "tortillas" with microwaved American cheese.

Emma, by contrast, had almost certainly grown up appliqued in Florence Eiseman apples to go with her gum-soled Swedish shoes. Her mother was a tall and slender blonde who always regarded me with quizzical but not unkind eyes, as if everything I said was impressive. Once, when I was a little older, she commented conspiratorially on the difficulty of finding Le Coq Sportif shorts like mine in pink, and I felt as seen as if she had asked me on a date. Surely Mrs. Blake was dressed by someone at I. Magnin, while Emma was down the street at Pappagallo (an expensive shop in Cherry Creek where you could buy interchangeable Bermuda Bag covers, "Alligator" shirts, Sperry Top-Siders, whale- and strawberry-printed turtlenecks, and grosgrain ribbon headbands decorated with gold scallop shells).

My goofy and clever friend Emily was of still another taxon. To an average Westerner, she was the real East Coast thing, exotic to us cowpokes. She had arrived from New Jersey with her parents and older sister late in the grade school game. Her real estate magnate dad and aggressively Republican part-time attorney mom had to have become the toast of Denver's society crowd (it is said that Colorado's capital has more deb balls than any other city outside the South). Emily's parents moved their photogenic family into an enormous house with a serpentine front lawn (great for sledding if someone watched for cars) and multiple bedrooms with their own bathrooms. In my mind's eye, the whole second floor was kitted out in matching Laura Ashley comforters with box-pleated skirts. Everything white with a spray of tiny burgundy and blue blossoms.

All around her mansion the grandest post–Silver Rush houses were being taken over by homosexual decorators (it was the early eighties) and other non-"native" Coloradans and upstarts who didn't mind being a couple of blocks from apartment buildings or unhoused people living out of shopping carts and collecting aluminum cans from their dumpsters. Emily's mansion was off the same numbered street as the one we lived on – but it was a mile deeper into the money and felt like a world away.

If Emily's Gilded Age manse was urbane and Emma's stucco palazzo was Country Club, our fourth friend, Sarah Becker's, enormous bloated bungalow was neither. But it was right in the middle of a very good block. My old neighborhood — or the one I eventually called my own — is one of the prettiest I've seen in any city. It's a pleasant few square miles of eclectic, curb-appealing, early twentieth-century vernacular architecture, with considerable variety on every street — from Georgians and Dutch colonials to faux French chateaux and soberly porched brick homes with no particular stylistic pedigree. After several blocks, the main avenue gets interrupted by a wide dog-and-jogger-friendly boulevard with flower beds tended by the city in the summer months. Sarah's house was not quite on the boulevard. It was four blocks from Emily's and ten from our apartment. If my old elementary school friends have passwords composed of their childhood addresses, they'd better watch out because I remember them all. I loved big houses long before I lived in one, which is probably why.

Emma and Sarah both came out (as debs) in our senior year of high school. I don't think East Coast Emily cared much about Denver's version of high society — in the end, it didn't matter who had Gloria Vanderbilt jeans or the coolest running shoes. The new and newer money had more pretentions than the old. Sarah Becker was a nice girl from a less-than-worldly cultural milieu and the social capital probably served her well later in life. Emily was a class act who didn't need the country club's imprimatur. And Emma quite simply looked great in a gown.

As a child, I had one goal on a typical school day and that was to go home after the last bell with one of my "friends." I could put it another way: My single, fervent aim was to find a way not to go home alone to the empty apartment. "Do you want to play?" kids would ask each other. This generally meant walking home together to occupy someone's backyard or TV room or kitchen. It could also mean prank calling from a spiral-corded wall phone dragged into the pantry or running errands in the Jeep or Volvo with a stay-at-home mom (filed under other painfully embarrassing memories, I sometimes accompanied my friends to their riding or piano lessons, where I waited on the sidelines like a maid or a babysitter until they finished). Occasionally, we'd join people's older siblings in a no-holds-barred form of neighborhood hide-and-seek called "Ditch 'em," which was fantastic to me for the access it granted us players to the strangers' backyards, where we were expected to take cover. I can't help but think now what that game would have been like had there been more (or any other) Black and brown kids doing the hiding between houses or in sheds or crouched beside stacks of wintering lawn furniture. As it was, there was nothing much worse to fear than a dad who pulled into the drive early, feigning irritation when some thirteen-year-old White boy surprised him from a perfect hiding place behind the covered grill.

How lonely I must have been. And how desperate. Because there I was making every attempt to look respectable and do things properly, when in fact I could only have come across as what I was – that sadly plump brown girl in the Top-Siders (too clever for her own good) who wanted so badly to have somewhere to go after school that she'd walk a classmate home and turn right back around just to avoid being alone.

When I couldn't find someone to go home with, the alternative was to stop by the grocery store for a cream horn or a Long John and take it home to the apartment like the latchkey kid of a hardworking single mother I was. Sometimes I forgot the key, which was only a problem until I learned (how did I?) that you could use a butter knife to easily jimmy that kind of lock (useful though frightening knowledge that has led me ever since, and should lead you, to insist on deadbolts).

Although I'm sure it's related, my love of architecture doesn't boil down to a fixation on stately old houses merely because I lived for a time in a modest apartment. I grew up in a family that cared about politics, education, language, doing things right, and something rarely discussed but incessantly cultivated – good taste. If connoisseurship is the art of comparison, I was born ready. It seems obvious that my affinity must have been intensified by hundreds of hours passed indirectly making my way home; by taking in the particulars of house after house from Denver's flagstone sidewalks during my most impressionable years. Psychology does what it does, but God has always been in the details for me. Herringbone brickwork, concrete lions rampant, red-tiled roofs, window boxes, trellised archways. I committed the whole neighborhood to memory door by door. "You know that house on Seventh with the cut-out hearts on the shutters," my mother will say these forty-five years later. And I always do.

Some days after school I would even wait stealthily in the stairwells until I "ran into" a friend and could basically coerce her to "play." Sarah, to this day a churchgoing Methodist, was the biggest pushover and therefore had it the worst. Sometimes I'd ask her if she could lend me a butter knife, figuring once we got to her house she'd be hard-pressed to send me away. She rarely did, though I cringe to recall a few exceptions.

Although it was on a different wrong side of the park than Emily's, our apartment was in a nice brick turn-of-the-century building, what in other cities would be called a townhouse. Thanks to my mother, it was stylish and comfortable in a pared-down, '70s way. I had my own room, we had an eat-in kitchen, and there were beautiful big windows. We had a stereo, and I was allowed to play records as long as I replaced them in their sleeves and the right covers. The refrigerator was modestly stocked as one might expect of a grad student with a youngish child. Microwaves were still sort of a new thing and we didn't have one. Not because we couldn't afford to, but because we were against them on principle (to this day I don't have one in Vermont). I rarely had homework or long conversations by phone at that age. Being by myself in the apartment wasn't scary or dangerous, it was simply boring. I got lonely playing and replaying Olivia's *Totally Hot* album until my mother got home from classes or working in a gourmet cheese store or a costume shop, which couldn't have been later than fiveish, usually while it was still light. We were dismissed from school at 3:20, but two hours seemed to stretch into forever as soon as I got home.

Once I was a little older, ten or eleven, I entertained myself by trying out the most intricate and least expensive recipes from Julia Child's *Mastering the Art of French Cooking.* My mother had been given all three cookbooks by her mother, and these are the same warped and loose-leafed volumes I use for occasional fancy baking today. If starting young worked with cooking the way it does with sports or playing the violin, I'd be an extraordinary chef by now. *Hélas,* I am by nature too imprecise and impatient to bake well; today's rough puff comes out only slightly more laminated than my early, inedible croissants did – though I'll admit my scones are pretty boss. My mother likes to remind me that in sixth grade, I was paid by some enterprising teacher to "cater" the school spelling-bee reception with cream puffs and deep-fried Rosette cookies.

Speaking of cream puffs, Emma, Emily, and Sarah were so uniformly blond and skinny and wholesomely dressed that Miss Radke and Mr. Potter liked to pretend not to be able to tell them apart.

This was a running joke in everyday gym class, but it was given the lie on birthdays. On birthdays Mr. Potter would sing to you. Just to you. In front of the whole class. It was a kind of serenade in the key of Bert Parks; very schmaltzy and drawn out. We all pretended to hate it. But what little kid doesn't want to be singled out as special even if it's only once a year?

As I remember it, every March, Emily got a warm, even affectionate version of the birthday song. And Emma got the same. But my song – and I know there were years when I did not get one at all – never sounded to me like theirs. It was easy to compare because my day came right in the middle.

"A fight! A fight! A Nigger and a White!"

Many people are now familiar with an enduring bit of gossip about Queen Charlotte, wife of the British King George III of Boston Tea Party fame, which turned out to be true. She was, it seems, descended from Blacks. Precisely, the Black African branch of the Portuguese royal house through one Ines de Valladares, herself of Moorish, that is, Muslim, ancestry. In her own day, Charlotte, who married the king in 1761, was and now is widely observed to have what a PBS website refers to as "African characteristics." African. Characteristics. I guess she resembles the give or take 1.2 billion inconceivably diverse inhabitants of another continent. You can see it in her portraits, people say, when you know what you're looking for.

Art and its interpreters are largely responsible for proving Charlotte's "mixed" heritage. As a student of portraiture, I've long been intrigued by the representation and reception of the German-born queen. But it's the cyclical nature of White supremacy and its willful forgetting, of history's ability to repeat itself, that brings the eighteenth-century British queen to my mind as I write about my own life as a passable Black woman. That and the advent of Meghan Markle.

Consider the notorious brooch incident of 2017: It's some 250 years since Charlotte's coronation when a member of the British royal family, Princess Michael of Kent, accessorizes the white coat she wears to a Buckingham Palace luncheon attended by Meghan Markle, the future Duchess of Sussex, with a large "blackamoor" pin. Anyone who studies "Blacks" in art is familiar with decorative objects of this sort. Carved of shiny obsidian or jet and festooned with precious stones and pearls, the heads and busts of Black Africans feature in elaborate jewels and reliquaries and sculptures from the fourteenth century on. In ancient Rome, much earlier, they can often be found as small intaglios and bronzes.

Which is to say, White people have collected and displayed and accessorized themselves with Black bodies for millennia. That a member of a historically imperialist royal family would own such a brooch is not therefore unique or surprising. The familial coats of arms (or heraldic "achievements" as they're rightly called) of several British nobles include a "Moor's head." A coat of arms is essentially a form of advertising for the family-owned business that is generational wealth; a multiplatform campaign for a heritable brand.

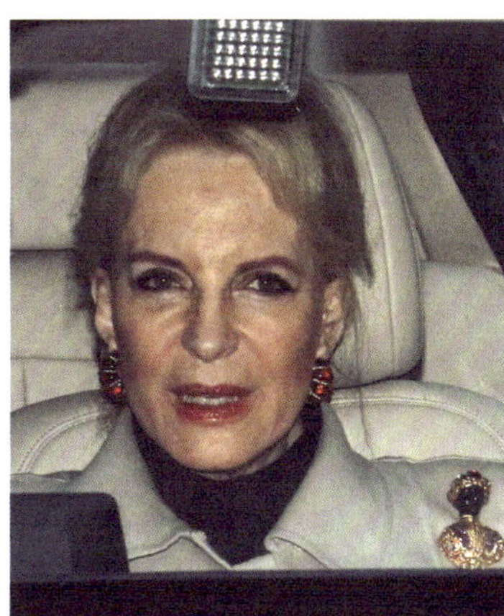

Princess Michael of Kent wearing a "blackamoor" brooch.

By way of illustrating intermarriage among noble Whites, heraldic Black bodies generally signify "Africa" or a Black-inhabited colony with a connection to the family who first claimed it for the British Crown. All across Europe, since who knows when, White aristocrats and cultural producers have asserted their identities through the symbolism of captured or conquered others.

What defies belief, however, is Princess Michael of Kent's choice on that specific day to wear that specific article of jewelry rather than any of the other boring and unobtrusive floral and nonfigural brooches in which she has often been photographed. Like the late Queen Elizabeth, whom she was obviously imitating, Princess Michael is a frequent wearer of dowdy jeweled pins.

The choice was not lost on paparazzi documenting the event through telephoto lenses. At first, the princess pleaded innocent, acting as if she were unaware that (adorning oneself with) certain representations of Blackness could be construed as offensive. In response, progressive media outlets dutifully pointed out that, as the fetishistic (at best) creation of White designers and/or patrons, the brooch is an unavoidably exoticizing object whose effect can only be heightened when worn by a White member of a royal family of former colonizers of darker-skinned peoples. So far, so good. The problem explained, the vilified White princess apologized in an ITV interview, describing Africans as "absolutely adorable." She'd also, she added, worn the brooch numerous other times without incident. This from a woman who, as later reported by *Vanity Fair,* named two of her farm's black sheep Venus and Serena.

So, sure, this is White supremacist behaviour, nothing else to see as far as that goes. Nothing else except the brooch, which consists of a glossy black head with a gemmed turban and baguette-encrusted gold jacket. Describing the explosion but not who placed the bomb and why only serves to normalize White supremacy. Imagine if, say, Venus and/or Serena (the female tennis GOATs, not the princess's sheep) were also guests, and you will soon realize that in a world of smartphone cameras, no one in the public eye would have made the same accessory choice. Even a royal would know that wearing a jewel in the form of a black head in the company of a Black person with deep brown skin closer to the tone of the jewel would have been too obviously suggestive and essentializing, way too on the nose.

That is not what happened. What disappointed me about the coverage of the brooch incident was not the media's immediate (correct) assertion that the wearing of the blackamoor jewel was evidence of garden-variety bigotry but rather the reporters' assumption that anti-Black racism is one-size-fits-all. This, and the failure to explain that where White supremacy is concerned, a picture or an image or an object can say what is highly unlikely to be expressed in words by a public figure. The fact is, the brooch's visual rhetoric relied on important if unacknowledged British cultural assumptions not only about skin color but also about the very American one-drop rule.

Merely by wearing what she did, Princess Michael of Kent had the capacity to remind any guest who might have forgotten that the woman who could (at that time) have become Queen of England was of African ancestry. Few would need to be reminded that Venus and Serena Williams are Black women, almost certainly connected, however distantly, to transatlantic slavery. But with Meghan Markle, a duchess, the danger from the White supremacist view, as always, is that the unwitting White observer might be duped by the paler, straighter-haired, irksomely attractive racial interloper only to later discover that (their) civilization is in decline as a result of miscegenation.

The subject visually and culturally broached by Princess Michael of Kent was not, therefore, Meghan's outward and visible similarity to the jeweled "African." Quite the contrary: The subject was Meghan's inward and invisible, that is, disguised, Blackness. And by extension, her perceived ability to pass. In this respect, the princess's ornamentation reads as a warning to other royals. As a far from clumsy means of exposing the reality "behind" Meghan Markle's appearance while rekindling long-standing European fears of what lies beneath the surface of the darker other. How many generations until an incontestably Black child is born to a descendant of this seemingly near-White mother? Remember the albinas; the Whiteness of the Whitest-looking Black woman is often compromised by her undesirably brown-skinned offspring.

By my lights, wearing the jewel was an even nastier form of prejudice than it might first have appeared, because it achieved two racist ends – aims that could only be accomplished when face-to-face with a real Mulatta. First, as noted, the jewel silently and socially reminded the royal family that what they were seeing wasn't what they, needfully obsessed with an heir, might ultimately get. Second, it suggested that their newest family member was innately, according to their own cultural and scientific legacies, subhuman: a kind of property rather like the property that was the decorative blackamoor brooch.

There is a chilling bedroom scene in *Suits,* the series that made Markle famous, where we watch her character, Rachel – who is known on the show to have a wealthy Black father and wisecracking White mother – lying in bed with Mike, her fundamentally dishonest and bro-ey White fiancé. Rachel has just received a showy engagement ring from Mike, and the two are presumably enjoying a moment of post-sex banter about the object on her hand.

Rachel: I can't stop staring at it.

Mike: Oh, I noticed.

Rachel: Yeah. So will everyone else.

Mike: Well, I mean, yeah. That's the point. For everyone to realize that you're my property.

Rachel: (laughs) O.K. Are you saying you own me now?

Mike: Oh, hell yeah. And this here is like a little collar for your finger.

Whether or not the same lines would have been written for a White actress or a White character, in the end, they were written for Meghan Markle. That the writer's words were spoken by a woman who would have been considered chattel property had she been born into the era of African slavery renders them especially ugly and pernicious — as if the denotations of enslavement belong to a bygone and incredible story of which fun can now be made. As if in centuries past, placing an actual metal collar around the neck of a kidnapped African person didn't mark her as a possession, most often of the White man who purchased her. Of the slave owner who, without being her husband, might force her into bed or anywhere else and rape her without consent or legal consequences.

Women like us catch hell from both sides when we explain that we, too, experience bigotry and racism. Because I know it can't be said enough, I say again: This is not about where we fit in a hierarchy of biases. Matching pain for pain at the hands of racists is, as the conceptual artist Adrian Piper writes, doomed to fail. Here, I want merely to note that our experience goes beyond being derided or distrusted for being too White to be Black by Black people or too Black to be White by White people. Inasmuch as we cannot be pinned down, we are judged not for being but for *seem-*

*ing*. Seeming to be other than what we are. By whatever beholder whose eye we are in.

And yet. Regardless of how I look (to others), I know who I am. There is no better way to keep the awful everyday machinations of White supremacy in motion than for a person of color to act as if it doesn't or didn't exist.

I once attended a prestigious writing workshop at which a famous Black Caribbeanist scholar gave a talk about slavery in Jane Austen's works, in which she said something like "Of course, Mulatta is a derogatory term," before going on to use it, derogatorily, for the rest of the talk. When I took issue during the Q&A with her acknowledgment that the term was a slur but nonetheless using it to suggest how inaccurately the *Bridgerton/Sanditon* characters were cast in terms of their racial appearance, she ripped me a new one – assuming, I think, that I was White and had no right to have an opinion. That those of us who may not look (to some) definitively Black or White are routinely, even publicly, dismissed for being unacceptably both and neither by those who are more readily accepted as one or the other is exactly my point. Go ahead and berate me as a half-breed who is less than you because of my supposed admixture of blood, but understand what that says about you and the way you see your own "purity" – especially within the context of a country, formerly a colony, born out of slavery, racial prejudice, and centuries of forced, but also chosen, miscegenation.

I consider whether I could expropriate blackamoor accessories for my personal style – embroidered turbaned heads on Stubbs & Wootton velvet flats, for example. But I think it's beyond taking back. Even worn by a person of color, a racialized symbolic form connoting the human commodities at the heart of the slave trade runs the risk of reifying that which the wearer seeks to destroy, giving it, some would say, even greater visual presence, ergo power. Then again, I reason, if I don't buy those shoes, some White woman in Florida will. And then a person like me will have to have their meal at a nice restaurant spoiled by seeing Black faces on her feet.

---

George Stubbs's *Zebra* of 1763 is the earliest likeness of an "exotic" animal by the famed English painter of horses. Smaller and more intimate in scale than many of his other works, *Zebra* depicts the "she-ass" received by the young Queen Charlotte as a gift from the governor of South Africa. Frequently caricatured in pamphlets and broadsides, the actual zebra was both familiar and unfamiliar to the English spectators who visited her. She might be viewed as a species of the Freudian uncanny, or *unheimlich,* always already a repressed double – in this case, a pendant to Stubbs's signature sleek-coated British Thoroughbreds. To relate the two animals within the cultural milieu of Georgian Britain, however, is to recognize the striped African quadruped as a darker kind of horse, not a foil but a specter. The zebra is not the domesticated English horse's African opposite but rather its haunting past.

Although Britain had led the slave trade since the seventeenth century, legal challenges and calls for the abolition of slavery began in the 1760s, precisely when Queen Charlotte received her animal gift. Throughout her life, the queen was frequently made the butt of a joke – prominent artists heightened what were deemed her "negroid" features. Numerous cartoons show the foreign queen calling for the boycott of sugar produced by enslaved people in the West Indies. The subtext is that Charlotte must have fellow feeling for Blacks "like her" laboring away for the empire in the Caribbean (sadly, as far as I know, we have no evidence of

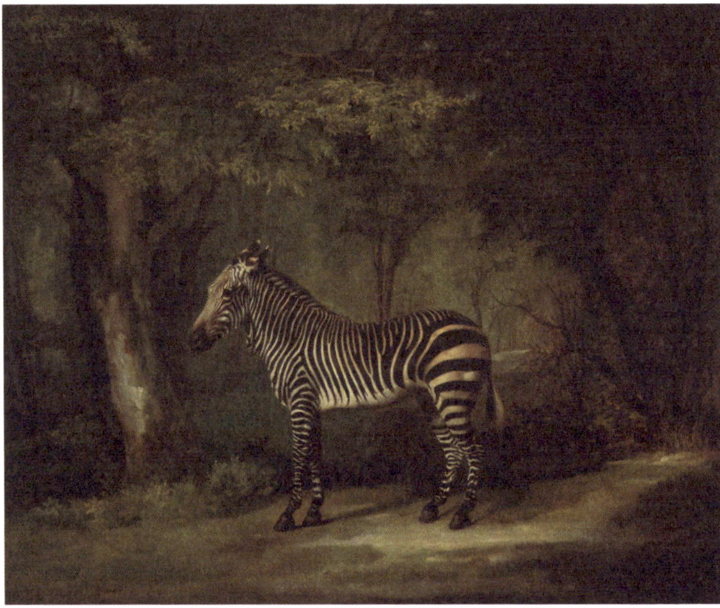

George Stubbs, *Zebra*, 1763

queenly sympathies of this kind). Nevertheless, with derisive portrayals of Charlotte in mind, Stubbs's *Zebra* can be understood as simultaneously a ghosting of plantation slavery and a stand-in for the much-painted queen, assumed by some contemporaries to be of mixed Black and White heritage.

Stubbs was a gifted observer and a highly skilled proto-realist painter. Through the lens of Enlightenment empiricism, his solitary, sweet-eyed *Zebra* was a contribution to natural history. This is what a real zebra looks like, the image seems to proclaim. It was painted in 1763, the same year Miguel Cabrera, across the Atlantic, made his *casta* series. In the Mexican works, Cabrera intends an individual figure to stand in for an entire "race." Stubbs moves in the opposite direction. In his painting a species of animal can be understood as representing an individual, in this case, I would argue, Queen Charlotte herself. The fact that eighteenth-century writers equated the queen's zebra with an "ass," implicitly a donkey, another member of the genus *Equidae* with African origins, would have racialized it further. Stubbs's portrait thus becomes a zoomorphic one, a likeness of the creature as mule-like as a Mulatta.

The neither-nor of the zebra has occupied artists and writers alike. Perhaps Charlotte's Anglo-German hybridity as well as her race/s is suggested by the zebra's pattern of distinct black and white stripes. Notably, the *Zebra-as*-queen is not "mixed." Her body cannot be construed as a gray area. Nor, though, as I have noted, it continues to be widely used, is the term "Mulatta" a neutral one. The word derives from "mule," the four-footed progeny of two entirely different species. "Mulatta" has always had a negative connotation in that it associates a certain kind of unnatural woman with the abnormality of a crossbred animal.

Mules are good for labor but cannot reproduce. Can be bred but cannot breed. Queen Charlotte had fifteen children. Five years after the *Zebra* was painted her name was bestowed on the largest city in North Carolina.

---

FURTHER READING

Hall, Kim F. *Things of Darkness: Economies of Race and Gender in Early Modern England.* Cornell University Press, 1995.

"The Real History Behind 'Queen Charlotte: A Bridgerton Story,'" *Smithsonian Magazine,* May 5, 2023.

Sorrell, Mark. "A Zebra, a Tigress and a Cheetah: New Light on George Stubbs's Exotic Animal Subjects." *The British Art Journal* 15, no. 1 (Autumn 2014): 99–109.

5

# BLACK BREASTS, BROWN NIPPLES

> At seven I had budding breasts. My mother would wrap them in tight cotton girdles so the kids at school would not think them strange beside their own flat brown mole nipples.
>
> — GLORIA ANZALDÚA, "La Prieta," 1981

I NEVER DATED in high school. Four years. No boyfriends. No girlfriends. And not because I wasn't popular. My prematurely curvaceous body, ineffectively curling-ironed hair, and increasingly obvious ill-will toward most boys hadn't done me any favors in middle school. But with the move to high school, the social butterfly that was and is emerged with a vengeance from her chrysalis. I got the character parts in the musicals. I skied. I played tennis. I sang in the supercompetitive jazz choir. I bought and drank gin for the White girls at their house parties. And though expressly forbidden while my parents were out of town, I drove to those parties in my mother's red MGB convertible, crossing my fingers that my new White Norwegian American stepdad wouldn't realize when they returned that the car was parked in a different spot on the street with a few dozen more miles on the odometer.

I had long perceived, probably from the age of four or five, that my sole and enduring attractions would be to other girls. A few years later, as I braved the congested corridors of my überdiverse inner-city high school, a thirties simulacrum of Philly's Independence Hall, I did wonder about sex. There were so many new people to think about, and it finally seemed like, given that the Emilys and the Emmas and even the Sarahs were never going to take me on a date to the new food court downtown, there might be other fish in the sea. For most of the hopeful teens I knew, there absolutely were. Immediately, all my straight White girl-friends had White boyfriends. Everyone was "with" someone. Everyone had a person to sneak upstairs or hold hands with in the bleachers at the football games. Even so, I can't recall any of us ever usefully talking about sex. Rarely in the abstract. Definitely not the act itself.

And there was so little to be learned from most of the movies I knew. My people were more *Breakfast Club* than *The Color Purple,* which I didn't see until years after it came out. Prior to the days when I was old enough to rent a VHS in a video store, old movies were such a critical part of my solitary and introspective development. Saturdays when my grandmother was mowing her lawn or riding her exercycle in the breezeway or walking her cart to the grocery store, I was lazily sprawled on the den sofa with my cold Pillsbury rolls and the movie matinees – usually a double feature from noon to four o'clock. I would watch just about anything, including Lon Chaney's grotesque filmography, but I had a particular attraction to fifties films. Grace Kelly, Connie Stevens, Patty Duke. I never liked Jerry Lewis in any of his guises, but I liked his confectionary costars.

Now, being a historian, I'm always looking at what was printed or reproduced or performed onstage at the time under consideration, what an artist might have seen or heard or otherwise been exposed to. But in reality, the seventeenth-century people I study were probably no more able to critically interpret the popular culture coalescing into history around them than most of us are right now. Today. Often people don't fully realize how retro they're being simply because these (youthful) tastemakers who believe themselves to be setting the trends weren't around when the original styles or aesthetics they prize last came into fashion.

Take *Grease,* for example. In 1978, owing in large part to a single movie musical (itself a filmic reprise of an earlier genre of entertainment out of fashion at the time), American teens became obsessed with the 1950s. The more radical among our former hippie boomer parents must have found this truly offensive. But nostalgia is as nostalgia does, and it nicely complemented Reagan's impending requisite backwardness. All of which is to say that when I was recently asked who my first queer celebrity crush was, I could easily answer without a hint of irony. Even before Olivia Newton-John stole my heart, there was Doris Day. "Que Sera, Sera" is a song I auditioned with at least once in high school. Unlikely as it sounds, I wanted Doris Day. Unlikelier still, I thought I could be her.

Surely the early teenage coupling taking place all around me must have required "Frenching" and giving head and being fucked, even of my new dishwater-blond BFF and *Oklahoma* costar Abby O'Grady, a Goody Two-shoes whose heartthrob tenor letterman was one of my grade school nemeses. She drove him everywhere in her Honda. But unless I've blocked it out, Abby never confessed to even the most venial of sexual acts.

Or maybe she rightly intuited that the details wouldn't interest me. It was all I could do to be in the same dark room with those horny high school hets when our group rented *Dirty Dancing.*

A few times a year, there were crepe-paper-and-balloon-strewn dances in the school's huge vestibule, which was bigger than the gym and allowed for some enviably grand entrances. I went to a few "Sweetheart" dances. Usually with some unbeknownst-to-him gay boy I could strong-arm. I was always the one to ask, knowing that a dress could be requested from my mother. My mother who to this day can sew truly anything on her high-tech machine, having once had a job making elaborate costumes for radio mascots and Restoration plays and the like. My mother who, relieved at the appearance of a potential boyfriend, happily indulged me with flattering takes on whatever Jennifer Beals or Kathleen Battle was wearing at the time. Does anyone else remember trailing their mother around fabric stores to buy patterns – those printed tissue-paper sheets that came in fat envelopes adorned with stork-like models? My dresses featured glamorous puff sleeves the size of a soccer ball, silky but structural in red fabric sold by the yard. Or they were triangular, postmodern shifts with square plastic buttons down the back. When people asked where I got them, I fibbed, of course. I never wanted it to seem as if we couldn't afford what they had. Junior year I got called out when a mousy frenemy grabbed one of the stunning homemade dresses out of my closet and showed a friend that it didn't have a tag. Those girls were always trying to catch me in a lie. I preferred distrust to pity every time.

There are pictures of my dresses. Suddenly, my stepdad was on the case, taking formal-looking solo photographs of me, usually before my date arrived. I stand on the house's pink stone steps, the sober concrete urn beside me overflowing with pansies, just the way I'd always imagined. However date-like I might have looked, I never kissed those callow boys at the dances. And I never went home with them after.

Up to that point, I'd had fleeting crushes on friends' sisters and the cynical, slightly older wannabe Madonnas who got leads in the plays. But it wasn't until senior year that I learned how to properly carry a torch.

Her name was Olga Larsen. And she was beautiful in that wholly singular way that makes a woman seem transported from another time or the pages of a classic novel. In Olga's case it was not least for being a green-eyed brunette. Her irises were the shade of a celadon glaze, like some magical hue formerly reserved for supernatural beings from Norse folktales. She was about as tall as me. Slender but never skinny. Her thick, glossy brown hair held the slightest natural wave, and she wore it most often with a soft pompadour widow's-peaking beneath one of those ribbon-covered metal headbands we loved in those days. Olga was possessed of the kind of White Northern European skin that tans evenly, without burning. She'd spent the summer before our sophomore year at a lake camp in Michigan, arriving golden for her first day of class in a public high school, where she stuck out like some princess from a Disney movie. In the first place, Olga showed up not with a broken-in JanSport like the rest of us. She carried her textbooks in a traffic-cone-orange synthetic fabric satchel with compartments and a big flap, like something a construction worker might need. I noticed her immediately, of course. But she was not my type at all.

Despite the iconoclastic book bag, Olga had been educated until that point at the exclusive and expensive, obviously conservative, local private school. Along with her sister, Birgit, who arrived a year later, she'd spent K through 8 just a few neighborhoods over—on a twee little campus in an all-White enclave to which parents living in other almost entirely all-White parts of Denver sent their children in order to prevent them from mingling with the more racially and ethnically and socioeconomically diverse student bodies in the pretty-darned-good public schools within walking distance of their own homes. No bus kids at Pineridge Country Day. (One supposes no standing in corners either.)

While it felt to me as if Olga came from another planet, I soon learned she lived only six blocks away. Two streets over from the Beckers. The house my mom and new stepdad had moved us into after they married, just after I started middle school, was like a dream. It wasn't much farther from my elementary school than the apartment had been. But it was on the opposite side of the blacktop. And that meant that even if I had nobody to play with, I now walked home in the same direction as the girls I had envied for most of my life thus far. Their neighborhood was now my neighborhood.

Our new old brick house had a backyard and two stories. It was big for just the three of us, designed around 1915 by an architect with a passion for foliate carving. When we moved in, every single wall except in the bedrooms and the kitchen was painted matte dusty rose, probably the original color, which sounds horrible but somehow in the very early eighties wasn't at all. Deep pink, not mauve, is my favorite color, and maybe that's where I came to love it. I worshipped that house. Especially the carved parts. Everywhere you looked there was warm tiger oak fashioned into flowering vines or egg and dart moldings or coffered panels set into the kind of pocket doors I'd seen on *Upstairs, Downstairs.*

This was respectable wood, lovingly routed into Ionic capitals and fluted pilasters for the glazed cabinets and matching oak mantel. There was a front parlor with high windows to which my grandmother contributed her mother's upright grand. Hulking and stained dark, that piano was like something from a saloon, its bench still stuffed with sheet music from the thirties and forties. Whenever I had asked as a child, my grandmother would play a rolling, slightly off-key barcarolle on its chipped, actual ivory, keys.

The mysteriously smelly tiled shower on the first floor didn't work and the entire kitchen was hideously indoor-outdoor carpeted. But all that was offset, in my opinion, by the presence, halfway up the stairs, of a suffragette-era phone booth with a built-in bench and desk for the telephone. For privacy, there was even a door with a small window through which the talker could see and be seen. To an avid reader like me, this old-fashioned nook evoked both the allure of the confessional and the space-time liminalities of Narnia and Madeleine L'Engle at a time when I was still young enough to crave the inexplicable. To want to be transported somewhere else.

In structure and scale, Olga's house was gratifyingly similar to mine. The same milk-carton dimensions with a short flight of steps leading to a long perpendicular porch perpetually in shadow. But unlike my bare wheat-colored masonry, every inch of the Larsens' brick house was painted a steely modernist gray. As far as the rest of the block went, the Larsens' house looked like someone had hung a mid-century monochrome on a wall of Victorian flower paintings. Inside, too, the place was stripped down to the minimum. It seemed that at some happier point in the '70s, the Larsens had gutted and lacquered their place into an open-plan white backdrop for a slew of Artemide lighting and Knoll furniture upholstered in comparatively playful Marimekko. Cold chrome and abstraction were undoubtedly just the right temperature for Mrs. Larsen, a tiny, straight-haired chain-smoking lawyer. When we met, she had recently divorced the aloof, vintage-Jaguar-driving, almost certainly alcoholic Dr. Larsen, a cardiologist who would later teach me how to order (and drink) vodka martinis.

That first year, I must have officially met Olga in concert choir. Like me, she was a soprano. But unlike me, she was a real one. Her Mozartean reach seemed only natural coming from such a long and gorgeous throat. Years later, as a senior, Olga would perform *Laudate Dominum* in the same symphony hall where I'd sat with my grandmother as a child. She won a prestigious singing competition just before graduation and headed off to college at a Midwestern conservatory.

I talked my mother into letting me take lessons with Olga's voice teacher soon after we started hanging out. So did Abby O'Grady. In time I became the spinto to Olga's lyric coloratura. A lesser but sturdier planet in her orbit. My new friend's outsize talent soon relegated me to the second or third chair from the choir director's piano, the better to adore her for being better than me. How fast and how hard I can fall for a woman who is better than me at something, preferably something I aspire to! A year later, we were side by side in the jazz choir, sharing the apron in the musicals, taking the same AP classes. As juniors, we were recruited as dressers for the opera. There, between acts, our job was to lace fleshy older women into their corsets. When that was done, we stole away to the parking garage to drink Baileys and hot chocolate from a thermos in my old Volvo or the new Toyota her father had bought her. I remember her mother's mainly off-limits wagon came with automatic seat belts that magically strapped you in when the door closed, as if to confirm Mrs. Larsen's control over anyone who invaded her glacial, post-Lutheran universe.

I invaded it. On one of my early visits to their house, we stood talking on the threshold with Mrs. Larsen. Olga informed her mother that I had been to New York on the high school drama club trip the previous year. She looked disappointed. And I, thinking it was a chance to show how cultured I was despite my looks, told her all about the backstage tour we'd had at the Met; how a circle in the floor turned like a record. Olga wanted to go on the next trip. And I was going too. A couple of days later she told me something in a manner that, however cruel, felt even then like a lifesaving tip-off. Reconnaissance for future encounters with a certain type of White woman. Mrs. Larsen had called me "pretentious." If you ever wonder what effect you might have on a sensitive young person with the weight of a single word, know that I think of Mrs. Larsen whenever I hear "pretentious." Whenever I wonder if I deserved it then, or if I deserve it now. I don't think I'll ever use that word to describe a woman of color, even if I dislike or resent her.

Did Mrs. Larsen, perhaps, intuit the pretenses under which I was operating with her beautiful daughter? How I ached during those operatic years for Olga's front-seat confessions to transmogrify into touch. To produce a physical intimacy worthy enough to run alongside our psychic kinship always firing on all cylinders – intoxicating but hardly ever hurtfully volatile. I didn't know what I wanted, exactly. Or how to make it happen. But I knew it would start by being alone with her. On a daily basis, I strove to be in Olga's presence whenever I could. My eyes scanned the world around me for that bright orange bag.

The next opera season saw the zenith of our flirtation. Alone together, we would tease and soulfully lament across the gearshift for torturous hours at a time, sharing the same maudlin humor and moodiness of the urbane seventeen-year-old girl who believes herself to be, and probably is, too prematurely jaded for her own good. Through beloved arias and standing ovations at sell-out performances of *Aida* and *Don Giovanni,* we talked around our feelings until we had steamed up the windshield and it was time to scale the underground stairs and strap in the chorus for the next act.

At home, when we were away from each other, I played my record of Kiri Te Kanawa singing one of Olga's least favorite numbers. She thought the song trite, but our voice teacher was no fool. Olga was the perfect girl to sing "O Mio Babbino Caro," the Puccini aria made famous in the Merchant and Ivory film *A Room with a View,* which we saw together as sophomores at our neighborhood indie theater. When *Blue Velvet* came to town and we had grown older and more curious about life's sinister underbelly, we became fanatical David Lynch fans. But that was still a few years off. Olga dated the goalie of the boys' soccer team until he graduated. A BMOC in training, he was a broad, hirsute, drowsy-eyed guy who sang a sardonic bass in our jazz ensemble, drove a motorcycle, and palled around with the governor's son, not the only one of our classmates with a parent elected to public office and a family ranch outside the city.

I carried around *Twenty-Four Italian Songs and Arias* in my new canvas tote bag, but none of them had the words I wanted to say to Olga.

"Vedrai Carina."

After we graduated, approaching the end of the eighties, when Olga went to music school, I, wait-listed at Sarah Lawrence and rejected by Vassar, or possibly the reverse, took what is now optimistically referred to as a gap year. During that unforeseen limbo, I embarked on piano lessons to no good avail, feeling too mature for "Twinkle, Twinkle" and too restless to bang out Hanon scales by the hour. Some days, I rode the city bus to Denver's enormous and excellent downtown library, checking out books about opera and the history of classical music. Some nights, I went to concerts at the symphony hall all by my eighteen-year-old Mulatta self, a pleasure I haven't since taken the initiative, or had the courage, to repeat. I remember the looks I got from some of the old guard during intermission, as if I were a prostitute. When Dame Kiri Te Kanawa, the tawny diva from New Zealand, came to Boettcher Concert Hall for a solo recital, I sat a mere few rows from the stage as she sang one of my favorite arias to drive to on a sunny spring or summer day: "Chi il Bel Sogno" from *La Rondine.* There was something about the elegant blondish singer, a texture and a tone, that felt familiar. Months later, when I discovered the singer's father was Maori and her mother was White, I felt quietly encouraged about my own future. In the spring I was admitted to Lake Forest College, north of Chicago. I'd applied with the declaration to study art. But after sensing that classical music connected me not only to the absent Olga but to something in me struggling to articulate itself about desire and longing (but for which I had no definition yet), I decided to become a musicologist.

I first saw breasts that looked like mine in an eighteenth-century print. I was learning about Sarah Baartman, sometimes referred to as "Saartjie," a nickname from the Dutch-derived South African language of Afrikaans. Baartman (1789–1815) was a South African Khoikhoi woman born in the Eastern Cape. After the father of her child was murdered by Dutch colonizers, she was apparently coerced into traveling to England and later Paris as a "servant." There for the remaining years of her short life she was displayed, nearly nude, as a curiosity on exhibit to paying customers. Billed as the "Hottentot Venus," Sarah performed/was made to perform as a sexual object whose "unnaturally large" buttocks and "pendulous" breasts provided European Whites with an exemplar of the African woman.

Baartman's exploitation and sexual violation came at the height of antislavery and abolitionist campaigns in Europe. In Britain, the act to abolish the transatlantic slave trade was passed in 1807 – though Caribbean slavery under British oversight continued in practice until 1838. Not unrelatedly, Baartman's representation to the public coincided with the print media heyday of scathing political satires and lithographed cartoons by artists such as James Gillray, Thomas Rowlandson, and George Cruikshank, who weren't afraid to amplify and distort the physical features of famous White parliamentarians and even kings and queens. But if what they did to Sarah Baartman seems no different than making fun of King George – or even Queen Charlotte – think again.

The invention of the artistic genre of caricature is often credited to the seventeenth-century Italian polymath Annibale Carracci, an enterprising painter of everything from elaborately classical ceiling frescoes to dynamic Counter-Reformation altarpieces. With its emphasis on features and physiognomy, early caricature was a logical

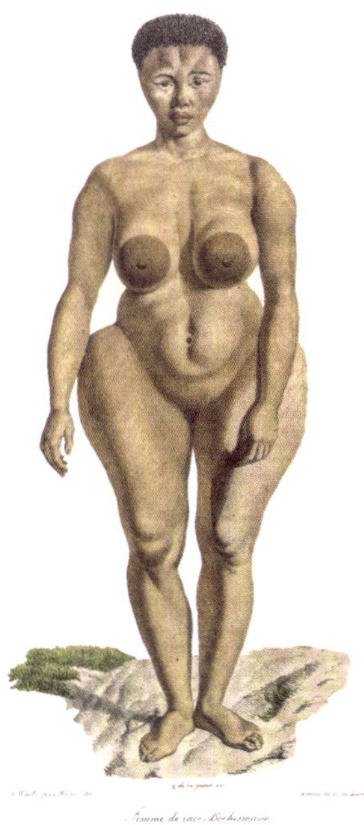

*"Saartjie" Sarah Baartman*, ca. 1790

outgrowth of the enduring genre of portraiture, still largely the purview of members of the nobility and clerics. In the sixteenth and seventeenth centuries, European portraitists devoted considerable attention to the sitter's costly clothing and accessories. But as time wore on, gestures, attitudes, and ultimately the face itself became the measure of a likeness that was true to the subject's essence. Like the Baroque era of its birth, caricature tends to rely on excess and overstatement.

In the minds of those who demeaned and reduced her to so many "exaggerated" body parts, Baartman was made for caricature. And she was certainly unmade by it. Renderings of Sarah Baartman's form by the White male European artists who were her contemporaries seek to rob her of a name and identity while simultaneously positing her as a monstrous exemplar of her race. As the Hottentot Venus, she was proffered not as a particular woman but, parallel to the visual rhetoric of *casta* paintings, as a generalized personification of a race and a gender. In life and in print, she was paraded before prurient audiences as an eager sex object, impervious to verbal and physical violence of any kind. It was comical, wasn't it? The very notion that a "black" or "sable" woman could ever be mistaken for the goddess of love herself.

Widely circulated and relatively inexpensive to obtain, prints of a naked Sarah Baartman were not meant for worship but for titillation. Or, in the guise of education, images of her body were meant to provide evidence for the claims of race science. Baartman's bare breasts and buttocks are nearly always the focal point of such depictions. I was introduced to these indelible visions of a Black woman's body in college. Sitting in a dark classroom of White students, I knew it was somehow treacherous to let my gaze return again and again to those brown breasts. To gauge the space between them and measure it against the inches that separate my own. Yet I couldn't stop myself. The sharp prick, the punctum, of recognition brought me up short. I knew the image was meant to offend. Yet I couldn't help think it might have been documentarily dead-on. Unimaginably unexaggerated.

Sarah's body was unlike anything I'd seen in a painting or an illustration or any kind of moving image. And yet I had seen it before. For my part, I had secret knowledge of Baartman's large areolas, spreading dark as syrup over the tips of her heavy breasts. Of those small, insouciant nipples. But how could I rejoice in that knowledge? Seeing the colored prints projected on the screen made me hunch in my chair for fear that my universally padded sorority sisters would suddenly realize that what they were seeing, what they were laughing at, was me.

—

When I came home from college following my sophomore year, I was an art history major. I had definitely given the musicology thing a go, starting freshman year with a class on the same Mozart symphonies I'd been reading about on my own. It almost seemed destined and should have been a perfect fit. Now, as a professor at a liberal arts college myself, I see how unlikely it was that one of my first college courses should have corresponded so closely on paper to my weirdo imagined academic plan. Throughout fall term, even on weekends, I dutifully checked out stacks of thick black record boxes, hefting them to the basement listening rooms, puffy headset in hand. Alone in my little bunker, I set and reset the needle for each movement of the symphony in G minor, searching for signs of melancholy in its unhinged frenzy of strings. Hours later, I was pleased to be able to identify the responsive woodwinds darting in and out of the horizon like hungry swallows at dusk.

The G minor is one of Mozart's last symphonies, regarded by many as his most interesting. He wrote it only after his uncharacteristically theological and genre-bending *Don Giovanni* crushed it in fun-loving Prague, only to be dismissed and derided in less libertine Vienna. This critical failure left Mozart feeling pretty low. A mature work ahead of its time, his symphony in G minor is often seen to anticipate, if not instantiate, the moody conflictedness of Romanticism, which is probably why I liked it then and relate to it now. A sucker for affect, I've always found comfort in uncategorizable art that mirrors my inexpressible feelings.

After the Mozart course, I signed up for a class in the history of jazz. Here was the same crochety, fedora-wearing, mustachioed old White guy standing before a handful of enrollees tapping out the measures, his tweed blazer sleeves pounced with chalk dust. Professor Crosby. He was great, really. From him I learned about Bix Beiderbecke, Coleman Hawkins, and Sidney Bechet. Bessie Smith and Ma Rainey too. I did well in that class. It helped that I had sung so many standards in high school. Much to Crosby's surprise – though we agreed it was best interpreted by Ella Fitzgerald and Annie Ross – I did a decent a cappella of Duke Ellington's "In a Mellotone." I liked studying music as much as singing it. But despite having taken AP music theory, I did not have the technical chops to go much further academically. Once again, the science or math of a thing had proved to be an obstacle. Olga, who had perfect pitch, scored a 5 when we took the exam. I think I got a 3 for my ear for intervals, which was generous, given that I failed to identify the famous Kabalevsky piece that sounded like a typewriter.

Olga and I didn't stay in contact during those early college years. I knew where her school was, but in an age without cell phones and email, what were we going to do, send letters?

Summers home were when you reconnected with your old

friends. By the end of high school, my infatuation with Olga had become an open secret; no doubt some people felt sorry for me, while others probably considered it "weird" or disgusting. Including both sets of our avowedly liberal parents. Lots of "tolerant" people felt sorry for gays back then. When I came out to my mom and stepdad that summer, seizing on a casual conversational digression about the probable lesbianism of a distant cousin, they reacted with shock and unconcealed disappointment (my mother) and anger (my dad). He assumed he had done something wrong. She said she was only upset because she "didn't want life to be hard" for me. Reactions like that were the hardest part, of course. Given their politics and our relationship, I hadn't expected anything but acceptance and support from my parents.

To be fair, I came out in the era of AIDS and the fierce homophobia that went with it. While I was still in my early twenties, thanks to the virulent reach of our homegrown hate group, Focus on the Family, Colorado was on the fast track to being internationally boycotted as "the Hate State." In 1992, the year I graduated from college, my state's legislature passed Amendment 2, an infamous ballot measure effectively prohibiting the protection of LGB people from discrimination. Six years later, Matthew Shepard, an out gay student at the University of Wyoming, would be beaten, brutalized, and left to die on a fence outside of Laramie, my grandmother's college town. The following year saw the release of Kimberly Peirce's *Boys Don't Cry* (1999), the story of twenty-one-year-old trans man Brandon Teena, raped and murdered in a Nebraska hate crime that had filled all us Western queers with terror when it happened back in 1993. Although *Brokeback Mountain* wasn't released as a film until 2005, Annie Proulx published the Wyoming-based *New Yorker* short story from which it was adapted in the fall of 1997. For the solidarity and bravery and creativity shown against all odds by homosexuals from all walks of life, it was an incomparable decade in which to learn to be gay. It was also a grueling one. Especially for queer people trying to make a life in farm and ranch country between the coasts.

Denver will always be what my grandmother called "a cow town." But it's also a big city in a state that boasts the country's first out gay governor. I'm scarcely more conscious now than I was thirty years ago of precisely how the shaming and the violence and the self-doubt and the fear that come of internalizing these emotions shaped me when I was younger. If we're paying attention to the world around us, feeling unsafe and finding life hard is probably inevitable for those of us who grow up (or grow into being) gay or queer. Or Black or Indigenous or disabled or Asian American or Muslim or female or trans or poor. What doesn't kill you the first time may well try to take you out again, no matter how strong you've become.

My young-adult performance of self was tempered in that hate-state forge. I couldn't always take the pressure. At one point, I went so far as to fabricate a serious, but unnamed, illness. I had fainted during one of our criminally long high school musical rehearsals. The next day the doctor said it was only exhaustion and dehydration from the spotlights and my twenty pounds of petticoats. But I exploited people's sympathy and played the bravely suffering invalid for keeps. My pathological dishonesty haunts me to this day. Because of course the sole intent of my performance was to attract Olga's concern, her attention, her tenderness. In the movies (*Beaches,* 1988; *Steel Magnolias,* 1989), being female while sick was a chance to be cared for by other women, something I got a taste of when my fellow concerned actors had surrounded me backstage. (I wish I'd seen *Desert Hearts* when it first came out in 1985.)

I didn't have much of a moral compass at that age, when so

much wrong was allowed to be right. And I certainly could have used some kick-ass lesbian role models beyond those who fell apart, fell off a cliff, or fell fatally ill, just when they'd finally found someone to love and be loved by (*Personal Best,* 1982; *Thelma and Louise,* 1991; *Fried Green Tomatoes,* 1991). But whatever the reason, I came up with some pretty wicked and soap-operatic strategies for loving another girl and seeing that love openly reciprocated. If someone had told me I was a queer romance writer in the making, I'm sure it would have helped.

As rising college juniors, Olga and I weren't girls anymore. When I came home again late my sophomore year, someone told me she'd started "dancing" just for the hell of it at the one old-school strip club everybody knew by name. Just down the boulevard from Target, it was only a couple of miles from her father's condo.

Something bad, I didn't know what, had happened at the conservatory. Olga's highs were higher when she came back, but her bottom-of-the-well lows were new to me. She didn't live with her mother anymore. I think she mainly slept at her laissez-faire father's bachelor pad, borrowing the black XJ6 to take us to day drink from time to time. Olga's relocation was a relief because her mother had spent the last year of high school informing me, no matter when I called, that her daughter wasn't home. "No, Vanessa. I'm not sure when she'll be back," she would sigh, her hoarse voice laced with disdain.

That summer, though, something was different. After a couple of weeks, Olga abruptly moved again, to Boulder. First, she shared an apartment with her sister, who was living there. But then she decamped to a crappy industrial space on the outskirts of the city. This wasn't Tribeca or Brooklyn. Boulder was in the foothills, as we refer to them, the shallower base of the mountains and open prairie apparent as soon as you drove a few miles away. Olga's new place was in the "sticks," as my grandfather would have called it. The middle of nowhere in the still-too-wild West. In the early nineties, this was not a thing one did. Even if you were a twenty-one-year-old classically trained operatic soprano and part-time stripper with a trust fund.

Home again for winter break, I heard that Olga hadn't gone back to school and was still living (I wonder if it wasn't technically squatting) in her "studio." I drove up to see her. We had dinner at Juanita's on the mall. We went back to her place. It was freezing. She had no kitchen. The bathroom was shared – with whom? – and at the end of an unlit, trash-strewn hallway. Gusts of wind rattled the building's metal siding. Ice-cold air whistled through the floors.

She lit candles. But the place was eerie, and it felt abandoned and scary to be there. Olga helped me with my coat and then she turned me around. Suddenly we were kissing. I was running my tongue across her smooth, perfect teeth, holding her. Feeling her press into me. Wanting nothing else but desperately hoping I would get it.

There have been a handful of times in my life when I have yearned for something impossible, knowing it was impossible, yet have still – intuitively, psychically, what have you – felt certain it will, in some mysterious way, come to pass. My unrepentant desire to be with Olga was like that. I knew how things would go with her the moment I let myself accept my lesbianism. Or maybe it was the reverse. Our friends. Her mother. My parents. None of them. Nobody believed she could possibly feel about me the way I so clearly and inescapably felt about her. And maybe she didn't feel exactly the same way. Maybe whatever happened at school changed Olga so much that her feelings for me had changed too.

She called me "Vivi." No romantic partner since has declared her love so unselfconsciously. Boundlessly. Epically. As if we were star-crossed wartime heroines doomed to come to blows with fate itself. We were barely of legal age. There were hearts and flowers and scarves inherited from her grandmother in Edina. Loopy, page-filling inscriptions in my John Irving paperback. And letters. Later that night on the nail-strewn floor of her horrid little hovel, with my face between her legs, one hand on her small round breast, the other on her goose-bumpy thigh, I found myself listening. Even more than I was tasting or feeling or finding myself surprised by the rough density of her bush, I was listening. Not for an aria but for sounds I'd never heard. The sound of Olga Larsen coming for me. Coming at my touch. Could there be anything more perfect, more blissful? Any better assurance that I wasn't crazy? Take that, Mrs. Larsen, you stuck-up Viking bitch. I wasn't pathetic or delusional or wrong about your otherworldly daughter. This was always going to happen. The two of us were meant to be together. I would have preferred to believe that being passionately loved by her when we became women was the just reward for my youthful constancy. But now my dearest was changing again. That has never stopped me from calling her the love of my life. Vindication is the recompense I value most.

---

Of the many classical depictions of the Roman goddess of love, the *Medici Venus* in Florence surely had the greatest impact on Renaissance artists. According to the Uffizi, where it is housed, the five-foot-high marble statue of a nude woman dates to the period between the second and first century BCE. The artist shows her in what is usually described as a state of surprise, of having been recently "discovered." The woman's reactive posture thus casts the viewer as an intruder, if not a peeping Tom. When I show the statue to students in my intro art history class, I ask how we might characterize the moral implications of her gestures. Is she a good girl or a bad girl? Modest or brazen? Eventually, we arrive at the answer I'm after: Hers is an ambiguous posture, so it's not so easy to say.

Which is itself surprising. Because Venus, or Aphrodite, is the goddess of love, one would expect her to try to seduce the beholder. By this line of reasoning, hands elegantly hovering over her left breast and pudendum (a useful word for undergrads) are meant to draw attention to these regions in an effort to arouse. Look at my breasts! Look at my pussy! Isn't that what you want? However. Putatively invited to explore these erogenous zones, the eye hits the barrier of her intervening appendages and is permitted to go no further. As art historians have often observed, Venus's revealing gesture is also readable as a concealing gesture. Confusion of this sort, with a respectable Greco-Roman pedigree, was tremendously useful to sixteenth- and seventeenth-century artists wishing to imply what many saw as (White) women's inherent Christian-virgin/pagan-prostitute duality. The marmorean rebirth of

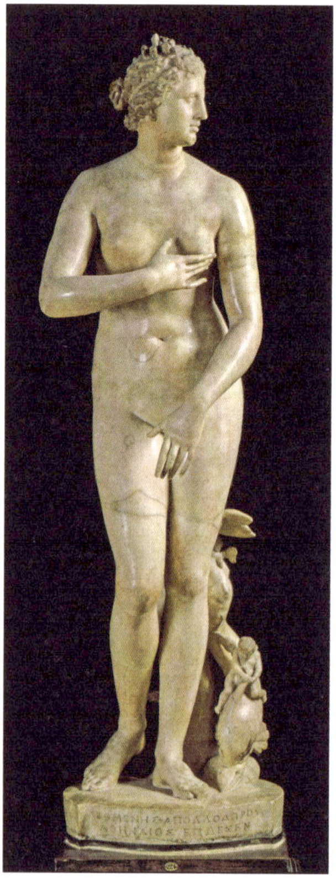

*Medici Venus*, ca. first century BCE

Venus as the ideal form of desirable womanhood is the end of Black beauty.

Although it's a story without a conclusion where Western painting is concerned, it does have a beginning. An important early and obvious case of a Renaissance artist appropriating the statue's composition is the National Gallery's *Venus with a Mirror,* painted by the Venetian Titian Vecellio in 1555. The compositional allusion is subtle. Not only has Titian reversed and gentled the position of the statue's arms (right is now down, left is now up), he has enfolded his goddess in a sumptuous swath of fur-trimmed red velvet that in its shade and substance suggests the qualities of the unseen part of the anatomy it occludes. In other respects, as in sculpture so in painting: Note the hair piled elaborately on a head similarly facing left. Even the tiny "Cupid" from the Florentine sculpture reappears in Titian's canvas, now child-sized and poised to crown his vain/modest mother with a garland of flowers.

A century later, no artist was more in Titian's debt than the cosmopolitan Fleming (Belgian) Peter Paul Rubens, an erudite artist if ever there was one. Rubens spoke at least five languages and preferred to write his letters in Italian. He was inconceivably well read, caught up on the latest science and philosophy, devoutly Catholic, and the artist of choice of powerful women sovereigns. Notably, his two most inventive large-scale programs (the Medici Cycle in Paris and the Eucharist tapestries in Madrid) were commissioned by art-loving female rulers. Even now, Rubens is dismissed as a vulgar specialist in "fat women." In any age, there is nothing wrong with representing women who defy today's anemic White mainstream beauty standards, which, importantly, did not exist in plague- and famine-besieged seventeenth-century Europe. More interestingly, however, Rubens's employment of the female form is far more subversive and sophisticated than he's

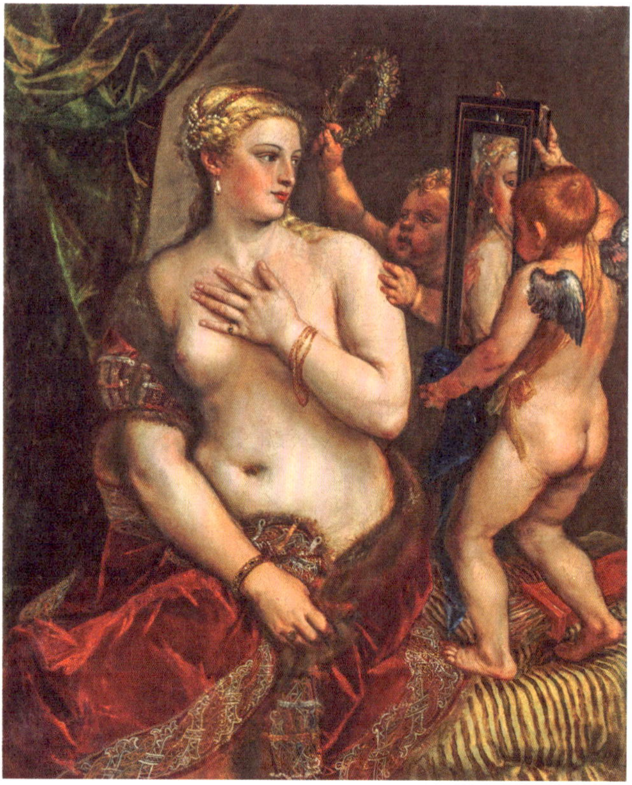

Titian, *Venus with a Mirror*, 1555, National Gallery of Art, Washington, DC

often given credit for by the many sexist, chauvinistic, and fat-phobic critics who write about his work. Like Titian before him (and Mozart, too, for that matter), Rubens tended to make art about art, both his own previous works and those that preceded them. His art is intended for an audience as well versed as he was. When he approaches a canonical subject or theme, he wants the viewer to see that he knows what's come before; and now he has superseded it.

Rubens's *Venus at the Mirror* is therefore a clever double take. First, on the original Greco-Roman sculpture. Second, on Renaissance painters' return to classical ideals. Innovative as it is, his version is self-consciously in dialogue with well-known earlier treatments of the mythological subject. Even his decision to show Venus from behind is based on yet another Titian – one where she clings to her lover Adonis. Rubens juxtaposes this Titianesque rear view of the goddess with a frontal view of the beveled mirror she faces, her head and truncated arms suggesting that the position of her unseen hands could, if they existed, approximate that of the Hellenistic statue. It's an inventively backward-looking and composite style of seventeenth-century Netherlandish "modern art," now known as Baroque.

At the height of the prudish Catholic Counter-Reformation, Rubens's painting seeks to deflect the viewer from what is already not on view, namely Venus's breasts as well as her hips and what is between them. In the case of a female beholder, as several of Rubens's patrons were, we look at the goddess, who is also a woman, looking at herself – as beautiful women are wont to do. Yet to take Rubens's conceit at even its surface level, Venus is not all we see, and we are not the only ones who see her.

There is a major development in Rubens's version of Venus, one without an obvious artistic source or precedent. Can you tell what it is? If you took seriously, or even noticed, the replacement of a White putto with a Black woman, you're ahead of many specialist art historians. Hence the painting's centuries-long designation as merely "Venus in Front of the Mirror," the title that currently appears on the website of the Liechtenstein Collections where the painting is on view. In fact, the Vienna museum's extended description does not mention the presence of a Black woman at all.

Which is odd because, according to the painting's internal logic, she has access to the goddess in a way that we on the out-

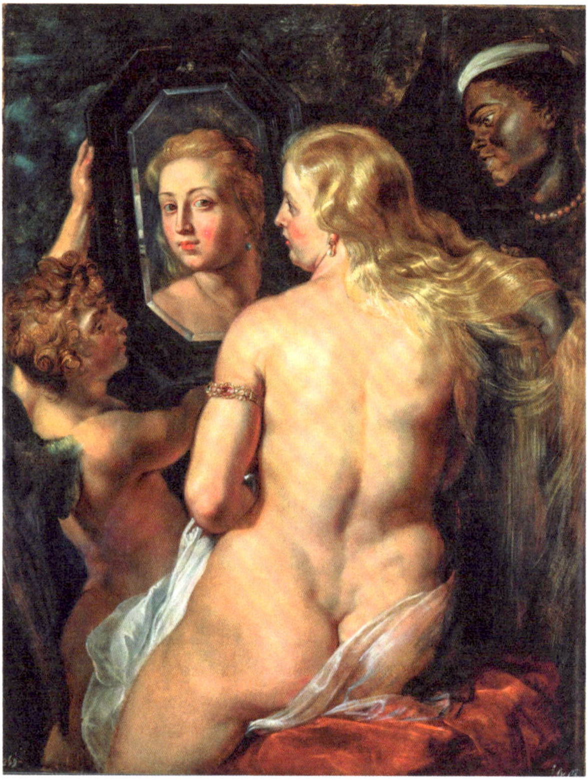

Peter Paul Rubens, *Venus and a Black Woman with Cupid Holding a Mirror* (author's title), ca. 1614–15

side never will. The Black woman alone is permitted the sight of Venus's naked beauty – both through a looking glass and face-to-face. The Black woman is also permitted to finger Venus's golden hair, skeins of which both envelop and visually crop her strangely massive hands, tethering her to the goddess's side. Here, as in a relatively small number of Renaissance paintings (see, again, Titian), a dark-skinned figure is intended to serve as a foil to the radiantly, chromatically White woman with whom she is paired, usually in what is understood to be a servile role. In the second decade of the seventeenth century, the transatlantic slave trade was at an early but active stage that included the Netherlands. It is not wrong to conjecture that, in the worst sense, Rubens has imagined the Black woman as an anti-Venus. That he has presented her attending the White woman as a slave to beauty.

In a catalogue essay from the 2008 Dutch exhibition *Black Is Beautiful,* an attempt was made to rename Rubens's painting the "Venus of the Night." Frustrated with the overt racism of so many early modern depictions of "Blacks" in the Netherlands, noted Rubens scholar Elizabeth McGrath encouraged museumgoers to recognize the ability of seventeenth-century artists like Rubens to produce "African images of real power and beauty." In her opinion, the Black woman as a personification of Night could, given Venus's love of things nocturnal, be considered as more a companion and "less straightforwardly a servant." Because she is so novel, she might, it was suggested, even transcend the confining contrast of "mistress/servant, white/black."

I love this idea, of course. The Black woman as Venus's significant other and equal – can we say inamorata? – running her fingers through her beloved's hair as they get ready to go out together, secretly alive to each other's presence in a manner they cannot be in public. But as far as I know, these are my fantasies, not McGrath's and, sadly, not Rubens's. The art historian intriguingly centers a figure formally marginalized by the artist. Her multicultural wishing for equality doesn't make it so, but at least she considers the represented Black woman a subject worthy of study.

One mustn't confuse representation with respect. Nor does the fact that Rubens seems to have viewed Whites as supreme mean he didn't find beauty in some Black bodies. Just as finding beauty in some Black bodies doesn't excuse him for using race to suggest where a figure or a character falls on the moral spectrum. In my own art histories, I've tried to push back on a trend in which White writers promote dangerously and anachronously post-racial magical thinking about Black figures created by artists for the consumption of cultures directly complicit in the slave trade.

However beautiful, no one would be less likely to model "real power" than an African woman in a Northern European city like Rubens's Antwerp. The Habsburg colony that was the Catholic Spanish Netherlands did not allow its citizens to keep slaves. But in the previous century Antwerp had rivaled Lisbon as a slave market, and the many wealthy Spanish and Portuguese who lived and traded there often owned slaves. For this population a perceived hierarchy of races provided a rationale for buying and selling the men, women, and children who occupied the lowest rung of a divinely ordained social and ontological ladder. In a nutshell, it would have been difficult for Rubens's contemporaries in Flanders not to equate Blackness with servility, if not enslavement—the notion of a Black Venus was already becoming an oxymoron, an impossibility, a joke.

That said, little is known of Rubens's views on race. Given the painterly attention he pays to Venus's straight and scintillating golden hair, one of his few known remarks on the subject may be useful. In speaking of Ethiopians, then a blanket term for Black Africans, Rubens dog-whistled that "excessively woolly hair betokens cowardice." There are no other relevant mentions of racial characteristics in the artist's extensive correspondence. But Rubens's scientific and artistic interests in color as both pigment and connotation are still possible to interpret in racial terms. Color was on Rubens's mind in the decade he made the painting I am hereby rechristening *Venus and a Black Woman with Cupid Holding a Mirror*. Together with his friend, the Belgian Jesuit François

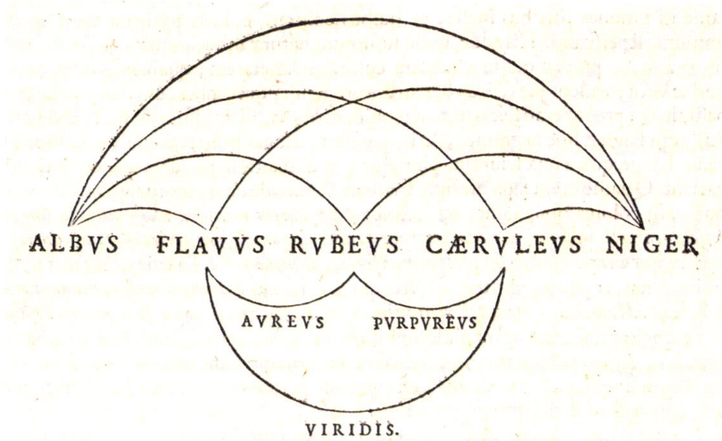


Aguilonius, Color Diagram, *Opticorum Libra Sex*, 1613

d'Aguilon, he had been at work on a Latin treatise called the *Six Books of Optics,* for which the artist provided complicated allegorical enactments of the mathematician's various theories. When the book was published in 1613, it was quickly recognized as a major contribution to the new science of color. In it, the author provides what Martin Kemp has called "the definitive version of the color scales." Simply put, it is largely to D'Aguilon, or Aguilonius as he preferred to be known, that we owe the concept of primary and composite, or secondary, colors. To explain how some colors can be mixed to create others, Aguilonius includes a simple diagram, positioning white (Albus) and black (Niger) opposite each other, with yellow, red, and blue between them, and the composite colors of orange, purple, and green below. It seems entirely likely, as Kemp and others suggest, that where color was concerned, Aguilonius learned as much from Rubens, who was known as a colorist par excellence, as Rubens learned from him. We can assume that Rubens agreed with his friend's theoretical claims, or he would not have contributed his own drawings to a treatise on matters central to his profession. Of the relationship between "opposites," the Jesuit author writes: "Among the primary colors the two having extreme positions are whiteness and blackness, they are maximally separated: of them whiteness is superior, it is similar to light; black is truly inferior, being near to darkness."

---

FURTHER READING

Chase-Riboud, Barbara. *Hottentot Venus: A Novel.* Doubleday, 2003.

6

# A PRAYER FOR OLGA LARSEN

When I next left Denver, during my college years, it was to fly to Italy for a semester abroad in Florence. I had never been to Europe, and I approached the adventure the way I approach everything: I researched the hell out of it, read the reviews, and tried to become as expert on the place as I could long before I arrived there. (I had already undertaken an Italian tutorial with the one Black faculty member, a German professor, I studied with in college.) My primary sources were Mary McCarthy's Baedeker of 1959, *The Stones of Florence* (a gift for the trip from my oldest friend Caitlin's Boston Irish mother), and the *Lonely Planet* guide to Italy – or maybe Europe – treasured and savagely dog-eared for its radical (for the time) inclusion of gay clubs and bars. Once in country, committing to memory the descriptions of such places from the flashlit privacy of a hostel bunk bed never failed to leave me feeling anticipatorily brave and deviant.

Keep in mind that travel was very different in the early 1990s, and European hotel reservations were generally made months in advance, often by agents, via expensive international telephone calls, if not by fax or written correspondence. Beyond and even in the big cities, Italians didn't always speak, or choose to speak,

English with Americans. A female college student, especially a brown one, traveling alone was looked upon by many Europeans with incredulousness if not open antagonism. Northern Italy was especially conservative at the time (as it is now).

Had I known this, I might have thought twice about reserving a single room in a pensione in Vicenza, a small bourgeois city about an hour from Venice that struck me as a good place to audition my Italian. I booked a flight into Milan and planned to arrive by train. I envisioned spending a few days taking in the architecture and legally drinking copious amounts of alcohol, before heading down to Florence to meet my nearly all-girl group of fellow juniors from various other member schools of the Associated Colleges of the Midwest.

I knew all about Vicenza from David Brinkley. Yes, David Brinkley the august anchorman. He and his wife, a dead ringer for Catherine Deneuve, were good friends of the remarried, DC-based father of Frances, a girl in whose company I spent much of my senior year of high school. Although Olga was my North Star, I was part of a large circle of outgoing girls in those years; it was also a time when parents not infrequently left their kids on their own. Frances had a mother who traveled internationally, and her daughter was often home alone – or would have been. Had we lived in New England about a century earlier, our arrangement would probably have been regarded as a Boston marriage.

Frances (or so I'm calling her). Granddaughter of a revered jurist and herself a future judge. I thought I knew WASPs after Emily became my friend, but Emily, Emma, and even Olga had nothing on Frances. Like Olga, she had attended private school before being folded into the batter of our public institution for urban finishing. Even prior to that, however, chestnut-haired, square-faced Frances – Frances of the retrievers and private dock in Maine – had done her time at Foxcroft. She'd taken me to see that horsey Virginia campus when we visited her father and stepmother on the way to our nanny jobs in Newport one summer. Frances with her quilted Pierre Deux bags and Liberty of London scarves and furtive Marlboros and tedious George Winston tapes. Frances of the Sunday-morning mimosas at the glass-topped table in her backyard. She is the one confidently ferrying her employer's new Range Rover up the coast to Rhode Island while I tailgate in mine's battleship of a silver Mercedes. I taught myself to make hollandaise sauce in Frances's kitchen. If she'd asked me to marry her at age seventeen, I would have said yes, though I'm glad she didn't.

We slept together under duvets heaped on her mother's puritanical four-poster bed. Our legs never so much as touched beneath those richly patterned coverlets; we never fooled around, never even kissed. But when her mother was on the road, I loved spending weekends at Frances's house in another nice neighborhood across town. I see now that we were training ourselves to be grown-ups based on what our parents watched on public television. Absent a murder to solve, we'd putter around like two old dykes, buying thick slices of pâté, drinking wine, and renting movies at the video store. Some weekends we held rehearsals at Frances's house for plays we were directing in drama class before driving to the boys' lacrosse games. Frances steadily dated at least one guy that year, as far as I can remember. She wasn't merely an ersatz Olga for me either. Frances was blazingly smart – too good at debate and forceful of opinion (she had a regrettable Ayn Rand phase) for most of the good-looking but dull boys at our school. From sophomore year on, she was effortlessly on track for Harvard, but really, Harvard Law, after which she went on to clerk at, shall we say, a very high level.

But none of that had happened yet when her stepmother, a

Georgetown socialite, invited the Brinkleys to dinner while Frances and I were passing through Washington. The eagle-faced anchor was getting up there in years even then, and honestly, what I remember most, aside from his slight Southern drawl and crepey pink jowls, is the sheerness of the crisp white summer pants he wore and the unavoidable outline of his briefs underneath. We didn't get to talk much. After an appetizer that seemed the height of sophistication, boiled new potatoes with crème fraîche and salmon roe, we were treated to the newsman's interminable Vicenza slide show. The Brinkleys, it seemed, had recently done Italy. He and Frances's dad shared a fascination with the architect Andrea Palladio, by every definition a Renaissance man. Palladio's buildings are ubiquitous in the Veneto, where several of his proto-Baroque villas can be found. Frances and I sat pressed close on a chintz-covered love seat for what seemed like hours while Brinkley narrated carousel after carousel of his joyless photographs of thermal windows and Roman arches and Corinthian – or arguably composite! – orders as if he were the first to discover some of the most reliable inclusions in any introduction to art history.

And now, here I was, sitting with a tall vodka *con tonico,* facing Palladio's basilica in Vicenza's exquisite town square. The next day there was a mishap with an overflowing shower – I flooded my sloping scagliola-floored room and rather than calling someone, chose to mop up the water myself with anything dry I could lay hands on, including the bedspread. Otherwise, my first Italian experience was *perfetto.* I was E. M. Forster's Lucy without a tiresome chaperone to slow me down. When I arrived in Florence four days later, having navigated the *stazione* and the strikes and the men, I felt worldly. (And I acted like it too, ordering *cappuccini* and *stracciatella,* superfluously gesturing to storekeepers with a blazer rakishly draped over my shoulders, that kind of thing.)

The second week in Italy, I received a thin red-and-blue-edged envelope from the States. It was a love letter from Olga.

---

There is a generally ignored relationship between Rubens's *Venus and a Black Woman with Cupid Holding a Mirror* of 1614–15 and a work that remains for many the most emblematic painting of the nineteenth century. Édouard Manet's *Olympia,* executed in 1863, shown in Paris in 1865, shares with Rubens's mythological subject/s the pairing of a White woman and a Black woman in an intimate, boudoir-like setting. Until recently, as is the case with the Baroque painting, most art historians, self-proclaimed feminists included, have generally ignored the Black woman standing at Olympia's side. If mentioned, she is mainly anonymized as the servant or "Olympia's" maid.

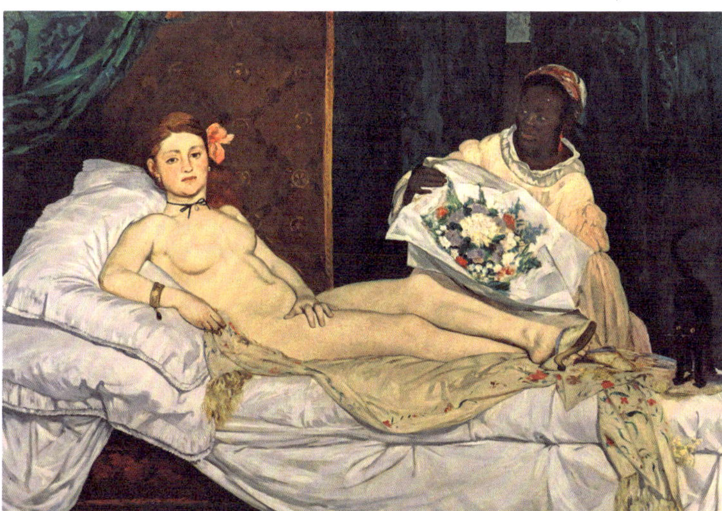

Édouard Manet, *Olympia,* 1863, Musée d'Orsay

Like her predecessor at Venus's side, she is cropped by Manet—though hardly marginalized. Yet as Jennifer DeVere Brody has observed, scholars who consider her at all have tended to classify the Black figure in Manet's painting as an accessory. For them, she is not a woman but simply "the Negress." When, at the end of the first quarter of the twenty-first century, I introduce my students to canonical (and still widely assigned) scholarship about Manet and *Olympia,* they're shocked by what they perceive as its overt racism, the authors' unapologetic unwillingness to carefully consider the splendidly rendered Black figure who takes up nearly half of the canvas.

For my part, I can't stop thinking about Manet putting these women together in that Parisian bedroom the same year President Abraham Lincoln issued the five-page Emancipation Proclamation, written in ink and tied up in red-and-blue ribbons under

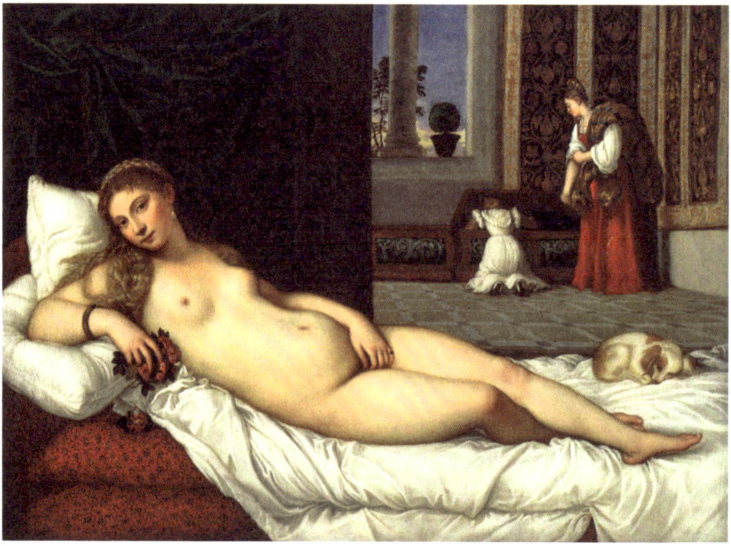

Titian, *Venus of Urbino,* ca. 1518

the US seal. As the National Archives summarizes it, the Proclamation declares that "all persons held as slaves" in seceded, rebel states were, from that day forward – January 1, 1863 – to be free.

Unlike his fellow Post/Impressionist, Edgar Degas, who had close familial, proslavery connections in New Orleans, Manet spent no time in the American South. Which makes it all the more fascinating that he was acutely aware of the battle over slavery unfolding across and beyond the Atlantic. We know this because Manet witnessed an episode of the US Civil War while it was happening. In France.

In 2003, the year before I leave Colorado to begin UC Berkeley's doctoral program in the history of art, where I will find myself in the same department as Manet specialists Darcy Grimaldo Grigsby and T. J. Clark, the Metropolitan Museum of Art produces an odd little exhibition. The museum's presumably donor-driven show is given the deceptively wide-reaching title *Manet and the American Civil War,* a piece of dishonest advertising for sure. In truth, it is an exhibition with a slim but richly illustrated, eighty-six-page catalogue devoted to a set of wildly out-of-character marine paintings and related drawings and sketches executed by Manet in France roughly between 1864 and 1868.

This wasn't the first time Manet had gone to sea. In an eye-opening bit of historicizing on and around *Olympia,* Brody cites a passage of the artist's correspondence that has since become the touchstone for his immature thoughts about Black women. In 1849, in hopes of passing naval officers' exams, the teenage Manet joined a merchant marine ship headed to Brazil as a sort of naval intern. While in Rio de Janeiro, he took in a slave market, "a rather revolting spectacle," where women and children were presumably being sold like other household objects to the highest bidder. The Negresses, he opined, "are usually ugly, though I have seen some rather pretty ones." For this pampered youth, the workings of slavery were, in other words, *rather* (*assez*) revolting, while enslaved women, some anyway, could be *rather* pretty. Black but beautiful.

By the mid-1860s, nearly two decades later and after he had finished *Olympia,* Manet felt the urge to return to the beach. This time, he ventured no farther than the coastal resort of Boulogne, where he painted what would be for him a rare suite of seascapes. It was time for a change. The painter had bombed at the official Salon of 1863. All three of his submissions, notably including the upsettingly flat and topically indecipherable *Luncheon on the Grass* (*Déjeuner sur L'herbe*), had been rejected by the jury. In response, Manet and a notorious group of other well-established artists, among them the American James McNeill Whistler, took the party elsewhere, effectively showing their work in the gallery next door. Their massive counter-exhibition was known as the *Salon des Refusés.* There, too, Manet and his revolutionary recent paintings were almost unanimously denounced in reviews and cartoons by critics as well as the public at large. Looking ahead to the next biennial Salon, the painter appears to have done what we often do when the reviews aren't good: He decided to go back to the basics.

As the authors of the Met catalogue, Manet specialist Juliet Wilson-Bareau and David C. Degener, explain in fascinating detail, the artist decamping to the seaside suddenly found himself in the wake of a decisive battle at sea. Far from the Mason-Dixon Line, it seemed the war over slavery was also being fought in France's neutral waters in the English Channel. Remarkably, Manet was unexpectedly and ideally situated to paint a previously unexplored dimension of Franco-American modern life.

I was astonished to learn that the US Civil War was waged as far from the mainland as the waters off Cherbourg, in Normandy, about 220 miles from Paris. As Wilson-Bareau and Degener relate, the USS *Kearsarge,* a Union warship under the command of Captain John Winslow, was sent abroad to destroy an approaching Confederate raider, the CSS *Alabama.* At the time, the *Alabama*'s captain, Raphael Semmes, was credited with burning or sinking dozens of Union ships and was therefore a serious threat to the steamship *Kearsarge* at a turning point in the Civil War. According to law, neither vessel was allowed to dock in the French port for longer than twenty-four hours. Adhering to this regulation caused an elaborate nautical dance to ensue. Each ship moved in and out of the calmer marine "roads" outside Cherbourg, Semmes claiming to need to come ashore for repairs, and Winslow biding his time. Eventually, on Sunday, June 19, 1864, the *Kearsarge* found a window and fired on the *Alabama.* The Confederate ship went down in a matter of minutes. In the absence of an intact mast, the Confederate Semmes (who may have misleadingly flown British colors until the very last minute) struggled to raise a white surrender flag.

According to the catalogue, there is no definitive documentary evidence that Manet visited Cherbourg, which is several hours down the coast from Boulogne. But whether or not he was an eyewitness from the water, as Proust's nephew had claimed, Manet began his studies for a painted representation of the naval battle soon after it occurred. From the comfort of his studio in the capital, he began and quickly completed a painting of the Union victory at sea. Far from a Titianesque reverie or an androgynous Victorine in drag, Manet's new work was intended as a respectable, subtly political, representation of an internationally significant current event — of a war story broadly reported in England as well as France. All eyes were on the *Kearsarge* as the dark destroyer of the rebel "pirate" ship *Alabama.*

Given the subject, it is an unexpectedly quiet, even somber painting, though not an unattractive one. Manet's harmonious gray-green palette is more evocative of porcelain glazes than a war zone. I am always moved by the way he puts paint on canvas. The manner in which the artist defamiliarizes a transparent vase of camellias or a style of Japanese prints or the sheen of silken hose on a well-turned calf. Thickly or thinly. In a screech of coal black or a patchwork of contrasting daubs. I can look at his waxen peonies, luminous in shades of yellow and green and gray and scarcely

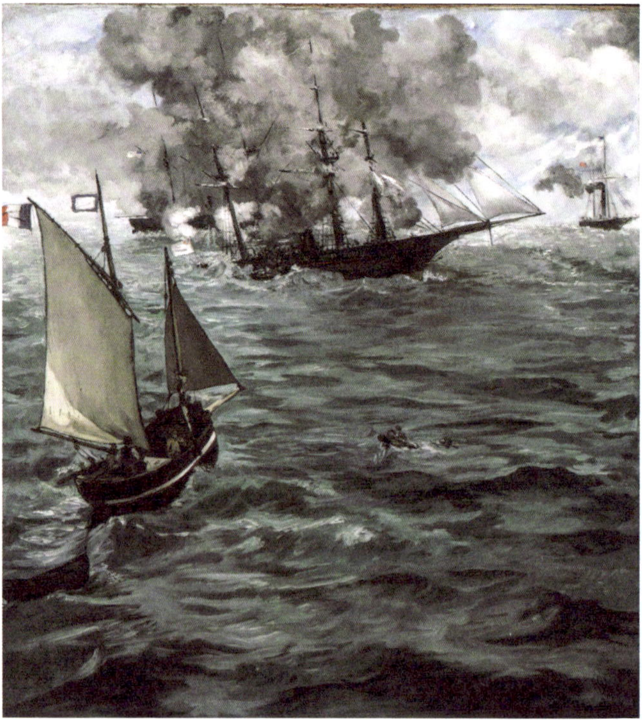

Édouard Manet, *The Battle of the "Kearsarge" and the "Alabama,"* 1864

any white at all, for hours. Voluptuous flowers and cross-dressed women are one thing, leaden sinking ships are quite another. Because Manet is the painter he is, I am captivated by these military vessels, the unlikeliest of his contemporary subjects.

In all but its gestural execution, in fact, the *Kearsarge* painting is rather old-fashioned. Among many similar ship paintings in the Louvre, Wilson-Bareau discovered a persuasive late Dutch Baroque model dating from 1690. Such earlier marine paintings were often executed by specialists in the genre — painters with a talent for making the wins and losses more obvious. In comparison, Manet's is a queer version of history no matter how seriously it takes itself — like me proudly donning a cheap Victorian Disneyland hat for the bus ride back through LA with my grandfather, unable to figure out why the California girls were sneering and laughing.

It may purport to report. But if Manet wanted his Civil War painting to come off as compelling journalism, he failed. Why, for example, is the jauntily white-striped French rescue boat in the foreground the star of the show? Why is the relatively small craft's foreshortened, partially sunlit sail afforded such centrality? If, as the Met catalogue contends, Manet might simply "have liked the idea of an anonymous protagonist who occupies the foreground," to what end? And if so, have we seen this compositional affinity in other works? Because it's true, the rescue boat's dominance means we can barely discern the outline of the mighty United States Ship *Kearsarge,* already eclipsed by the vanquished Southern man-of-war. Manet has made the supporting actors (the distant boat in the upper right will rescue the Confederate captain and crew and take them back to England) far more visually interesting than the downed *Alabama* or the heroic but scarcely visible *Kearsarge*. I will admit the fated Confederate ship does look appropriately sinister (and Turner-like) with its needle nose, spiderwebby rigging, and spindly masts engulfed by black clouds as it plunges, stern first, into the deep. But is this the moment when ominous cannon smoke erupts suddenly from walls of choppy water? Or is it simply the part where layers of patinated turquoise meet thickly laid passages of black?

Olga sent me several letters while I was in Florence. She had been there too. There was always that music between us. If it wasn't the arias, it was the operatic feeling of being destined for no good end, simply because we were two young women in love with each other in a time when that wasn't okay. Before I left, she gave me her copy of *A Prayer for Owen Meany.* The book (like James Taylor's "Sun on the Moon," Rickie Lee Jones's "The Horses," and Bobby McFerrin's entire *Medicine Music* album) was our shared language. We talked to each other through the apocryphal references and fateful plot of that book. She liked Irving's dry, patrician humor and maybe, it occurs to me now, the idea that there is a purpose, even a meaningful destiny, for misfits. For people who are tragically ill at ease in this world. For shining, brave, wise, and gifted children who haven't been warned what's out there or what's coming. I liked the novel for its run-of-the-mill mysticism, coded as Episcopalian, the denomination of Protestantism I call my own.

It's a book about providence. When I came home to Denver the next summer, we spent time together, but not as much as I wanted. She was still in Boulder and I was waiting tables, and after, going out with my restaurant friends to the gay club under the viaduct. Falling asleep on my parents' sofa in my work clothes because upstairs was too far to go to pass out. Waking before they did, creeping up to my bed to sleep until noon, and doing it all over again. But the distance between Olga and me was more than miles or schedules. She was becoming flighty, excitable, hard to pin down. I had always loved her spontaneity and wanted to think this was that. But it wasn't. Sometimes now she wasn't where she said she'd be. She canceled plans. And when we were together in public, she signaled the desire for intimacy but wouldn't always allow it when we were finally alone. I packed us a picnic for Tracy Chapman at Red Rocks. But she wouldn't eat the turkey croissant sandwiches. And she wouldn't drink the ingeniously smuggled-in wine. She held my hand as we stood on our rocky ledge of a seat bravely swaying together for "Baby Can I Hold You." I thought: It will never be better than this.

*Years gone by and still.*

It wasn't until several years after college that I saw Olga regularly again. I'd graduated from the North Shore to the big city of Chicago, working at a bookstore, then an auction house, before I moved back home. Soon after I returned, we were back in touch. Wonderful Wednesdays. Dr. Larsen had wisely concocted a way to see his daughters – Olga and her sister, recently out of college – on a regular basis. He hosted a standing dinner to which I was always welcome, at a very good restaurant about five blocks from my new apartment.

Dr. Larsen was a circumspect man with a molten hot intensity that flashed terrifyingly to the surface on more than one occasion. He worked at a high level in various institutions, I never knew exactly what kind. He had an Alan Arkin quality, like a man portraying a spy who is super fucked-up in ways you'll never know. But who is still very good at his job and so you trust him. Even though he drinks. The two of us would order dry vodka martinis with dinner, then another with dessert; Dr. Larsen welcomed a partner in crime. His girls uniformly abstained. After we ate, Olga and I would sometimes go back to my place and talk. But not often. Sometimes in the middle of dessert she would get up from the table and inform us that she had to be somewhere. She'd leave me there with her sister and her father, as we all shared a knowing, embarrassed laugh. As we pretended that this was typical atypical behavior when we were each beginning to know better.

A mutual high school friend who had stayed close to Olga when she first got to the conservatory – when she and I were not yet romantically together – told me this: There had been a night in an office with a teacher. Someone she respected and cared about. A mentor. A genius. A maker and breaker of futures. Something had gone very wrong between them. After that she'd started stripping. After that she'd seemed less and less like herself. After that she'd fallen in love with me.

Manet's political outlooks are not easy to determine with certainty. Though an avowed republican and anti-Bonapartist, he may not have been as activist as some of his admirers would have liked. The historian Philip Nord has described him – citing the teenage distaste for Brazilian slavery voiced in that single line of Manet's letter from Rio – as an abolitionist. In fact, this letter was at least as much about the relative physical beauty of Negresses and (non-Black) Brazilian women as it was about the morality of slavery. In service of his claim, the historian also nuances Manet's words, for which Darcy Grigsby provides the original French: "*C'est un spectacle assez révoltant pour nous*" (she translates "assez" as "somewhat," while I prefer "rather"). Nord alters Manet's (rather) blasé qualification: "a rather revolting spectacle" to, in his more affronted translation, "a spectacle, utterly revolting to us." Nor does Nord provide the passages preceding and following Manet's comments about slavery, quoted at length in Brody:

> In this country, all the Negroes are slaves; they all look downtrodden; it's extraordinary what power whites have over them; I saw a slave market, a rather revolting spectacle for people like us. The Negresses are generally naked to the waist, some with a scarf tied at the neck . . . they are usually ugly, though I have seen some rather pretty ones . . . Most Brazilian women are very pretty; they have superb dark eyes and hair to match . . . they never go out alone but are always followed by their black maid or accompanied by their children.

Enslaved or not, it is how these women look that matters most to the young Manet. Indeed, who can say if Manet the artist wasn't more revolted by the sight of naked ("ugly") Negresses – their breasts and their bellies on view – than by the commodification of human beings. Still, following Nord's logic, it seems accurate, given the arrival in 1867 of Manet's most overtly political painting, *The Execution of Emperor Maximillian,* to see that painting, along with *The Battle of the "Kearsarge" and the "Alabama"* of 1864, as critiques of current Bonapartist policies. Where the US Civil War was concerned, France's Napoleon III and the Bonapartists were pro-Confederate South and Manet's republicans were pro-Union North. It only makes sense to read Manet's muted marine battle scene as a form of abolitionist propaganda, albeit a super subtle one. Yet in the Met's catalogue, the conditions of bought and sold Black people in Confederate states like, say, Alabama seem to be irrelevant to a museum exhibition about "the American Civil War." The reason for the conflict between the states is only mentioned on the fly, with typical art historical hedging and obliquity: "Manet may also have shared the opposition's awareness that the basic issue in the American Civil War was slavery. The sixteen-year-old Manet had seen slavery in Rio in 1849 and disliked it."

From "utterly" revolted, to "somewhat" revolted to "disliked." Manet "disliked" slavery. Perhaps he "unliked" slavery.

Did he unlike slavery enough to make a painting deriding it? I'm still unsure. But I do believe we need to keep thinking about Manet's nautical side. In the first place, he painted the USS *Kearsarge* at least three more times. As the catalogue relates, in late summer of 1864, as luck would have it, the ship docked several times in Boulogne, where the artist was vacationing. Manet may even have boarded the *Kearsarge* at some point. As if to make up for its near absence in the battle scene, he painted a giant oil portrait of the American steamship at anchor, also in 1864. By then the ship had become a tourist destination, something of an American celebrity. A sleek but massive sloop with a distinctively sharp profile, the color of the *Kearsarge* was unusual. According to Wilson-Bareau and Degener, unlike most gray-blue Federal vessels, the ship was painted glossy black. And not only before it set sail, but frequently mid-cruise. During its prime, the USS *Kearsarge* was affectionately known as "the Stovepipe Black cruiser of the Isle" as well as "the Black Spirit of the Western Isles."

As Grigsby is keen to note, Manet once described Laure, the model who appears in *Olympia*, as a "very beautiful negress." The art historian finds this an important contrast with the more typical White supremacist view of Black as inherently ugly. Personally, I don't give a good goddamn whether Manet thought Laure, as a possible exception to the racist rule, was beautiful. I don't find her face "clumsy" in the studies the artist made in 1862–63. And I have never been one of the "we" who read the standing and formally prominent figure of Laure in the painting as Manet's idea of a "subservient foil."

I am not dismissing the obvious pictorial binaries in Manet's paintings. Far from it. As in *Olympia,* there is a rhythmic play of unmediated contrast and chiaroscuro in Manet's equivocal Civil War canvas. In formal terms, the chromatic push and pull between the *Kearsarge* and the *Alabama* mainly plays out between blacks and whites. Whatever suspense there might be is activated by the advancing rescue boat and the half-sunk Confederate raider. Here and elsewhere, counterpoint is a structural principle for Manet. I find myself viewing the French painter's peculiar mid-century battle at sea as a (more interdependently Hegelian) rejoinder to Grigsby's provocation – that Laure serves *Olympia*'s beholders as a reminder of French colonization of Blacks in places like Haiti. Regardless of their intent, such readings reduce the Black woman to an ahistorical embodiment of slavery and universalized subjection (France permanently abolished slavery in 1848) in a manner that I, personally, do not believe the painting or its creator suggests. Which is not to say that *Olympia*'s mise-en-scène doesn't prefigure, for example, the bedroom homosociality of the famous "fiddle-dee-dee" scene in *Gone with the Wind* (1939), where a head-wrapped Mammy dresses Scarlett after carrying in her breakfast tray.

Might we, then, read the lightly bellicose *"Kearsarge" and the "Alabama"* as another sort of Creole allegory? As a Frenchified and painterly abstraction of a brazen American Southern belle – a fallen enslaver – in deserved decline? *Recline.* Only to be attended by the picture's unignorably upright, black-bottomed protagonist—whose contrasting screen of sails might be compared to the angular white surfaces of Laure's proffered bouquet. Dark and light in eternal engagement. If representation is not always positive, neither is Blackness always negative; like so many artists, Manet would be lost without it.

---

FURTHER READING

Brody, Jennifer Devere. "Black Cat Fever: Manifestations of Manet's Olympia." *Theatre Journal* 53, no. 1 (2001): 95–118.

Grigsby, Darcy Grimaldo. "Still Thinking About Olympia's Maid." *Art Bulletin* 97, no. 4 (December 2015): 430–51.

Nord, Philip. "Manet and Radical Politics." *The Journal of Interdisciplinary History* 19, no. 3 (Winter 1989): 447–80.

O'Grady, Lorraine. "Olympia's Maid: Reclaiming Black Female Subjectivity." 1992, 1994. Reprint, Routledge, 2003.

Wilson-Bareau, Juliet, with David C. Degener. *Manet and the American Civil War: The Battle of U.S.S. Kearsarge and C.S.S. Alabama.* Metropolitan Museum of Art, 2003.

7

# COTTON TALES

"Tu'n me loose, fo' I kick the natal stuffin' outen you," sez Brer Rabbit, sezee, but de Tar-Baby, she ain't sayin' nuthin.

— JOEL CHANDLER HARRIS, "The Tar-Baby," 1881

Now the stupid rabbit becomes the clever one, pretending that the punishment he fears most is being returned to his own neighborhood.

— TONI MORRISON, Foreword to *Tar Baby,* 2004

WHEN I WAS little I drew rabbits instead of people. My "bunnies," as my family called them, appeared in many guises and locales. I made rabbit-shaped patterns out of paper bags. I cut them out of double thicknesses of fabric and sewed them together on my mother's small Singer machine with the electric pedal. She taught me to leave an inconspicuous opening on the animal's side (where it would soon be covered by the dress she made). Once I turned the stitched-up shape inside out it was time for the best part. Inserting the filling made the dimensionless shapes into something real, with feelings. Grabbing handfuls from a plastic bag, I pushed the fluffy cottony bunny insides inside. A knitting needle worked well to fill in the pointed tips of the ears. In this way I learned how to stuff my own stuffed animals.

By the age of ten, aware I had been drawing for an intimate audience of biased admirers, I decided to go bigger. *Westword,* Denver's ubiquitous free weekly newspaper, had an ongoing contest of sorts for getting your art or your poetry printed on the paper's highly visible and widely distributed back page. Under the heading "Last Words," your thing would be circulated to readers across the Mile High City. In return, you received a check for forty dollars.

My mother encouraged me, as she has all my life, to send something in. If you shoot enough arrows out, one of them is bound to hit the target. At the time I was very interested in the "traditional costumes" of peoples around the world. We had been trained by some of our teachers to think of the globe as a small world after all. Whether you wore your long wavy hair in braids like the Mexican girls or shaved it short to go with your loincloth the way they did in "Africa" or wore it in a shiny black bob over in China, everyone was interesting and valuable in their own way. The lie of multiculturalism. Everyone wants you to win. You can do and be anything you want! At that time, I wanted to be an artist. But wanting to be chosen was part of it too. I didn't so much want to become famous, because I was terrified of being grilled about my father and my mother by the press. That was the conflict. What would happen, I often forced myself to consider, if I got famous enough that someone would want to interview me? What would I tell them when they asked me what I was? As a child, I lived in absolute fear of having to answer this question with any specificity in some kind of official context, not knowing, as I knew I didn't, anything about my father besides his race.

We bought a large manila envelope, found some cardboard for

protection, and sent in my drawing. It was accepted! I counted down the days, and finally, at what I was told would be the approximate drop-off hour, I ran down to King Soopers, the big grocery store two blocks away. Two shiny red metal newspaper boxes stood like sentries outside the store's automatic doors. With the weekly's yellow sans-serif masthead splashed across their fronts, you couldn't miss those *Westword* boxes near strips of businesses and theaters and restaurants. It seemed like they were on every corner. Can you imagine a child's euphoria at being able to reach in and grab a copy of this newspaper that EVERYONE would see—with her very own drawing taking up the whole back cover!? Forty dollars was maybe thirty times my allowance. In that moment, I didn't even care about the money. Walking home, staring at the thick stack of newsprint held against my chest, I realized something. Not only had the editors published my submission, they had also reproduced a portion of my handwritten (and illustrated) cover letter. Which was really more of a cover *drawing*. They had a lot of nerve doing that. I found it completely unacceptable. The letter was supposed to be between me and them. It wasn't cute. I wasn't a baby. This was how the professionals did it, my mother had assured me. It was business. I felt that by superimposing the handwritten letter on my art, the *Westword* people were basically vandalizing it. Would you frame a Saul Steinberg with a handwritten letter from the artist partially obscuring his art? Plus, I had spelled a word (the name of our school) wrong, as Mindy Barnstable pointed out to everyone's glee the next day.

Here is what the letter said:

> Dear Editor,
>
> This is a drawing of bunnies playing croquet. They are celebrating their First Anniversary. I am sending it to you thinking you

could use it in your "Last Words" page in "Westword." I sometimes draw bunnies from other lands. I am in the fourth grade and going to Dora More [*sic*] school. Thank you for looking at my drawing. I hope you like it and I hope I hear from you soon.

*Vanessa Lyon*

(Next to my signature I appended a full-length drawing of a bunny in a kimono with "syonara [*sic*]" printed in a word bubble over her head.) It's a mystery to me how I correctly spelled "croquet" but not the name of the school I had already attended for four years. Never mind knowing what *sayonara* meant.

Several aspects of the drawing, the letter, and the fact that I

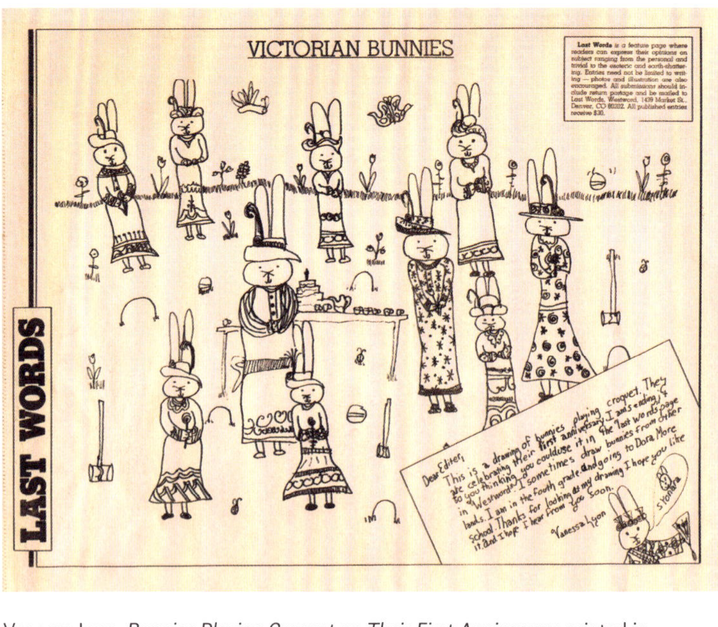


Vanessa Lyon, *Bunnies Playing Croquet on Their First Anniversary*, printed in *Westword*, 1979

am trained now to analyze art in the first place strike me as eerily predictive of who I would become. When I say that I've known since I was very young that women — as friends, as lovers, as muses, as obsessions, as demons — would be the center of my life, I'm not kidding. Already in the fourth grade, I was representing for myself a thoroughly feminine subjectivity and same-sex sociality. I don't think I'd ever played croquet at that time. But three decades later I would do so daily and competitively with my fellow summer research residents at Yale's suburban Lewis Walpole Library in Farmington, Connecticut. It was there, in the course of a heated match, that I met the woman, currently my most recent ex, who became my partner of seven years.

In my *Westword* drawing, nobody appears to be actively playing the game. Even so, one of the croquet balls (in the upper-right corner) is depicted in the "*air.*" Apparently, I was already aware of the boundless signifying power of quotation marks, which, to this day, editors consistently encourage me to remove. "Is this ironic or reported or what?" they write. I like quotes because they ask the reader to contemplate the source and the legitimacy and the subtext of the word or phrase between them. I am Black, but I'm not "Black."

Elsewhere in my drawing, hoops are planted in the soil, but mallets lie lifeless in the grass. Not so the peppy flowers, randomly and unrealistically interspersed across the pitch. In this world the flora, whether tulip-like or swirly in form, is uniformly long stemmed. The one exception are the berries of a single, perhaps too labor-intensive, grape hyacinth. Regular trumpet-blossomed hyacinths were a favorite of my grandmother, who planted pink and white and Delft blue ones in the shallow brick beds affixed to the garage. Like lilacs, the hyacinth's hopeful Eastertide scent will always remind me of my grandmother, cigarette in hand, surveying the post-divorce plantings in what was, un/happily, her very own yard.

As to "Victorian." One source of my discontent with the editorial choices made in reproducing my early work was the page's caption. I can't say whether I had memorized the dates of Queen Victoria's reign (1837–1901). Or if I knew that, although King Edward only ruled for the next nine years, his name was often associated with fashion until the beginning of the First World War. I was nonetheless intuitively attuned to the stylistic differences between Victorian and Edwardian dresses. Already at that age I could easily identify what distinguished those awkwardly unconstrained styles from what followed them, but predated Pearl Harbor. From all those solitary weekends at my grandmother's house sifting through a deep cardboard box full of family pictures, I had gained a sense of what White American ladies of a certain merchant class had worn in their youth. Tossed in with cracked and yellowed fifties and sixties snapshots of my sullen mother and her blond, hedgehoggishly cute little brother, I'd pretend to myself to "discover" the occasional brittle sepia photograph from a much earlier time. In these images, the ghostly, bleached-out figures are most often my White great-grandmother, Lillie, and/or her sisters, Mary, Nellie, Annie, and Maggie, seen occasionally with friends. It was all girls in that Price generation. Three schoolteachers with the exception, according to my mother, of Nellie and Maggie.

My grandmother spoke of her aunts as if they were a secret coven of good witches. She even adored Mary, a hard-ass, which you can see pretty well from her fierce black eyes and sprung steel trap of a mouth. Maggie (not pictured), described by my mother as "the down-to-earth one," eventually opened a bar with her husband, Arthur. In the photos taken in the first decades of the twentieth century, my Welsh American great-grandmother, née

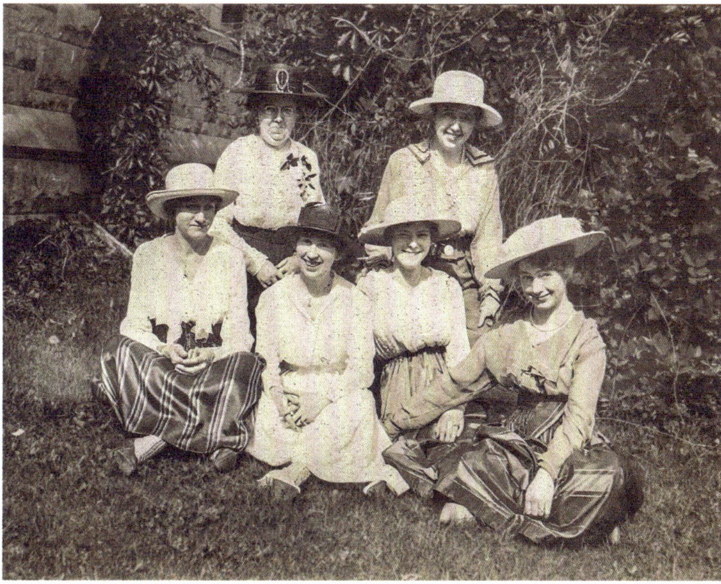

Lillie May Price, far right, with Aunt Mary (in black hat) and friends, ca. 1915

Lillie May Price, never fails to give the camera a flirty cock of the head or lift of her chin. Perhaps in an attempt to lessen the impact of her stand-out beauty, she hams it up a little, looking as if she's the only one posing, whereas the other less-cute friends have been caught off guard. Possibly taken before or after lunch on the grass, the snapshot shows Lillie looking the most stylish with her flattering, cake-like hat. My mother recently gave me a reticulated silver spoon that belonged to my great-grandmother. It seems to me chicly modern for the time. Lillie May Price Caldwell wore heels for so long, her daughter, my sensible-shoed grandmother, would tell me in a pitying tone that as an elderly woman, she couldn't wear anything else. Anatomy was destiny for those girls. Over decades, her tendons had shortened so much that she was condemned to tottering around in ladylike pumps until she died.

Nellie, short for Eleanor, decorated houses when she was

younger. Later in life, family lore has it, she became the "companion" of the Quaker Oats heiress. I wonder what that entailed, of course. Just as I wonder about the younger sister of my White great-grandfather (my mother's grandfather). Unlike her siblings, Lucille Caldwell was a woman too brass tacks to need a middle name. In the family, and I remember this from the time I was very young, she was simply referred to as "the Colonel." And a military woman she was. Born in 1909, my never-married great-great-aunt served in the Air Force during World War II. Fifteen years later, in the JAG bulletin of 1959, she is the only woman officer of the Judge Advocate General's Corps listed as newly promoted to the permanent rank of lieutenant colonel. "Lou," as she was known by her familiars, was stationed at Kirkland Air Force Base in New Mexico. She was buried at sixty-eight, in the National Cemetery in Santa Fe. In 2024 I visited her grave for the first time while I was renting a small casita in the hills off Tano Road. The Colonel must

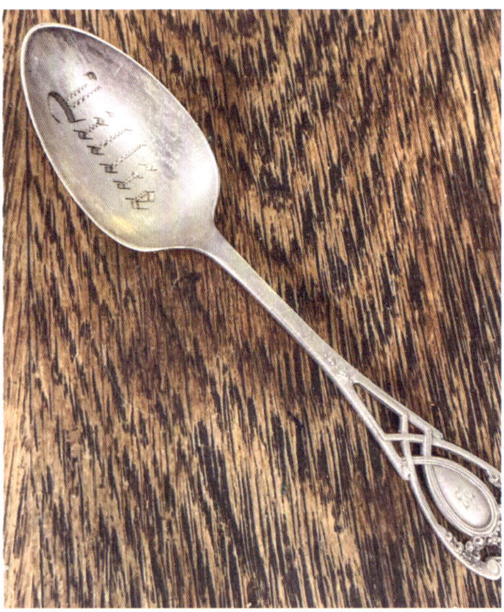

have died right around the year I made my *Westword* drawing.

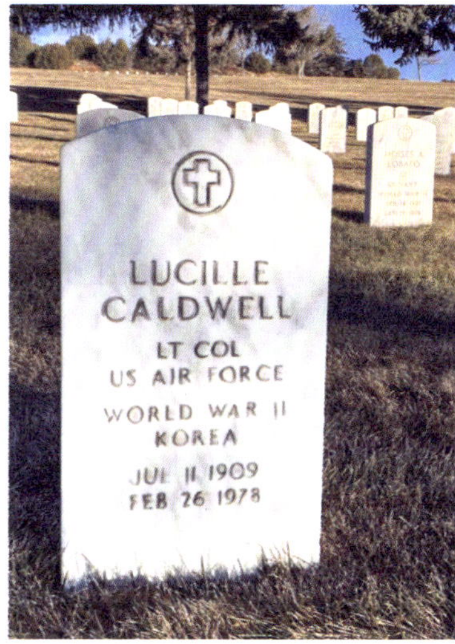


Grave marker of Lucille Caldwell (1909–1978), Santa Fe National Cemetery, 2024 (author's photo)

I recall exactly what she was wearing the first time I met her. We were still living with my grandparents, so I was three or four. I see her in crisp Air Force whites, which made an impression on me, though I can't say if she was in a skirt (more likely, given the era) or trousers (cool to think about in any case). Thick, snow-white hair, cut lesbian short, with a hank of bangs over one eye. There are colorful striped bands of ribbon pinned across her sizable bosom. The cane the Colonel walks with is off to the side, and she is stern with me as I sit across the dining-room table stealing looks over the grown-ups' iced tea glasses.

If I'd had photographs of my barrier-breaking, decorated, probably a dyke, power attorney great-grandaunt to lose myself in, my notion of (queer) femininity might have taken a different turn. Instead, in their lace collars and below-the-knee dresses, the inhabitants of the bunny realm I drew suggest the Colonel's conventionally cis-het sisters-in-law. Still, I'm happy to see a range of body types in attendance at my fantasy same-gender garden party. These are not, I think, young rabbits or bunnies of my own age. But then, I don't think I was ever a little girl. I was never into princesses or glitter or ballerina tutus. At the age of ten, I was into grown women. Like-minded women who dressed impeccably and gathered for sport on the occasion of their "First Anniversary," whatever that meant to me. Women as rabbits. Rabbits as women.

John M. McBryde Jr. was an English professor at several Southern colleges prior to his death in 1956. His father, John McLaren McBryde, turned down the University of Virginia's offer to be president in order to assume that role at Virginia Tech. McBryde Sr. was a Confederate veteran, present at the rebel army's bombing of Fort Sumter, the inciting incident of the Civil War in 1861. Writing while editor of *The Sewanee Review,* a post he held from 1909 to 1919, McBryde Jr. opens his 1911 article, "Brer Rabbit in the Folk-Tales of the Negro and Other Races," with the following passage, which bears, or brers, quotation in its near entirety:

> In the character of the old negro, Uncle Remus, is embodied one of the most lovable creations in recent literature and one of the most valuable contributions our country has yet made to the literature of the world. Both young and old, as they read these tales, feel themselves draw very close to the old man, whose humble cabin and warm heart were ever open as a haven of refuge to the little boy; and with the youngster come to share in the venerable negro's ready sympathy, to enjoy his quaint and genial humor, and to admire his simple, child-like faith in humanity and in God. If older readers have sometimes smiled at his assumption of affectionate superiority over his little companion and friend, at his social prejudices, his class distinctions, and his family pride, they have nevertheless been filled with admiration for his courtly manners and his loyalty and devotion to Ol' Massa and Ol' Missus, and to all the principles of conduct

> he imbibed from his free and familiar, yet very respectful intercourse with them. . . . Not for its individual traits alone, is the character valuable, but for its representative qualities, summing up the best characteristics of the negro race at a special period in its history – the time of slavery – the very traces of which have almost entirely disappeared. If *Uncle Tom's Cabin* set forth to the world the darkest aspects of slavery, *Uncle Remus* represents its brightest side, for the book makes clear to every thoughtful reader that the system of slavery, pernicious as it may appear to us now, took the dusky savage from his haunts in the African jungle and made of him a Christian and a gentleman, something which freedom and the most improved methods of education have thus far failed to accomplish.

Where to start? With the "brightest side" of slavery, that "special" time in a race's history? Or with the "venerable negro's" laughably "affectionate superiority"? The coded language is both pointed and subtle here. Perniciously so. For example, the author anticipates the discomfort of the "older" reader (i.e., original Confederates like his father) faced with the representation of even a fictional Black ex-slave effectively providing a moral education to a young White boy. McBryde thus prophylactically defuses the White reader's resentfulness, if not imminent outrage, into condescension and amusement. He overrides, or really, oversees, the usual violent responses to an uppity N-word by making a joke, at his expense, of Black Uncle Remus's silly pretentions. As McBryde sees it, Blacks born after the Civil War ended had missed out on experiencing slavery's "benefits," since its very traces had "almost entirely disappeared" by 1911, the year the piece was published. In an attempt to demolish Reconstruction, McBryde portrays Uncle Remus as a comforting reminder of times gone by – as a living, breathing instantiation of brighter days in the fugitive past. He is, to be sure, a movable type, the next generation's Uncle Tom.

Consider the writer's wily projection of slaveholder "traits" and insecurities, of White people's "principles of conduct," onto the vacuous Black character. (McBryde's strategy is familiar from the first reviews of Manet's *Olympia* about fifty years earlier, when French critics suggested the dirtiness and animality of the White "prostitute" through descriptive stereotypes normally reserved for Black women.) In a variation of this racializing rhetoric, McBryde criticizes Black Uncle Remus for acting (too) White. The son of a Confederate soldier scolds the formerly enslaved (fictional) Uncle Remus for taking on White airs, with his "social prejudices," "class distinctions," and "family pride." But here's the twist: McBryde Jr. then informs the reader that the Black man's best qualities were "imbibed" or taken in through the osmosis of "free" intercourse with his White master and mistress. Uncle Remus can't win for losing; either he's uppity on someone else's terms or feckless on his own.

There's a devilish internal coherence to McBryde's racism. To his way of thinking, having been enslaved — indeed, as the result of slavery — Uncle Remus was transformed into a Christian and a gentleman, capable even of instilling moral sense in a youthful White "companion" through his colorful plantation tales. But there's always a bigoted back stab: Despite their origins in Black oral history, Uncle Remus's stories are not the products of his or any other "negro" imagination. Rather, McBryde goes on to argue, the tales are lifted from other traditions, above all Native American trickster animal legends with which they do share a number of tropes and traits. (This is unsurprising given Black and Indigenous interrelations and, eventually, intermarriage going back well prior to the founding of the United States — what, as

Arica L. Coleman notes, Oklahoman Ralph Ellison referred to as the "Negro-Indian confusion.") By claiming that the South's Blackest folklore wasn't originally so Black after all, McBryde was clearly less interested in protecting Native American intellectual property than in framing the formerly enslaved as copycats and thieves. By his estimation, credit for the "most valuable contributions our country has yet made to the literature of the world" should therefore go to the White author Joel Chandler Harris, who "discovered them and preserved them in posterity," and not to the enslaved people from whom Harris stole the tales that made him, and a good bit of Southern culture, famous.

Born the same year as Édouard Manet, Joel Chandler Harris spent his teenage years in Georgia. He became a printer's apprentice at Turnwold, home of *The Countryman,* said to have been the only weekly newspaper published by and on a Southern plantation. When he wasn't honing the craft of journalism as the plantation owner's protégé, young Harris spent his free time in Turnwold's slave quarters. Stowing away in those small and drafty rooms, he supposedly (over)heard the stories that would become *Uncle Remus, His Songs and His Sayings: The Folklore of the Old Plantation.* While we're on the subject of theft, here are the concluding words of Harris's introduction to his first edition of *Uncle Remus,* issued in 1881:

> If the reader not familiar with plantation life will imagine that the myth-stories of Uncle Remus are told night after night to a little boy by an old negro who appears to be venerable enough to have lived during the period which he describes – who has nothing but pleasant memories of the discipline of slavery – and who has all the prejudices of caste and pride of family that were the natural results of the system; if the reader can imagine all

> this, he will find little difficulty in appreciating and sympathizing with the air of affectionate superiority which Uncle Remus assumes as he proceeds to unfold the mysteries of plantation lore to a little child who is a product of that practical reconstruction which has been going on to some extent since the war in spite of the politicians. Uncle Remus describes that reconstruction in his "Story of the War" and I may as well add for the benefit of the curious that story is almost literally true.

Note the many similarities in Harris's introduction to the opening salvos in McBryde's scholarly article for *The Sewanee Review,* published some thirty years later with no attribution or citation of its obvious source. As a plagiarist, the English professor is less gifted than some college first-years I've known. Moreover, the rest of the content of McBryde's "study" of Negro folklore was also previously outlined in Harris's remaining prefatory remarks to *Uncle Remus.* Perhaps McBryde felt it was a takeable risk, since Harris had been dead for three years when he published his article in the prestigious Southern journal of which he was also the editor.

What goes around comes around, even in a rabbit hole.

Wouldn't you know that Beatrix Potter, beloved British author of twenty-three Peter Rabbit stories, found herself similarly inspired by the "Folklore of the Plantation." Unlike McBryde and Harris, however, she was quick to identify her source when she chose to illustrate portions of *Uncle Remus* for her personal drawing practice and edification.

The first edition of *Uncle Remus* was accompanied by only a handful of illustrations by two artists: Frederick Stuart Church and James Henry Moser. Harris wasn't especially happy with either artist. He says as much in a letter quoted in Joseph M. Griska Jr.'s "Uncle Remus Correspondence: The Development and Reception of Joel Chandler Harris's Writing, 1880–1885." Says the "creator" of Uncle Remus: "The animal illustrations of the folk-lore are made by F. S. Church, and they are good as to artistic execution, but are uniformly bad as to spirit and intention. The illustrations of negro characters are by Mr. Moser of this city, and while the spirit is good the art is crude."

To my eye, Church's agitated linear drawings give his Brer Rabbit *au naturel* a suitably scrappy, creaturely, wild-eyed look. His raggedy panels are workmanlike, yet stylized and playful, a mild take on Art Nouveau. Moser, on the other hand, merely provides gross caricatures of Harris's "venerable darkey." His Uncle Remus smiles broadly, his bulbous peanut head trimmed with a hide of woolly white curls indistinguishable from his beard, glasses pushed up on his forehead as if he might not know they are there. Or need them to read what he cannot.

It wasn't until 1895, with the release of a new and extensively illustrated *Uncle Remus,* that the more familiarly anthropomorphic version of Brer Rabbit made his debut. In artist Arthur Burdette Frost's hands, Brer Rabbit gets a makeover. He also gets dressed. We first see the full-length rabbit in three-quarter view, from behind, as he's described in chapter 1. There Brer Rabbit appears to Brer Fox "ez plump, and ez fat, and ez sassy" as can be—but also as nattily attired. The old-man rabbit now wears cottontail-accommodating trousers rolled up to reveal his long hind paws. Above the waist, he sports a waistcoat or vest over a blousy shirt with the starched collar jauntily popped. His pants are patched at the knees, and he is without the walking stick and the riding coat that will become part of his fancy-pants look later on. With this second edition, "new and revised with one hundred and twelve illustrations by A. B. Frost," Harris was well pleased. While his original self-aggrandizing introduction is left more or less unaltered, the preface concludes with an expression of gratitude to the artist: "The book was mine," he writes to A. B. Frost, "but now you have made it yours, both sap and pith."

Beatrix Potter had begun making her own uncommissioned illustrations for the first edition of *Uncle Remus* at least two years before Frost gave Brer Rabbit and friends their new appearance. In a drawing from 1893, Potter shows us her Brer Rabbit from behind as he happens on Brer Fox, who is up to one of his usual subterfuges playing possum. Not surprisingly, it's difficult not to mistake this "naked," long-eared and oh-so-soft animal for the bunny known as Peter. Potter's approach is somewhat more realistic than Frost's, keeping in mind that differences in ear length and leg-to-body proportions might also align with American versus British types (there are more than fifty species of rabbits).

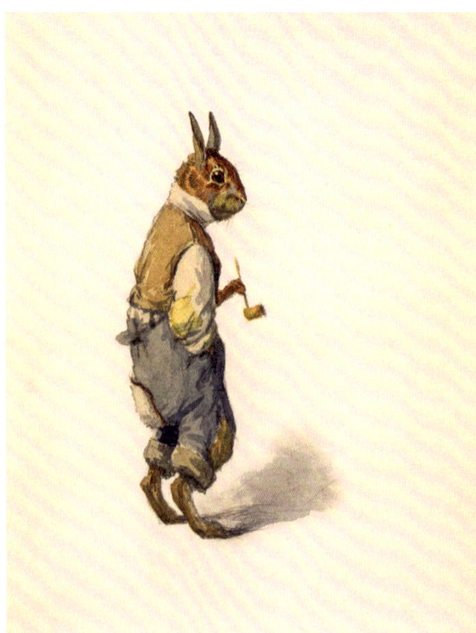

A. B. Frost, *Brer Rabbit*, 1895

Although Brer Rabbit *goes without* in some of Potter's early images, she experiments in others with elaborate hats and short waistcoats and jackets of a more Victorian than Edwardian type; the clothes her rabbits wear are generally quite old-fashioned for their time. According to the Victoria and Albert Museum, which holds the largest archival collection of Potter drawings and ephemera, the tale of Peter Rabbit was conceived in September 1893, the same year Potter made her Uncle Remus drawing – the first of several she penned in the period.

Potter accompanied her *Uncle Remus* drawings with captions from Harris's book, as, for example, in the case of Brer Rabbit from behind: "Mighty funny. Brer Fox look like he dead yit he don't [*sic*] do like he dead." Despite the "Negro dialect," there is little visual evidence of rabbit racialization in her drawings. Potter's quotations from the American book seem at odds with the highly naturalistic, and in terms of plants and settings, distinctively British, watercolor scenes. Potter was a meticulous observer of nature. Even some of her storybook marginalia assume the objective and empirical quality of botanical illustrations.

The British artist's whimsical and ingenious mixing of graphic genres can be seen in the Brer Rabbit and Brer Fox encounter, where Harris's words appear on an enclosed *cartellino* held in the mouths of two convincingly lifelike bunnies in the *bas-de-page*. Potter had been studying art, copying other artists, and visiting British museums for years by the time she turned to *Uncle Remus*. (Nor was she the first British artist taken with the American stories – as my thesis student Bailey Yarbrough informed me, William Morris's beloved "Brother Rabbit" pattern, first produced around 1881, is said to have been inspired by his nights reading *Uncle Remus* to his children.) Beatrix Potter also amused herself by making drawings for *Alice in Wonderland* and other popular children's books.

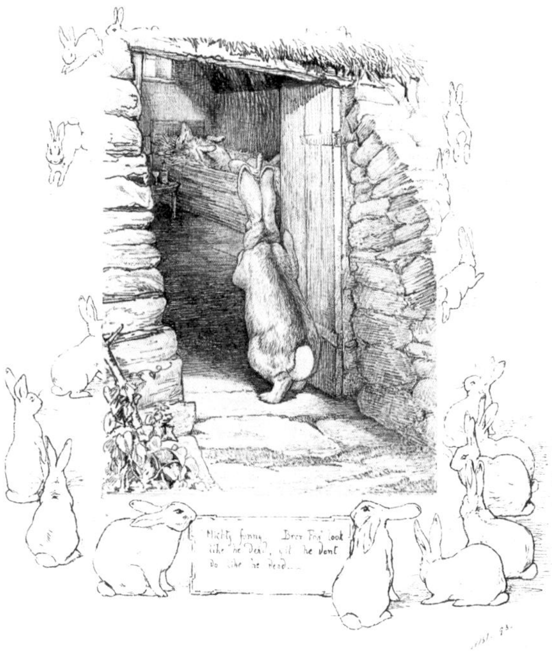


Beatrix Potter, *Brer Rabbit*, 1893

Formally, these Arts and Crafts–era precursors to Peter Rabbit were influenced by medieval illuminated manuscripts.

Prior to the widespread use of movable type printing in the West from around 1450, the illustrated pages of breviaries and devotional books of hours often combined two distinctive image worlds. Typically, in these compositions, the main narrative or sacred scene occupies an enclosed box or a larger, historiated, letter – think "Once upon a time" – while the subjects on the margins of the page are usually both conceptually and narratively distinct from the central one. Marginalia can also differ in scale, artistic technique, and even ontology from the "real" story—seeming to exist in another world. Like Potter's, sumptuously illustrated prayer books were often small enough to be held in a woman's (or child's) hand.

Detailed watercolors of Potter's own rabbit, Peter Piper, who died at age nine in 1899, convey her affection for the little animals. Her naughty (and hungry) fictional Peter may have a bit of Brer Rabbit's mischievousness, but he is also youthful, cuddly, and cute. Even when clothed, as many of Potter's creatures are, the impression is somehow of an intelligent animal-like animal who just happens to be wearing "human" clothing rather than an animal who, "deep-down," is human and dresses accordingly.

Overdressed not only for an animal, but for an animal always on the run, Frost's dandified Brer Rabbit, by contrast, is freighted with a haberdasher's subtext. Along with his preposterous hand-me-down clothing, this ridiculous animal from the American South has a mind and manners of his own, for which he is worthy of ridicule. Who else in Harris's era might be accused of such conceited and unnatural behavior? Certainly not the docile Uncle Tom. Brer Rabbit's human analogue is, rather, the strategically deceitful would-be runaway. For it is the oft-hunted animal's enslaved double who negotiates and prevaricates and schemes in order to survive the constant threat of brutal violence and separation from his s/kin while confined to a plantation like Joel Chandler Harris's Turnwold. When Brer Rabbit gets away with murder on the page, he is also vicariously outfoxing the plantation overseer. Many before me have acknowledged the appeal to subalterns then and the underrepresented now of a crafty, underdog Brer Rabbit who, with the odds squarely against him, nevertheless manages to get the better of his betters—in this case, the cruel and immoral Ol' Massa gussied up by Frost in literal wolves' clothing.

Hang on, though. If these appropriated "trickster" tales are so subversive, why have they also appealed to White people, even – or maybe especially – White supremacist Southerners, for so long? McBryde, and Harris before him, provide answers to this question, I think, in their admiring introductions to *Uncle Remus*. It all goes back to the observation that Whites of the old guard will rightly feel sympathy or affection for a pathetically proud and "prejudiced" Uncle Remus, who foolishly believes he holds the moral upper hand over his White charge. And why shouldn't they approve of him? Remus, who shares the name of one of the legendary twin founders of Rome, is the ex-slave who stayed on the plantation long after 1865, when the war officially ended. In one of the book's last illustrations, Remus visits offices resembling those of *The Atlanta Constitution,* where Harris's tales and sayings were first published. The old man looks laughably out of place – and time. This "venerable negro" has been (pitifully) conditioned by his White master and mistress to misrecognize his position in the halls of a Predominantly White Institution as honorable, even trusted and respected. Depicted in his master's cast-off clothes, as house slaves sometimes wore, the Black storyteller and mentor becomes a clownish caricature of the enslavers who once legally owned him. With his patched pants and dandyish walking stick, Brer Rabbit, too, was meant to engender Whites' laughter. But given the rabbit's crafty escape strategies and sheer endurance, the joke may be on them.

---

My family tree, like that of many people in America with a Black parent and a White parent, is as old and established as it is chopped and pruned. Branches beget branches on the White side.

And then there is a stump. Maybe I am the stump. Maybe I am where the Black growth ceases. Maybe I am where the trenching starts and what's left below ground of formerly enslaved people and workers and freedom fighters from my mother's old neighborhood gets dug up and ferociously chipped into pieces that cannot be reconstituted.

I know quite a bit about my mother's family. But I know nothing at all of my biological father's. So much life writing by BIPOC authors in this cultural moment pursues a lost parent or a lost genealogy or a place of origin never before visited by the writer. It's tempting to make this my story's trajectory too. In writing and in living what remains of my life, I want to interrogate and explore what my own Blackness – but also my own Whiteness – has meant, and means. I have to figure out my racial identity. And I want to. But to come to an understanding of myself in the present, tracking down my Black father and his past is not something I feel I have to do.

Let's be real. Nor is it something I *can* do. I don't even have a name. We do not speak of this man who is or was what I am beginning to think of as the other half of my mother's teenage hookup. NB: America's bureaucratic, patriarchal protocols for keeping and accessing legal records require that you have not only your mother's but also your father's full name in order to request and receive a copy of your birth certificate. If I knew *that,* of course, I wouldn't be making the request in the first place. The electronic age and, most recently, the rush to digitize has made archival research infinitely more doable. Relatively democratic. Anyone with access to a computer and the internet can worm his/her/their way into databases and libraries and legal records of all kinds. I am trained to do research, but without a name, I don't know where to start. Why doesn't she just ask her mother, you might wonder. After half a century, you'll just have to trust me when I tell you it's not that simple.

But anyway, in memoirland, if you do have a name, locating and meeting your long-lost parent is often upheld as the key to finding out who you really are. As if merely laying eyes on someone, or sitting over coffee with a stranger for an awkward twenty minutes, will render you and your self-knowledge whole. A reunion of this sort might have that effect on some people, especially younger ones. But I don't see it working that way for me. Or maybe I do, but I don't see it happening anytime soon. For now, the promises made by Ancestry.com-style gene hunting strike me as complicit in promoting false notions of something called race "mixing," the same false notions unwittingly grounded in the kind of wrong-headed race "science" that continues to empower racism, essentialism, and bias. Notions implying that miscegenation is a genetic truth containing two materially different strains or racial types of genes. Which it is not. "White blood" and "Black blood" are human blood. According to the National Institutes of Health (NIH), "in 2003, Phase 1 of the Human Genome Project (HGP) demonstrated that humans populating the earth today are on average 99.9% identical at the DNA level, there is no genetic basis for race, and there is more genetic variation *within* a race than between them" (italics mine). Race is a construct. Race is a taxonomy. Get down to it with the people in a random classroom or at a football game, and you'll find there is probably greater genetic variation among the Black people than between Blacks and Whites. Imagine.

I am no scientist. But as I understand it, genetics—with a basis in the pea cross-breeding experiments of Austrian botanist Gregor Mendel, published in 1866, a year after the American Civil War ended—has to do with heredity at the gene, chromosomal, or DNA level. Where claims about race are concerned, biology, of which genetics is a part, can, nonetheless, be another matter. According to the NIH, our health and our bodies themselves can be affected by "social determinants" such as income, education, and occupation. That is to say, your biology, as a racialized or Black body, can be affected by external factors having to do with perceptions of your race – you might, for example, endure more pain (or have your pain ignored) as a medical patient. Per the NIH, a 2016 study (Hoffman et al.) reported that of 222 White medical students and residents asked "true" and "false" questions, 40 percent of first- and second-years believed Black people have physically thicker skin – and feel less pain – than White people. But again, neither genetics nor racialization in relation to social location, economic status, and nurture are what I'm talking about when I reject the language of "mixed."

I'm talking about the one-drop rule. The concept that race is determined by the proportion of one "type" of blood in another. In the United States, racial categorization has always been about protecting the "purity" of the White race from being tainted by the colored ones. The first blood-fraction rules in America date to the early eighteenth century. In 1705, if a person had one Black great-grandparent, he/she/they were considered Black. Two hundred years later, seeing, in the sense of visually identifying, Blackness had become an additional criterion for believing Blackness. For example, prior to 1911, according to the Encyclopedia of Arkansas, that state's railroad segregation law declared "Negro" as "one in whom there is a visible and distinct admixture of African blood." As we all know, the mere perception of visible and distinct Negritude has had and continues to have legal as well as social implications. At least since *Plessy v. Ferguson* legalized (Jim Crow) segregation in 1896, the principle of "hypo-descent" has determined American Blackness. Hypodescent means that one's race is decided by that of the racially and culturally "subordinate" parent. In 1910, Tennessee became the first state to make the one-drop rule law. "One drop" refers of course to the assertion that any Black African ancestry whatsoever renders one a member of the Black (or Negro) race.

In the United States of America, "blood" is what makes us who we are for most legal, and educational, and medical, and political intents and purposes. But, I ask, how – to one familiar with such markers – is my genetic Blackness *not* distinct and visible? Shouldn't the hint of Negroid characteristics in my physical appearance – a prominent nose, freckled and spotted olive skin, dark brown eyes, coarse dark hair – and underneath my starched shirts, brown breasts with dark, uncircumscribed nipples – confirm my status as a member of this category long established by my country in accordance with both appearance and parentage? I've spent a lifetime observing how Blacks and Whites and anyone else in my presence talk about passing, and Mulattas, and what it means to be truly African American, knowing (regardless of whether they do) that they are talking about me. I like to think my Blackness bleeds through in the decision to write this book.

It's certainly why "mixed" or "mixed blood" or "half black," or "biracial" are the terms with which I take issue. I'm warming to "Mulatta," but "tragic" definitely has to be there. The longer I live, the more I want to revive rather than blot out this much-derided moniker, if only for my own use. I'm no fatalist. I'm not even a Black pessimist. But there is to me something potentially irredeemable about a culture that cannot find a way to comfortably and voluntarily incorporate the one who is many or both. My lived experience is of having no people. Of being very much without community. Even among others "like" me. They do not like me. I am not like them. We are not like each other to each other.

A recent example: Admitted to a prestigious New England writing residency and seeking refuge from a majority-White participant atmosphere, I eagerly attend the BIPOC writers' panel and pose a question to the "faculty" women of color onstage (both of whom have just noted that they have a White parent). Is it, I ask, still worth pursuing Toni Morrison's critical investment in how Blackness – her word is "Africanism" – operates in the work of White writers? What followed – in the very venue where Morrison herself had given numerous readings – was sufficiently mean-spirited that total strangers came up to me afterward to offer words of consolation. I was willfully misunderstood, performatively scoffed at, and verbally shut down by both writers, who told me my question was of no consequence, "flat," "White," and irrelevant. By implication, "real" people of color aren't interested in White writing anymore, and who was I (a White woman?) to ask.

The nineteenth-century trope of the morally tainted "dusky" woman doomed by her incommensurable Black-Whiteness or White-Blackness does not originate in the Confederacy's rabid anti-Black bigotry. No, it was born out of (Northern) antislavery crusades. During, before, and after the Civil War, miscegenation was deemed the first and worst unwanted outcome of slavery. Under the peculiar institution, the rape of enslaved Black women by "their" White masters was a common form of torture, debasement, and discipline, a power play of the most heinous kind. As Annette Gordon-Reed, Heather V. Vermeulen, and others have argued, whether or not there was some twisted version of "consensual" sex between White slave masters and overseers and the enslaved Black women under their control, it is a sick travesty to characterize these routinely brutal displays as "Plantation Romance." Within the historical imaginary of American slavery, to be "mixed" is to be the product of a de jure criminal, but de facto unpunished, act of sexual violence between one's parents. The grafted hybrid – that is, the human being born of such intercourse – is poisonous fruit of the tree.

I am not the result of such a nonconsensual commingling. Nor can I imagine answering the existential questions that might beset me if I were. I hope I would realize that regardless of how I came into this world, I am me and I have value and purpose and promise. I hope I would find a way to believe that having a sadistic or criminally violent father didn't mean that those same characteristics were in my blood.

And suddenly I've written my way into the hard places. Into the quandaries and questions. Into the intersections, the ontologies, the ethics. What is this *being* neither between races nor existing as a mixture of them? Why is my inborn Blackness all that matters in an America where to be Black is not to matter? And how, at the very same time, does my inherent Blackness, this Black inheritance, not sufficiently signify or count?

---

The earliest White ancestor from whom I am known to be directly descended was a fellow born in England in 1670, named George Griest. Griest was the husband of Ann Butt. He was the grandfather, through John Griest (b. 1710) and Martha Baldwin (b. 1710), of Willing Griest of Pennsylvania (b. 1736), husband of Ann Garretson (b. 1750). Ann's mother, I am happy to report, was named Content Hussey (b. 1716). The Griests had thirteen children, one of whom, Jacob Griest (b. 1770), married the Dutchly named Esther Van Scoyac (b. 1771). These two had only three children, including Jonathan Griest (b. 1793). Jonathan married Mary Davis (b. 1796) and had nine kids, including Lucinda Griest (b. 1822). Lucinda married Parkerson Longerbone (b. 1821) and the two had a daughter named Mary Ann (b. 1849). Mary Ann Longerbone married Levi Griffith Myers (b. 1846). Their daughter, Merta (Murtie) Mae Myers (b. 1874), married James Addison Caldwell (b. 1867). Murtie Mae and James (then in Iowa) had eight children, of whom one was my great-grandfather, Edgar Fay Caldwell, born, like Potter's Peter Rabbit, in 1893. Edgar had one younger, unmarried, sister Lucille Caldwell (b. 1909), the same Lucille who would also be known by her family as "the Colonel." Edgar Fay Caldwell married Lillie May Price of Iowa. One of their three Wyomingite children was my grandmother Dorothy Elizabeth Caldwell, who preferred to be called Betty.

My grandmother was quite proud of the fact that she had been asked to join the Daughters of the American Revolution as a young woman but had declined in view of their racist stance on segregation. I'm not entirely sure where the Griests were during the Revolutionary War—they may have been royalists, for all I know. William Penn was a "Friend" who owned slaves, this much is true. But the Griests, having settled at York very near the time the colony of Pennsylvania was founded in 1681, are said to have been good abolitionist Quakers.

We have always known something about our family's Civil War history through the exploits of the husband of Griest descendant Lucinda Longerbone, Levi Griffith Myers, who would, if I'm doing the math correctly, be my great-great-great-grandfather. Of Levi Myers of Polk Township, Iowa, a helpful account was compiled about sixteen years before his death in 1928. The details appear in a book-length history of Jefferson County, Iowa, published by S. J. Clarke in Chicago. Iowa is the traditional, ancestral, unceded land of the Báxoǰe (Bah Kho-je) or Ioway, Sauk (Sac), and Meskwaki (Fox) peoples. Myers's parents were some of the early settler colonists (that is, thieves) of their land. This part of Iowa was originally "created" by piecing together tracts of Wisconsin Territory acquired in the Louisiana Purchase of 1803.

By 1912, Levi and Murtie Mae had rented out their prosperous farm and moved into the more townlike village of Packwood. Their property of some 250 acres was, in the words of the Jefferson County historian, "one of the most attractive features of the landscape." Levi's parents, who had moved the family there from Pennsylvania in 1855, would die suddenly, within a week of each other, in 1872. Growing up, Myers attended local schools, then purchased part of what would be called the "old homestead," converting the land into "one of the fine farms of the county." All this before he turned eighteen. Then, on February 22, 1864, he enlisted at Abingdon, Iowa, as a member of Company K in the 7th Volunteer Infantry. He was immediately sent to the front and took part in many engagements across the country until the end of the war. He marched in the grand review in Washington on May 23, 1865, where 145,000 troops were greeted by President Johnson and the "Battle Hymn of the Republic" as they made a triumphal procession through the streets of the District. Not a single soldier from the "colored" Infantry was invited to march in that parade.

In 1864, however, before the war's conclusion, Levi Meyers, led by General Sherman, fought in the battle of Lay's Ferry, Georgia, near the town of Resaca. Although estimated casualties of that engagement total more than five thousand, the drawn-out Lay's

Ferry battle apparently ended in what was basically a draw, albeit one giving an edge to Union forces.

Resaca is about 150 miles from Eatonton, Georgia, home of the Turnwold Plantation. This means that in May 1864, while cub reporter Joel Chandler Harris, also *The Countryman*'s "printer's devil," lingered among the enslaved people with his ears open and his pen at the ready, my teenage ancestor Levi, two years Harris's senior, was mired in mud and blood in what must have felt like a futile battle, given that the rebels were just a few towns away.

With scarce documentation of his father, Joel Chandler Harris, the "creator" of Brer Rabbit, is almost always described by historians as "illegitimate." Scholars argue over his birth date, since he may have fudged it once he became a famous writer. Early biographies incorrectly claim that Harris's father died when he was a baby. If, as seems likely, he was born as early as 1844, he would have been eligible to fight in the Confederate Army, which he did not. Harris's possibly Irish father, it is generally accepted, "seduced" his mother, a poor, uneducated girl, and deserted her. When it came time to take control of his own narrative, Harris wrote a short account entitled "The Accidental Author"—an allusion, according to an article by W. J. Rorabaugh, "When Was Joel Chandler Harris Born?: Some New Evidence," from which I learned all of this, to his unplanned birth.

Nobody wants to be an accident. But being called illegitimate is so much worse. There are happy accidents, after all. And in fact, "accident," in its Aristotelian sense, is merely a property or a feature, an adjectival quality, it is sometimes said, of something more noun-like and substantial. "Legitimate" derives, more decisively, from "leg" or "lex," as in one's legally married parents. Growing up, I was often asked why I had my mother's name and not my father's. I see now that such inquiries were almost certainly motivated by the desire to prove or disprove my legitimacy. It's odd to think that this kind of unlawfulness is something I share with Joel Chandler Harris, the liar, the thief, the White supremacist. I don't have a single nice thing to say about the man. But I don't blame him for trying to rewrite his own life his way.

---

FURTHER READING

Morrison, Toni. *Playing in the Dark: Whiteness and the Literary Imagination.* Harvard University Press, 1992.

# 8

# PROVE IT ON ME

Wear my clothes just like a fan
Talk to the gals just like any old man
'Cause they say I do it, ain't nobody caught me
Sure got to prove it on me.
— MA RAINEY, "Prove It on Me Blues," 1928

I HAVE DATED only White women. Though I don't know that what Olga and I did would count to some people as dating. This was still the flux-filled period near the end of my senior year of college, and we were only in the same city for a few days at a time after we started having sex on the fly. We only slept through the night together once. She had taken me to a big dinner at one of those unavoidable hippie mountain pizza restaurants Colorado used to have by the dozen. Not the first places you'd see when you pulled off the highway, but the ones in the middle of Main Street. Inside, you could count on thickly shellacked tables made out of roughly hewn tree parts. Grateful Dead music. Wheat or even bulgur crusts and pitchers of beer and ski-bum servers with shaggy beards and greasy hair pulled back in bandannas.

We ate at one of these places, or I did, and then Olga got it into her head that we should go to her favorite hot springs before heading back down into Denver. It wasn't really even out of the way, she said, green eyes full of mischief. When I was probably seven or eight, my grandmother had booked us on a train to the hot springs in the mountain town of Glenwood, an unglamorous place at the time, to "take the waters" in a bathing suit. When we went there, the remotely Italianate Hotel Colorado, a rambling complex of sandstone towers and turrets, had fallen on hard times, sold to outside interests by the family who had once turned it into a world-class spa. If *The Shining* (1980) – filmed at Estes Park's Stanley, another haunted Colorado hotel – wasn't a few years from release, I have no doubt I would have had nightmares for years from that childhood trip. There was something viscerally evil about these labyrinthine resorts carved out of Native land and secreted among the evergreens and the mountain peaks. Even the resolute Colorado sun failed to brighten up their lobbies; the thought of venturing in the middle of the night to the "water closet" at the end of the hall would put any bladder to the test.

However atmospheric, the Hotel Colorado would have seemed too expensive to my penny-wise grandmother. Instead, she reserved us a room across I-70 in a musty little Victorian hotel that hadn't been renovated since the Depression era. With twin beds and roller shades, it was plenty depressing to me. Like most of the town's saloons and shops and restaurants, our place had been left to fend for itself after the demise of mining. Unlike California, Colorado never had enough gold worthy of a rush. In the Rockies, silver was the precious metal on which to speculate. In order to mine silver, you need coke. The bounty of immigrant coal miners' life-threatening underground labor kept the high life going in

Glenwood from around 1880 until 1920, when the coke wells ran dry, a few years ahead of Prohibition and the stock market crash.

To a kid who'd spent many an ennui-filled Saturday afternoon half watching black-and-white Westerns where the streets were made of planks and the bars had swinging half doors, our hotel looked a lot like a brothel. While my grandmother donned her Kelly-green one-piece with the bullet bra, I stood at the window trying to mask my anxious feelings (she was the avid swimmer, not me) about the enormous rectangular pool of dark water glinting with reflected goggles and bathing caps.

Glenwood's geothermal springs are nestled between two rivers on Ute ancestral lands. The pizza place where Olga had taken us was closer to Idaho Springs, which turned out to have a hot spring and a cool one that were only accessible via a tunnel of slimy, painted-rock showers. The whole place was embedded in a mountain, so the pools, which were really subterranean baths, were indoors, not out.

It is a mark of my complete devotion to and unbridled lust for Olga that I was open to anything hot springs related. I hate being seen in the nude. Always have. Since visits to the pediatrician who told me to lay off the cookies. Since yearly scoliosis exams in elementary school. Since sleepovers at Sarah Becker's when I'd find the optimal moment to quickly sneak into my nightgown alone while the other girls were talking about boys or brushing their teeth. My ever-larger breasts were a constant source of shame to me, and nobody, especially my relatively unendowed mother, seemed to have a clue that, beginning at a very early age, my sense of self had been severely diminished by constant taunts and jeers about my body, for which the synecdoche was my bosom. Nobody in my circle of skinny White girls had skin or a shape even remotely like mine. Not only were none of them brown, none of them were as tall as me. No one had a stomach that went out rather than in. Nobody had hips. Nobody's mother had hips. Except Mrs. Becker, and hers seemed almost immeasurably wide beneath her plaid circle skirts. She was a mother of six, after all. Those White girls were in training bras for years. Their negligible pink protuberances were gently padded with opaque white cotton, effortlessly cantilevered by thin stretchy straps. They would reach back and spring open their brassieres with a single gesture I hoped to master myself. And not for the lightning-fast removal of my own unpretty undergarments.

By the time we went to the hot springs, I was a grown twenty-something and Olga had seen me in a bra and partially out of one. With my shirt open over my breasts. She'd seen my soft belly and the long centipede-like scar on my arm from when I was hit by a car at age five. She'd seen the perpetual tennis, and now, golf, tan that leaves my torso beige and turns the rest of me deeper brown. She'd seen what I convinced myself was a gross and unacceptable voluptuousness, though thinking back now, after full summers of dieting on canned mandarin oranges and plain yogurt, I was probably about a size 8. I had somehow grown accustomed to being naked with Olga in the flickering light of her studio. But I had never, ever, been fully naked in public.

I'd had some wine at the restaurant, which got me in the mood. We left our folded clothes in an open cubby. I wrapped as much of myself as I could in one of the nearly pileless white terry towels you could rent for fifty cents. Olga casually draped her towel over her arm as she exited. Under the yellow light she was pale and toned from her other life as a dancer. I wish I remembered better. I know I had a possessive feeling about her body because I had previously held her breasts in both hands when I kissed her from behind. But that was a private thing. Much as I longed to, I couldn't do it there in the baths.

The steam pool she chose was, to my immeasurable relief, for women only. Post-dinner was an unpopular time to go, and it was not crowded. But to stand at the edge of the water with even a few strangers casually glancing up at me as I quickly unveiled myself was – well, it was amazing, actually. Olga was smiling from the steaming gray water. And I was suddenly in there with her. Naked. Seen by people who didn't gasp or giggle or stare or make a face. Even if the two or three older ladies (who had pretended not to hear Olga's endearments as she cooed to me) now began to bristle at the sight of us together. Surely they felt the desire radiating between us, even as we submerged ourselves to the neck in those mineral-inundated waters that were meant to be healing.

We stayed in for too long. Once out, I became violently ill as soon as the cold air and sulfuric rotten egg smell hit me. Not enough hydration. Too much wine and pizza. My head was throbbing so hard I couldn't see. I genuinely believed I was dying.

Not for the first time I thought, if I die, let it be with Olga. With the friend I had dreamed would someday become my lover portioning me sips from a plastic water bottle. Unfortunately, I was too far gone to derive much pleasure from her ministrations. I was probably undergoing a near lethal level of cleansing, my pulse racing, stomach seizing, and shards of pain shooting into my eyes. All the bad things inside me were fighting to see who could get out first. A little while later – I don't remember how we got there, though I think I paid – we ended up in a very cheap motel near the springs. Just the two of us. In bed.

The thing was, I was leaving to go back to college in Chicago the next day. Which was surely why my prescient parents hadn't wanted me to go out that night with Olga; I was supposed to be home with my family. In my own twin bed on my last night in Denver. Instead, here I was, mortally ill in the mountains. Vomiting so violently and continuously, I had trouble getting to the bathroom in time. Between runs, Olga held a cold cloth to my forehead, and it was divine. In fact, though barely able to keep water down, what I wanted most before I departed this life was for us to have what I considered real sex. Not on the floor of her hovel. On a mattress. More than once. One last time. Before I flew back to the iced-over lake on Chicago's North Shore for the rest of the winter, if not before I left the planet entirely. I couldn't stop the room from spinning. My heart was beating faster than it ever had. I couldn't call my parents like that. So I didn't. But she did.

When we were "just friends" in high school, my mother had absolutely adored Olga. Her humor, her intelligence, the outlandish way she dressed. The rebellious nature that was such an obvious consequence of Olga's snotty mother failing to grasp what made her eldest daughter unlike anyone else and truly brilliant and talented, because of, not in spite of, her oddness. But once she gleaned that Olga was becoming the Thelma to my Louise, a ride-or-die friend in what I'm sure was a frighteningly imaginable sense, my mother didn't like us being together any more than Olga's did.

Thirty years later, I'm remembering our night in the motel as I sit in an architecturally significant library gazing at a copse of feathery, once lime-green ferns gone wheat color or chocolate brown. It's the first week of October and I am on a coveted residency not only to revisit my past, but having promised I would do so in writing. A text pings from my most recent crush, a woman almost twenty years younger than me. I prefer to imagine she's been fatefully thrown in my path in the course of this woodland retreat. She is sharp but serrated. Funny. Sad. Religious. Fearfully (to me) aware of her own sexual energy, which I find familiarly entrancing, of course. I can't tell if she is aware of the effect she's having on me; I choose to think that she is. Just as I am aware that she has been broken and is more likely to indulge that brokenness, to put her hand in the flame, than step away from it. My opposite in this respect. She is drawn perhaps to my apparent empathy and steadiness. She is seeking those qualities in a friend rather than a lover. And me, feeling all the old feelings, suddenly alive to my inclination to chase and my willingness to wait. I can be exceedingly patient if I think you could be the one.

*Are you in the library?* reads the screen bubble.

---

In Louise Nevelson's pen-and-ink drawing of 1934, a statuesque woman sits sideways in a high-back chair. Her broad torso twists outward. Head slightly tilted, one knee bent beneath her, she turns to the side, resting both wrists together on the chairback. This serpentine gesture torques her posture into something less frontal. Sitting this way makes her seem slightly less available to the gaze, more dynamic. In turning, she appears to shield her breasts from view, their disguised doubleness nonetheless suggested by the rounded contours of her two arms.

Nevelson runs pen over paper in swift, mostly unbroken, gestures. Her drawing hand moves across the beige newsprint sheet with few signs of hesitation. A handful of tiny pools of ink, like visual punctuation, are the sole indications of a breath or a pause in her mark-making. If you look closely, you can see one of these saturated dots at the end of the gently arcing, left-to-right line that forms the belly beneath the figure's navel. There is another dot at the intersection of the woman's cleavage and the crease of

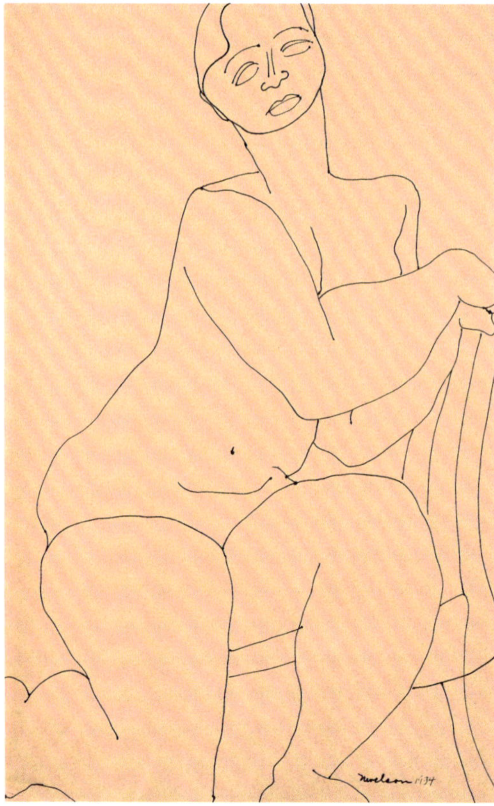

Louise Nevelson, *Seated Nude,* 1934

her elbow. Near the top of the sheet, a heavy black dot shows a rare recalibration of the diagonal line that forms the woman's long, cylindrical neck.

If her neck is a cylinder, what we see of her head falls somewhere between egg and sphere. The masklike face is an almost geometrical enclosure within which the woman's features are indicated with the artist's graphic shorthand. Three lines for the nose; three for the eyes; three for the mouth. Eyebrows: one arch each. Hair: a single ogive.

As an act of drafts(wo)manship, Nevelson's drawing is effortlessly characteristic and accomplished, pure *sprezzatura*. Like most drawings or sketches, it suggests immediacy. Because it was made relatively quickly, even impulsively, on something as ephemeral as paper, we, the viewers, feel ourselves as close as possible to the *première pensée*, the first thought, of the drawing's creator. It is as if we have caught the artist in the act because — what else can a drawing be but a stage of practice on the way to the final, rehearsed and perfected, performance? The ease and speed with which Nevelson conveys a conventionally female form, her economy of line (in the sense of the prudent management of resources) is nothing short of irritating if you've ever tried to draw with a pen. Things done both well and fast never cease to amaze us.

But in addition to the impression of speed, Nevelson's drawing offers the frisson of intimacy. If the image was taken from life, as they would have said in Rembrandt's time, there is the presumption that the model and the artist were once together in a studio, most likely in 1934. The connection intimated between the viewer of a sketch and the artist who made it is here compounded by the imagined physical, emotional, or at a minimum, spatial closeness of the artist and the model who poses for her. An insightful literary critic and art historian named Harry Berger Jr. famously theorized drawn and painted portraits as "fictions of the pose." Read as a portrayal of a real person, Nevelson's drawing implicates three subjects: the posing sitter, the artist, and the beholder.

Ten years before Louise Nevelson drew a nude woman in a chair somewhere in Manhattan, a lawsuit for the annulment of a marriage between the White descendant of an old New York Huguenot family and a working-class woman deemed Black received sensational coverage in local and national newspapers. In 1924, Leonard "Kip" Rhinelander married Alice Jones, a former chambermaid. When a New Rochelle paper ran a scandalous story about the marriage with the headline RHINELANDERS' SON MARRIES DAUGHTER OF A COLORED MAN, Kip took the bride to court, claiming that she had hidden her race from him. It is a matter of debate whether Kip himself, or his father, was truly behind the legal action. When the case went to trial, Alice's attorneys were tasked with building a defense of passing; the legal complaint against her was essentially an accusation of "racial fraud."

The ins and outs of the lawsuit are complex and appalling. "The Rhinelander Case," as it was known, is the subject of a compelling book preceded by a 2007 article by law professor Angela Onwuachi-Willig, the dean of Boston University School of Law. As Onwuachi-Willig explains, Alice Jones's lawyers (rather shockingly) changed their strategy about a year into the case. Attorney Lee Parsons Davis had first argued that Alice, whose mother was White, was also herself White. About twelve months in, however, Davis reversed course. Now he was claiming the opposite, that Alice was indeed "colored" and that her husband had known it all along and had married her anyway. Onwuachi-Willig's inexhaustibly documented book and article, on which I'm drawing here, argue that while the case is not a landmark in the sense that *Loving v. Virginia* was, it has just as much to tell us, if not more, about how US law has reified false notions of biological and "inexorable" race, White purity, and the real-world legal and cultural purchase of the one-drop rule.

It may surprise you to learn that, in 1925, an all-White, all-male jury decided in favor of Alice Jones and she won the case.

The newlywed Jones would nevertheless lose her marriage. In the eyes of a White supremacist "public," Alice proving herself Black also proved that her White socialite husband was an N-word lover. Following the trial, even in mid-1920s New York, the home of the Harlem Renaissance, it was impossible for this interracial marriage to survive.

I am fairly obsessed with this case, a clear demonstration of intersectional bias and bigotry, for one detail only. In the middle of the trial, Alice, who gave no verbal testimony, was forced to undress before the jury.

It's a horrific, enraging, and heart-wrenching story. One I've thought about leaving out of this chapter simply because, as Saidiya Hartman has argued, repeatedly showing and telling these devastating stories of emotional, physical, and sexual violence perpetrated against people of color, regardless of the author's supposed intention, has a way of giving these heinous tales a new and undeserved life. Under the premise of information or education, violence is perpetuated when, as in the original circumstances of Alice Jones's case, Black bodies are re-represented as a racist spectacle for the White gaze.

One possible response to this abolitionist-derived manner of exploiting Black pain, however, is to bounce or deflect violent White looks back onto themselves, like a mirror to a laser beam. Kerry James Marshall's harrowing 2002 triptych *Heirlooms & Accessories* achieves this end. From the White mob photographed at the much-reported double lynching of Thomas Smith and Abram Shipp in 1930, Marshall makes a focal point of three expressionless female faces. Screening back the rest of Lawrence Beitler's original image until the scene of the crime is whited-out and barely visible, the artist frames the monstrously placid female onlookers in oversize three-dimensional, rhinestoned lockets.

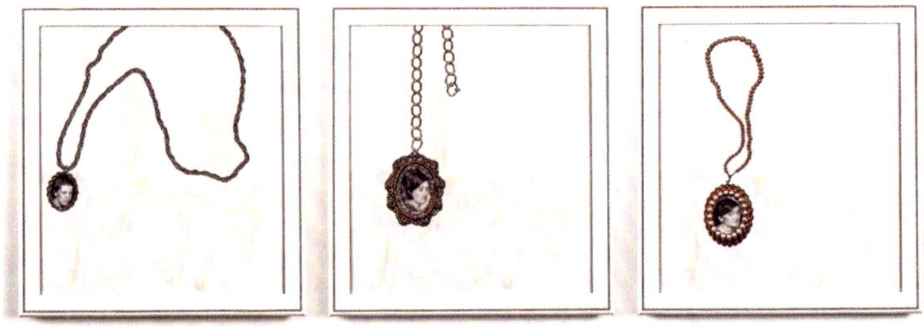

Kerry James Marshall, *Heirlooms & Accessories*, 2002

The result is a blown-up allusion to the common practice in the '20s and '30s of cutting out – literally beheading – a face to wear as a keepsake. Marshall has spoken of his desire to implicate the memorialized women as both "accessories" to the crime of murder and the source of normalized race prejudice passed down from heir to heir.

As a scene of double martyrdom, Marshall's large-scale triptych pointedly evokes the hinged altarpieces that became a fixture of the Northern Renaissance, especially after the Reformation, when Catholics and Protestants alike were killed for their religious identity. By visually indicting those demonic White watchers as complicit in the execution of two innocent Black men, by keeping the women continually judged and hanging in suspense, the artist creates the conditions for a retrial. For a new verdict. Here, in a similar way, I want to deflect the white-hot gaze from which Alice Jones Rhinelander never escaped back on her enemies and their heirs. Like Marshall, I want the context of the crime to be known. I want more people to see what happened not for the sake of art, but for the sake of truth.

For Alice's sake, I will keep it short. Onwuachi-Willig, working from legal transcripts, reports that at one point in Alice's defense, her husband, Leonard, was asked first if he was "color-blind." Then, if he could "distinguish between black and white." Then, if he could "distinguish between brown and white." Following these questions, the attorneys, the plaintiff, the stenographer, and Alice were removed from the courtroom. They were accompanied by the all-White-male jury. In an adjoining bathroom, Alice was made to remove her clothes before returning partially naked to the group assembled outside. "Weeping" when she did, she was asked by her attorney to expose her body, first the upper portion, including her breasts, then her legs with her breasts covered. Wishing perhaps to spare Alice Jones Rhinelander the posthumous shame, Onwuachi-Willig does not make what happened in that room explicit in her *California Law Review* article. She does not suggest or come right out and say what most writers make a point of reporting: When the jury was shown Alice's breasts, it was her nipples that decided the case.

It apparently goes without saying that a Black woman's nipples give her away. To an expert jurist like Onwuachi-Willig, the court records tell us all we need to know. Yet it is what they do not say that matters to me. As Onwuachi-Willig writes: "Davis [Alice's attorney] did not engage in extensive questioning about this 'piece' of evidence. Rather, he left the jury with the notion that 'the thing speaks for itself.'" She goes on to write, "Indeed, after seeing Alice's bare shoulders, arms, legs, and breasts at trial, no all-white jury in 1920s New York would have determined that Alice was *purely white*" (my emphasis). At the trial, prior testimony against Alice's Whiteness — or *for* her Blackness — was presented in the form of the "dusky complexion" of Alice's testifying West Indian father. I think I know what Onwuachi-Willig is trying to do by couching the incident in decorous vagueness. But good God, how it pains me to read this matter-of-fact assessment. Would my collarbone give me away? Would my thighs? What did the all-White jury know about Black breasts back then, what did a Mulatta shoulder look like? What does "purely white" even mean?

In his 2004 book *Interracial Intimacies: Sex, Marriage, Identity, and Adoption,* Harvard Law professor Randall Kennedy spells it all out explicitly, in a way I believe we need to hear. The purpose of asking Alice to disrobe, he writes, "was to demonstrate to the jurors that there were aspects of her physiognomy, including her nipples, that would have put Rhinelander on notice about her race." Someone had to say it.

Were Alice not an im/passable Black woman, she would not have been made to show her nipples to a roomful of White men. In this sense, her experience is unique to having the kind of "unreadable" body women with Black and White parents or grandparents or great-grandparents are said to possess. What happened at Alice's trial may be very loosely related to Sojourner Truth's choice to bare her breast to show that she was a woman, as Miriam Thaggert and others have suggested. But it is certainly not the same.

Three years into grad school in 2007, I was awarded a yearlong Fulbright scholarship to Madrid in order to conduct further archival research for my dissertation on the powers of women in the paintings of Peter Paul Rubens. The letter was very clear that I'd need to pass a physical examination comprising dozens of mandated tests. The Fulbright Commission is "the flagship international exchange program" of the US government. A Fulbright Scholar is an unofficial ambassador of the United States, and the commission needs to know you're of sound mind and body before they send you abroad.

At the time I had access to health care at Berkeley, so I made an appointment at the busy clinic on campus. The ponytailed woman doctor who saw me was athletic-looking and probably in her early forties. I remember my age at the time because the certificate I eventually received described me as a "healthy, 38 yr-old woman." The examination included blood tests and the usual knee-knocking for reflexes, palpitating, and pulse taking, and a gynecological check. It was at this point that the woman, with whom I'd been easily conversing, asked me to lower my paper smock for a breast exam. More than fifteen years later, as I look back on that moment, I instantly feel the sharp edges of its impact both in that room and since. I feel it cut to the quick of my self-image as I sit there on the cold metal table getting ready to be examined by a White woman.

The doctor was seated on a wheeled stool at my feet. As soon as I shrugged off the smock, she looked up and blurted out, as if I had been concealing a second head: "WOW! Gosh. Have you never considered having a reduction?"

I assumed my doctor would catch herself and apologize. She hadn't even touched me yet. Instead, she began describing happy women who had had their breasts made surgically smaller. "Is there any medical reason for me to do that?" I asked. I was shocked. Too shocked to explicitly call her out on what seemed to be a fucked-up reaction to a body type common among Black women and women of color – toned, muscular legs, round belly, strong arms, and full, even "pendulous" breasts – a body type with which she was perhaps unfamiliar. From the expression on her face, I could see plainly that my shape was abhorrent to her. She was truly embarrassed for me. Her involuntary response was based on what she believed good breasts should look like, regardless of their health. "It's great for your back," she said. I told her that I maintained a regular Bikram Yoga practice in San Francisco, which I did. I was in great shape at the time, in fact. Not thin. Never thin. But fit, with a strong core, to use the language of the mat. Still, I was a 36F. "It's just something you might want to consider," she went on. "Why?" I asked, increasingly indignant. "Like I said, it's just something I wanted to make you aware of as a possibility. It definitely makes exams easier." I'm sure I wanted to cry. But I didn't.

She stood up and placed her chilly hands on the unacceptable parts of a body that made her job more difficult. I looked down as she worked her fingers across the surface of my palest beige skin, forever untouched by the sun. Long before that experience I was doctorphobic. I've always felt judged by White GPs, as much for my weight as anything else. I don't remember what came next. Only that at some point before she finished, I forced myself to say something like: "I guess I'm just happy with the body God gave me." It was a half-truth, but at least it shut her up. I left that appointment so riddled with shame I'd nearly forgotten the achievement that brought me there.

"To each her own, said the old woman as she kissed the cow" was a favorite expression of my vegetarian grandmother, who wore jeans and Clark's shoes and read the L.L.Bean catalogue the way I read *Harper's*. As she often pointed out: Men's clothes are generally better made and less expensive than women's – most dry cleaners used to charge more for women's shirts, which they could identify by which side the buttons were on. These days, now that I've soft-butched it up, I am comfortable with how my belly and bust look in jeans and the Brooks Brothers shirts I've worn for decades. I've lived long enough to see how notions of what counts as a valid performance of queerness or femininity or Blackness are as susceptible to change as any other style of being. Coked-up-skinny, androgynous masc, and sparkly Barbie haven't always been in. Like a well-fed Rubensian noblewoman, I am perfectly fine with the space my robust body takes up in the world. Barring medical imperatives and in accordance with my personal variant of Black lesbian feminism, I have no desire to alter my shape in response to misogyny, the inescapable male gaze, or White supremacist conventions of female beauty. I do not equate masculinity with inherent strength or power or freedom, and my butchness has nothing to do with notions of being "masc." In fact, nothing about the way I embody my sexuality or express my gender renders me a candidate for top surgery or reductions, though I think I can begin to imagine how life-changing and life-saving these procedures are for people who need and choose them. There can be plenty of good reasons to reduce one's breasts. And there can be plenty of good reasons not to.

My partner while I was in Berkeley remains the woman with whom I've been the longest. She had only or mostly dated Black women when we met. She was seven years older than me and culturally Jewish enough to prefer a deli for Sunday brunch and detest my parents' fetishization of Christmas, though she didn't much practice her religion. Out as a lesbian since her pierced and tattooed teenage years drinking and drugging in semi-suburban Denver. Who can say what drew her to a professionally ambitious partier in her late twenties, moving through the world at the time as simply herself? As an unqualified woman of color who was by implication unraced.

Had Rachel (not her real name) known as soon as she saw me something I had not yet come to terms with myself? She first set eyes on me when I accidentally walked into a meeting she, from a different organization, was attending at the Colorado AIDS Project, my workplace at the time. Did she, as someone who had seen her share of Black women's bodies, perform a racial profile when she first glimpsed me and mine? Making an unintentionally grand entrance, I had swung open the door to what I believed was an empty conference room. I was wearing my shoulder-padded red '90s blazer and requisite pencil skirt. I'd interrupted the director's multiagency confab, at which point all eyes had turned my way until, flustered and freaked out, I excused myself and ran back down the hallway.

Rachel got my number from a coworker and called to ask me on a date a few days later. I thought it infinitely romantic. Love at actual first sight. Destiny. I, too, had felt the crackling charge of our meeting eyes at what was, for me, a very embarrassing moment. I hardly ever made it to Wonderful Wednesday dinners with Olga and Dr. Larsen anymore, having reluctantly admitted to myself that our tortured relationship was predestined to be over. That was tragic, not romantic. Romantic was a very hot woman – long, wavy, prematurely salt-and-pepper hair, stonish butch in demeanor but brushed-silk butch in presentation. Rachel's closet was full of plain but expensive women's button-down blouses in muted fruit shades and just as many sets of tailored black trousers to go with them. She wore softly masculine ankle boots and liked to pluck her frequently waxed eyebrows standing in front of a curtainless window, where the light was harshest.

We were both early in our "real job" lives, though Rachel was years ahead of me in responsibility. She was considering a master's degree in psychology and she already managed a clinic on the edge of downtown. At the time she drove the sporty white Honda coupe that predated her black BMW. She still wore the simple but heavy gold ring her ex had given her – a round black stone where the diamond should be. The adoring previous girlfriend was born in the British Virgin Islands. She was much, much darker than me and always very nice when we ran into her at the club. Rachel and I were together for thirteen years, but we might never have discussed my race at all if it weren't for a barbecue in Denver one hot summer afternoon.

We had taken things slow until we took them fast, making good on the stereotype after dating less than six months, and moving into a sweet little carriage house with a peach tree in the back. My grown-up fundraising job as a development officer for an HIV/AIDS nonprofit had come at a time when protease inhibitors, the first of which was approved in 1995, were a very new, truly miraculous development. Unlike my cube at the auction house in Chicago, in Denver I had my own office with a window, two chairs, and a big metal desk. I had a phone and files. I went to meetings. I took minutes. All within a very gay, albeit very male, workplace environment. It felt like a triumph to be respectably employed where I grew up, plus it seemed I had a talent for raising funds. I plied that talent to good end until the director fired me for insubordination, which, having tried to get my supervisor dismissed, I probably had coming.

After that I went into a kind of tailspin. When I landed, it was on the idea of opening a store with my mother. This we did, and although the Paris Flea Market, as we named it, did not turn anything close to a profit, it kicked off what was to be a uniquely simpatico period for my mother and me. Back then we would get up early on the weekends and go to estate sales and auctions together, driving into neighborhoods neither of us knew existed to find quirky but utilitarian vintage stuff to fill our converted alley house. Our creative hodgepodge of a store was on a cute street in what would become (but wasn't yet) one of Denver's most high-rent and weed-centric neighborhoods. We had so much fun together, pricing our little finds and celebrating the months we made rent with a little to spare.

My parents had waited to travel to Europe until I left for school. But once I was away, they started taking yearly trips to small towns mostly in France and Italy. Separately, all three of us had made pilgrimages to real Paris flea markets outside the 18th, from which we had brought back small gifts for each other. A vintage enameled silver Eiffel Tower keychain from me for my mother. A pair of eighteenth-century beakers for me from my dad. The trips to Europe came only after my parents closed their own retail outlet, Lillie Price Antiques. For most of my high school and college years, Lillie Price was known for top-of-the-line tiger oak rolltop desks, French country "china" cabinets, stacking legal bookcases, and mammoth Victorian dining sets, often meticulously restored by my dad.

My mother and I love front-of-the-house retail. Maybe it's in our genes. But there's also something in the culture of our family that makes buying and researching and selling feel like a reasonable use of one's time. Not unlike teaching, with which it shares the excitement of discovery. It goes back at least to my mother's grandfather, my great-grandfather (Edgar Fay Caldwell), who helped James Cash Penney open the first of his American department stores in a barren and isolated Wyoming town called Kemmerer. We used to have a postcard sent by J.C. from his mansion in Florida to his trustworthy, cigar-smoking store manager in the Wild West. My mother and I are both similarly energized by the breezy, good-faith small talk that expert salesmanship requires. We are gratified by transactions that feel more like making friends, and we derive genuine happiness from leading people to objects that we obtained because we appreciate them too. Our

Paris Flea Market store sold pristine floral waxed-cotton pillow shams from the forties and deco ice crushers painted lemon yellow and Depression glass lamps and mid-century botanical prints in Venetian mirrored frames and packs of old photographs. What we couldn't part with, we kept.

Inside, we left the house's three little spaces to their original purposes – displaying just the right accoutrements for one's dining and living and bedroom. Martha Stewart was as yet unincarcerated and shabby chic was a newish thing, and the idea was you'd pull a picture off the wall, a dish off the table, or a rug off the floor if you liked it. Edith Piaf and jazz standards echoed through the house. When my mother baked cookies four at a time in a toaster oven in the tiny kitchen, the scent of burnt semisweet chocolate wafted out the door to lure shoppers inside. We opened at noon so we could shop in the mornings. But one of us was ALWAYS there. Store slaves, my mother used to call us.

One unexpected outcome of this intergenerational business was socializing together with my parents and some of the customers we jointly came to know. Flora and Bev were a lesbian couple who lived on the other side of town with their two small children. They were serious of personality but nice, and easy to talk to. We liked them and they loved the store and shopped there often. Flora, French and small, had straight dark hair and sincere, animal-like brown eyes. She was thoughtful and warm but also a ready source of sometimes disarming non sequiturs; you never knew what to expect from her. Bev was a borderline humorless, otherwise typical outdoorsy Colorado dyke with thick waves of light brown hair under a baseball cap. Both were White, their ages somewhere between my mother's and mine – late thirties at the time, I'd guess.

Flora and Bev had invited my parents, along with Rachel and

me, to their house to grill and drink. The summer beverage of choice at that time was the French Kir, refreshingly ruby-colored and made of inexpensive white wine infused with a shot of the blackcurrant liqueur known as crème de cassis. Rachel liked Flora and Bev well enough simply for being lesbians. And my Francophilic dad, who still didn't seem all that comfortable having a queer for a daughter, also got along with the couple. Bev was the kind of stoical butch some straight men can easily connect with through their obviously shared interest in women. *Così fan tutte.* It was a hot, dry Colorado day and we were stationed around the fish charring on a grill behind the house, laughing with our glasses in hand. I had gone inside for some reason and headed back out to join the five of them in the grass. Flora turned to look at me as I approached, her gaze newly hungry and eager.

In fact, all their eyes were on me as I approached. In a way I couldn't read.

"Ah, but what was her father then, unh?" Flora asked in her Marseillaise accent, searching my features for the answer even before my mother could provide it.

"He's Black," she said.

Rachel looked at me.

I stared at my mother.

I felt the heat of tears rising in my throat. I felt the fury of betrayal and the roil of rage along with it. How dare this woman broach the subject of my birth? In front of everyone – everyone except me, had I washed my hands for a few seconds longer. How dare she ask so very rude and so very French a question? I turned abruptly around and sprinted back up the stairs and inside. From the kitchen window, I stared at them for several minutes as they gestured to each other sympathetically.

When I returned, Flora took me aside. *Mais non.* She hadn't meant anything by it. I was so beautiful. So exotic. She only wanted to know what made me that way. It was nothing to be ashamed about.

---

In 1932, at the age of thirty-three, Louise Nevelson was hired as an assistant by Diego Rivera. The Mexican artist had been commissioned by the Federal Art Project to make a mural for Rockefeller Center. Nevelson prepared the paints and walls and research for Rivera's brush. But two years later, the finished mural was chiseled off and plastered over when Rockefeller objected to an unflattering family portrait and the inclusion of Lenin, definitely an unwelcome guest at Rockefeller Center. Nevelson is said to have had an affair with Rivera while she was working for him, greatly angering her (former) friend and roommate Frida Kahlo.

In 1934, Nevelson began studying with the sculptor Chaim Gross. She had been moving surely and steadily from painting and drawing to making work in three dimensions. Soon after her time with Gross, Nevelson became a sculptor herself, fulfilling a prediction she is said to have made as a child about her future career as an artist. Born in Ukraine, Nevelson was the daughter of Jewish immigrants who had settled in Maine. In 1920, she married. The couple moved to New York and had a son two years later. In 1931, Nevelson left her husband, who had prohibited her from making art, and sent her son to live with his grandparents.

Which brings us to the circumstances under which the drawing described at the beginning of this chapter, the image signed and dated 1934, was created. Nevelson's graphic works from the mid-1930s have come up at auction not infrequently in the 2020s. She was prolific in those Great Depression years—a little surprising since she would have been occupied with the Rockefeller mural debacle (and an irate Frida), as well as her new sculpture studies with Gross.

Personally, I have long considered working, in the sense of doing work, to be the best, maybe the only, productive distraction from worry or sadness. Perhaps Nevelson felt that way too. Whatever the reason, her most recent art on the market is mainly figural sketches and drawings, of which she appears to have made dozens if not hundreds in the thirties. The drawings are of varying complexity and quality. Some are obviously preparatory and notational, lacking the fluidity of line and compositional interest of the "woman in a chair" drawing and others like it from the same year. Nevelson's sketches of women are especially abundant. One can only imagine that, being in close contact with dance studios and the Art Students League, where she had begun studying in 1929, while working in the studio of a figurative artist, Nevelson must have had access to a variety of paid female models.

But what "kind" of models?

In 2018, the Whitney Museum's Clarence White assembled *The Face in the Moon,* a small exhibition of Nevelson's prints and drawings from the museum's permanent collection. Many of these works on paper from the late twenties and thirties feature female forms whose contours consist of a single confident line but whose heads have been left out of the frame by the artist. In the 1934 drawing, by contrast, we see most of the model's face as well as her nude body. We see, I think, that she is a Black woman.

But how can "we" tell?

For me the most frustrating and maddening reality of writing about passing as White or Black is that this project of engaging visual representations of race forces me, the author, to undertake some of the same highly subjective, book-by-the-cover appraisals against which I'm rallying. If I want to suggest that a figure who has previously been read as White is "really" Black, I have to prove it on her. I have to tick off a list of her Blackisms over against her Whitisms in order to make my highly circumstantial case.

But there I go, there I go, there I go.

As we have seen, the wonderful drawing of 1934 — which I bought at auction as a present to myself after I sold my second novel — features a nude woman seated on a chair. In it, Nevelson hints at a belly and broad hips. But mainly she emphasizes the woman's, or should we say the model's, thick, muscular-looking limbs. The seated figure's forearms are nearly as thick as her calves. Her thighs are similarly substantial and rounded. As I noted before, the model's posture denies the viewer access to her breasts. If they are conspicuously Black breasts, with the dark nipples that presumably convicted and exonerated Alice Jones Rhinelander, we cannot see them. I might argue that the emphasis on a kind of "unfeminine" muscular sturdiness could indicate Nevelson's interest in (attraction to?) the woman's "Black" body for its divergence from conventional ideals of slightness and Whiteness. But what remains to help determine the woman's race is her face.

And here, we have only fifteen drawn lines to go on. Conventionally, with Black faces, it is not the eyes but the nose and the lips that have it. Accordingly, art history asks: Is this a flat nose? Are these full lips? Even a cursory survey of Nevelson's female nudes from the 1930s sold at auction over the past decade soon makes this racial guessing game unplayable. In a self-portrait circa 1935, Nevelson has abstracted and distilled her own features, particularly her slightly flaring, bracketlike nose, into shapes that might easily be mis/read as "negroid," or at least "mixed." This possibility in itself is interesting. But it may tell us more about why the

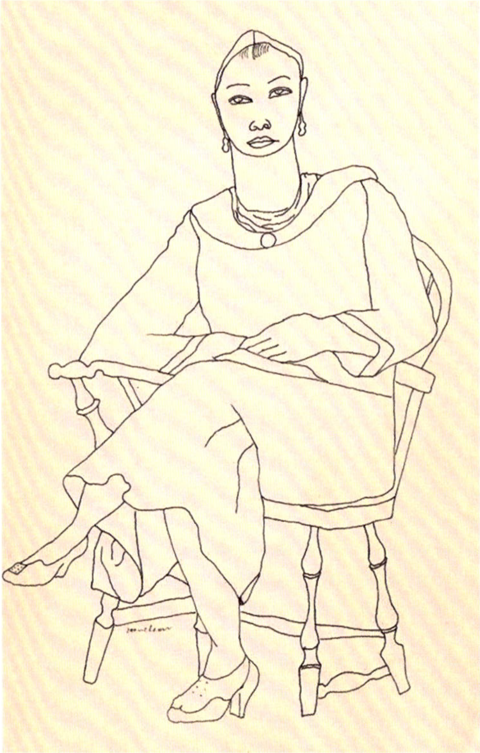

Louise Nevelson, *Self-Portrait,* ca. 1935

alterity of Black models appealed to Nevelson than about the kind of woman she saw herself as – given the penile appearance of her head and neck, the phrase "phallic mother" comes to mind.

In my drawing, Nevelson made the model's nose out of a pair of parallel lines perpendicular to the same kind of bracket that forms her nostrils in the self-portrait seated in a chair. One sees immediately that a significant difference between these women (as portrayed) is the rendition of their eyes. In my drawing, the woman lacks both pupils and irises, a choice that inevitably endows her visage with an emotionless, masklike quality accentuated by the non-natural geometry of its outline. In Nevelson's Nevelson, the sitter has pupils. (She also has ears.)

Rendering the model's face like a mask could be a means for evoking a physical "Africanness," or Blackness, along the lines of Picassoesque "primitivism" still very much of the moment (Man Ray's celebrated modernist photograph of *Kiki with African Mask* is dated 1926). Then again, the drawn faces by Nevelson, whose sharp noses, tiny waists, and small areolas read more stereotypically White, also commonly possess blank eyes. Hairstyles aren't much of a help either, as most of Nevelson's women are merely given vaguely pageboy-like or bunlike helmets rather than detailed coiffures expressing color and texture.

Nothing I write will prove beyond a doubt that Nevelson's model was a Black woman. The harder I argue for her face or body to register as Black, the more I invite the exceptions that prove absolutely nothing. White women have thick arms and broad hips and muscular thighs and pooching bellies too.

As an unintended interwar catalogue of the "female" form, the best of these drawings are compelling to me both individually and as a series. This is because there's no way around Nevelson's palpable need to look at and represent naked women. Women of a wide variety of body types and sizes and of different "races" as well. Nevelson decided to make three-dimensional figures out of a flat surface, using pen and ink to provide something close to the minimum of graphic information. The living bodies represented were inevitably sculptural. But Nevelson's investment in abstraction is clear. For her, the models boil down to a handful of suggestive lines decisively edited and executed.

According to the Oxford English Dictionary, to ab-stract is to take out of, to remove something from its (or her) context. To forgo the specific for the general. But also: to convert the sensual and vital into a concept or idea. To make, or try to make, a universal from the particular.

I can't help but think that when Nevelson began to make sculpture in three dimensions, like her abstract forms of aluminum (1933) and terracotta (1934), her expert knowledge of the bodies of women gained over the preceding years played a role in this conceptual turn. White bodies, Black bodies. Nude bodies whose race and femininity stubbornly defied reduction. Drawn, and drawn, and drawn.

A few years later, in 1941, Nevelson has her first solo show. Then, in 1945, she makes three blockish terracotta forms and incises them with the barest indications of human features before attaching the chunks to a spinelike rod and painting the whole thing black. By the late fifties, Nevelson — like Barbara Hepworth and Ruth Asawa, the rare woman sculptor working in nonfigural idioms — was starting to be known for her monochromatic cabinet-like assemblages. Soon her name would be synonymous with towering wooden sculptures made of bulbous banisters and shapely spindles and newel posts and discarded geometric cut-outs uniformly covered with paint. From women in chairs — to disembodied legs. I wonder if the fragmented furniture and domestic objects Nevelson endlessly reconfigured, beginning, essentially, in the civil rights era, were a way of turning her previous sketches of women into abstractions of both gender and race — in black, in white, in high-yellow gold — drawing on those minimalist Jim Crow–era studies to reconstruct new forms of modern art.

# 9

# BIG SHOULDERS

After I was outed as Black at the backyard barbecue with the lesbians and my parents, Rachel and I went back to our little bungalow. I was quiet on the drive home. I was quiet for the next few weeks. But there was something new with us. We'd never talked explicitly about my race. And now she had heard my mother inform two nosy relative strangers that my biological father was Black. Rachel, who often assumed the role of therapist to her unhoused clients, was an exceptional listener. She could see that my mother's frank disclosure had upset me. Perhaps because she had known all along that I was in some way Black, Rachel must also have realized that I had not truly faced that truth myself until the words were spoken aloud in my presence.

I'm reminded of the archetypal delivery-room utterance described by Judith Butler as the "girling of the girl." The moment when the all-powerful doctor speaks a gender into existence according to convention, constructs, and convenience. The physician's words are the ultimate performative speech act. Whether his/her/their determination of the baby's sex is felicitous for the infant body in question, only the future will tell. At the time, of course, the tiny body's own opinion doesn't matter. Though it was pronounced well past the hour of my birth, my mother's speech act, her "Blacking of the Black," made this identity incontestably mine. And now there were witnesses to prove it.

In retrospect, I can only have been in a mild state of shock as I turned to exit the scene. To know something in your head or your heart or the marrow of your bones is miles away from hearing it plainly stated as fact in front of other people. How can I explain? Had I been passing for the years and weeks and days prior to that summer afternoon in my early thirties? I had never claimed to be White, never written that down. Nor, when I was coming of age, was "woman of color" in use in the way it is now. Though I did not and still do not like it, I had been called "mixed" by both Black and White kids at school when they wanted to shame or insult me. Where I lived, being called "mixed" was something like being called "mongrel" or "half-blood" a generation earlier. To my younger self, I was always an *other*. But on principle I had never, ever, checked solely the box marked "Black."

So visceral was my response that afternoon, two or three years must have passed before my race came up again with Rachel. Meanwhile, I was midway through the second year of what they called a "Joint PhD" program between the Iliff School of Theology and the University of Denver. Although I'd won an award for distinguished scholarship as a master's student, I hadn't received anything close to full funding for the doctoral program. According to my application, I was working toward teaching at the college level. In reality, I was surreptitiously pursuing ordination. I, a partnered lesbian of color, was edging in my uncertain way toward the process of becoming an Episcopal priest in a somewhat conservative Western diocese that, at the time, prohibited the ordination of "practicing" homosexuals. But also, in the eyes of my denomination, even straight people could get in trouble for trying to get into the Church through the side door. Officially, obtaining the master's in divinity (rather than in the more academic and less practical field of religious studies, as I had) was a path pursued by the candidate for holy orders only once she had the backing of her parish, the Diocesan Commission, and, provisionally, her bishop. My bishop was not supportive of ordaining gay Episcopalians, though he had already done so (perhaps) unwittingly; a few single, undeclared gays had slipped through. One of these was our deacon, Mother Eileen, a highly regarded, beloved, and deeply spiritual woman who became my mentor and friend. But Eileen had been married to a man when she took holy orders – it was only later that she fell hard for the business-savvy former Catholic nun Amy, with whom she shared a life, a fierce commitment to service, and a wonderful house, until Amy died of cancer. Theirs is a love story for the ages. Knowing wise and spiritually generous Mother Eileen, from whom a laugh feels like the highest achievement, is like encountering a divine instrument in the form of a human being – whether saint or guardian angel time will tell.

Our conservatively progressive little inner-city church, designed by Ralph Adams Cram, the same architect responsible for New York's Cathedral of St. John the Divine, was known for its exquisite but never precious High Church liturgy and vital, comparatively young if childless, congregation – almost entirely White, largely professional, but also sincerely welcoming to anyone who was not a social-climbing "cathedral type." The splendor of worship. Smells and bells. Tallis. Evensong. A lesbian deacon. How could we not have attracted a solid core of devoted queers? Still, my homo church friends unanimously agreed that, for the gays, being faithfully partnered to someone you loved rendered you well nigh unordainable in Colorado. (It wasn't until the succeeding bishop, the Right Reverend Robert O'Neill, came to the state that an out and partnered lesbian was made a priest of the church. Mary Catherine Volland was ordained in 2009 after what *The Denver Post* grossly termed "several years of restraint" on the part of my former diocese.)

My parish priest in Denver at the time of the barbecue outing, whom I'll call Mother Barbara, is another churchwoman for whom I hold immense respect. Though I was never attracted to her as I often am to smart, elegant women who know their minds, a Eucharist presided over by Mother Barbara filled me with a depth of admiration and fealty I have rarely felt for a woman I'm not dating or trying to date. She was, in fact, the first woman ordained in our state. In her early sixties at the time she was my rector, Mother Barbara was intensely ethical, thoughtful, dry of wit, and innately well mannered. So coiffed, manicured, and outwardly of her era as to be likened to Debbie Reynolds by certain gay men I knew. She was the most unabashedly intellectual preacher I'd ever heard – the most literary, the most rhetorically gifted. Teach, move, delight, says St. Augustine. Imagining there might be others like her, I wanted to be one of them. In the twenty-five years since I first saw her in the pulpit, I have, however, never heard anyone – at cathedrals in England, in New York, in Chicago, San Francisco, or Washington, DC – preach more spiritually demanding, more artful, or more convicting sermons. Sermons that broke my heart open and made me aware of having a soul that could go either way depending on my actual words and deeds. And doing all that by means of the English language.

Just before and during my seminary years, I went to church several times a week. Often, in small gatherings of five or six. Morning prayer, evening prayer, compline. I served weekly in the altar party; became a member of the vestry. Pledged some of my small recent inheritance from my grandmother in a way that depleted my grad student coffers. Any good priest is aware when hearts among her flock are strangely warmed. Mother Barbara sensed my vocation. We spoke of it. But I have come to see that in her subtle, though somewhat faithless way she was trying to signal the difficulty, if not the impossibility, of my heeding what I then perceived as a calling.

None of this means I was meant to be, or would have become, even under different political circumstances, a priest. The fiery words come easily enough. The devotion is pure. For better and for worse, a preaching strain runs through me whether I have a congregation or not. You don't have to be holy, or even good, to become an Episcopal priest. But you do need to make yourself smaller and more docile before the ecclesiastical polity. Not only did I lack the necessary humility and selflessness, I lacked the patience and perseverance. I gave up far too soon.

In so many words, Rachel told me we could no longer be together if I pursued the ordination thing. Being Jewish, she understandably never attended services with me or followed the rhythms of a Christian calendar. Nor did she wish to be the spouse of a priest affiliated with a homophobic religious tradition. Convinced I saw the writing on the wall, I shut the door on that vocation and applied to a handful of doctoral programs. Again, I asked the woman I considered my partner to remain with me as I started a new life for both of us. This time in California, where I was accepted by Berkeley's doctoral program in the history of art.

The University of California was a proudly democratic public institution in those days, so nobody got into Berkeley's PhD program in art history without full funding. We were told our fellowships would cover the duration of our seven – six if your cutthroat drive knew no bounds – years. But those of us without highly paid partners or personal wealth had to take out loans and look for research side hustles just to cover rent. Between 2000 and 2015, which includes the six years I was living there, the East Bay's consumer price index (CPI) rose 78.4 percent, making the region one of the most expensive in the nation. Our annual stipend, less than $20K, remained the same term after term, from start to finish. But I convinced myself it didn't matter. I was being paid to read and research and write about Baroque painting; paid to take classes with the kind of actual geniuses who made you wonder if your brain was made of the same squishy pink stuff, whose revolutionary books and *Art Bulletin* articles changed the face of the field; who received standing ovations at the end of a regular weekday class. It was almost paradise.

Except that my partner was still back in Denver. After selling the small house Rachel had bought, we'd downsized her into an apartment in her old Capitol Hill neighborhood, not two blocks from my elementary school. She at least had an apartment with a kitchen she could wander into in her underwear and a living room with her own couch. My private, quasi-cloistered existence in North Berkeley was confined to the four walls of a rented bedroom. The built-in desk in front of the window. The cheerfully cornflower blue plastic Ikea chair. The single bed pushed flush against the wall. The blessedly en suite bathroom and the spider I considered a friend staked out between wall and toilet. I was delirious with pride and excitement to be a student in that program. But I was so very lonely.

Eventually, around the beginning of my second year, Rachel found a really good job managing a UC clinic in the city. She packed up her apartment and all our larger things, and moved to the East Bay. At first, we lived in a small first-floor apartment with frosted-glass street-facing windows on College Avenue in

Oakland's Rockridge neighborhood. About a year later, wonder of wonders, the San Francisco housing gods smiled upon us when a gay guy Rachel had befriended at work fast-tracked us into his soon-to-be-vacated, hardwood-floored, bug-free, one-bedroom on the bright second story of a four flat. Right in the bleeding homosexual and Hispanic heart of *La Misión.* Paradise gained. From the comfort of our living room, we could monitor the line for the original Tartine as it wound around the corner of that unparalleled French bakery. The late and legendary Lexington Club was our neighborhood (lesbian) bar. Dolores Park Café (the real-world equivalent of *The L Word*'s "Planet") was less than two blocks away. On Pride, a raucous sea of leathery dykes on bikes revved up their rides directly beneath our bay window. It may have been the closest I will come to finding myself at the center of the cultural zeitgeist of a given era, my life's version of Gertrude Stein's Paris or Bessie Smith's Harlem. We were out and proud lesbians living in what felt like the epicenter of queer San Francisco. When my girlfriend wanted to go to a movie, we walked down to the Castro Theatre, for crying out loud. I didn't care what was playing as long as we got there in time to see the gothic Wurlitzer rise onto the stage so David Hegarty could play his rousing version of "San Francisco" while the audience clapped along like the believers at a rainbow revival we absolutely were.

It was in San Francisco that Rachel returned me to my race. One morning she leaned against the wall outside our bathroom while I twisted my hair into a ponytail for school. I can't remember how the subject came up. What I do recall is Rachel catching my eye in the mirror from her spot in the hallway. "It's your culture," she said, looking at me doing what I daily did to smooth my hair into femme manageability. "I just think you could get a lot from it if you wanted to."

Girlfriends, I've had my share. Sometime around 1992, late in my senior year of college, I went to a "country night" on the second floor of a bookstore on Chicago's North Side. It may be news to millennials, but two-stepping and line dancing to mainstream country music were very popular among some segments of what was called the gay community in the nineties. Being from Colorado, I had already learned to two-step at some point. What was funny, though, is that I'm sure I'm not alone in having first practiced this form of partner dancing – to ideologically conservative and politically reactionary, if not populist-racist, music – in a bar full of men with their arms around men and women with their arms around women. Impossible as it sounds, Denver had maybe fifteen gay and/or lesbian bars and clubs in those years. And while I can scarcely believe it now, my hometown was home to no fewer than two *exclusively country* gay bars. For guys, there was the big and glitzy uptown country-only Charlie's. For gals, there was the more modestly appointed "Miss C's," which, though also on gritty, sex-club-strewn Colfax Avenue, was barely within Denver's city limits. Regardless of Charlie's coat checks and musclebound shoe polishers and mirror-encrusted cowboy boots majestically spinning overhead, or C's bare bones and typically lesbian lack thereof, both bars provided local homosexuals with a slick and sizable parquet dance floor. They also offered visiting rodeo and stock-show queers a downhome venue where they could safely cut a rug and show off their buckles without the fear of redneck aggression or, worse, violent hate crimes. There were often police stationed outside the entrance to Charlie's; I cannot recall seeing them at C's.

In my post-college adopted city of Chicago, I don't think there were any gay bars solely devoted to line dances like the Circle Jerk or the Tush Push. But several of the regular clubs subbed out Madonna and the Eurythmics once a week for popular hits from Dwight, Trisha, Clint, and then patron saint of cowgays Garth Brooks. Whether they were doctors or postal carriers, stockbrokers or high school teachers, most people dressed to the nines on those frigid Midwestern nights. Skating arm in arm down icy, unshoveled sidewalks in their spanking new Luccheses and Justins, some of those dancing queens even wore spurs.

Chicago has a huge Mexican community. Alcala's, even then a West Town fixture, is the best Western-wear store I've ever encountered, and I felt welcome in a business that started out serving brown people and immigrants from the neighborhood. Even penniless, at the height of my youthful obsession, I had three pairs of boots from that place: shiny and sharp black lizard, a vulvic pale-pink leather with darker pink trim, and an ivory pair of snip toes with brown contrast stitching. For dancing, as in civilian life, I only occasionally wore jeans. In girly mode, I was more likely to show up in a short denim skirt and tights with maybe a black velvet blouse and some heavy Indian turquoise and silver I'd stolen from my mother or been given by my grandmother.

In those early stages of my about-to-be-professional life, like many if not most urban working queers in the '90s, I had a split identity. At the auction house, employed as a junior account executive, I had been a blazered, Hermès-wearing baby appraiser, giggling in the back seat of the company van with the latest gaggle of hungover, dyed-blond denizens of Miss Hall's or Miss Porter's. Like art galleries and museums, auction houses were then and remain a common premarital holding tank for pretty, gregarious, hard-living White girls of this ilk. Girls who will happily labor for free in exchange for a blue-chip name on their résumés and access to potential husbands. Girls born to make blasé chitchat with potential consignors with penthouses on Lake Shore Drive or gated estates in Kenilworth or Winnetka. My primary job, as it had been in my sorority, was that of debutante whisperer.

Initially at least, when two or three of us were sent out on an appraisal appointment, the girls in pearls would provide the entrée by casually dropping the names of their fathers and brothers at Goldman Sachs or Merrill or recounting their exploits at Bailey's Beach Club or the Head of the Charles. Surveying the clients' property but scarcely interacting with them, I was in charge of knowing what we were looking at and, more importantly, whether it was worth our time. A few steps into a room, we'd send each other speculatively positive or negative signals with our eyes as I flourished my tubular silver scale, calculating value per troy ounce of silver (ten dollars then; much more if it was Tiffany or Gorham) in my head. Being so new and so young, I was initially sent on the B- or C-level one-bedroom-apartment-type appraisals. The auction house's senior account executive, a tall, auburn-bobbed closet smoker in her thirties with an extensive repertoire of Campbell plaids and luxurious butterscotch knits, was sent to net the big fish. As I began to learn from my coworkers (one of whom I was sleeping with) how to spot the sleepers—a cache of pristine geometric-patterned Kazak rugs rolled up in plastic sheets in a policeman's basement like so many corpses (they would later sell for tens of thousands apiece) or a neglected lakeside patio outfitted with a huge suite of rare aluminum furniture by the industrial designer Warren McArthur—the boss started to send me to the more obviously profitable estates.

By day, it was two-tone Ann Taylor (boutique chic at the time) skirt suits and my lone and cherished pair of Ferragamo Vara Bows. By night it was Tony Lamas and white denim snap shirts. By day, it was keep your sex life to yourself (I was judiciously out only to my closest friends and my Republican but tolerant employer). By night, it was write down your number on this napkin and/or meet me in the bathroom. Answering machines. Missed connections. Friend of a friend. Fate.

A couple of years later, I would be deliriously present at one of the first Chicago showings of Rose Troche and Guinevere Turner's *Go Fish* (1994) while working part-time for the Film Festival. In 1991, the two women had started shooting their breakout lesbian feature film in the Wicker Park neighborhood. Though I never witnessed it in action, this groundbreaking bit of filmmaking corresponded with the time I was attempting to escape the frat bullies at school with a term-abroad program in the city called "Semester in the Arts." Each week, we took the bus from our Gold Coast State Street SRO to our classes on Damen in the same pregentrified corner of Chicago where the lowest of low-budget lesbian films was being made.

On screen, everything about *Go Fish* felt validating and accurate. It's hard to convey how shocking it was to see two regular women from the neighborhood kissing like they meant it in a real movie theater, with tickets and Twizzlers, in the inescapable company of row upon spiky-haired row of dykes to watch out for. I don't think I noticed how diverse the cast was because Wicker Park was just like that — Black, brown, immigrant White, Spanish-speaking, artsy, working class. It was a neighborhood of diners with slashed vinyl booths, pregnant stray dogs in stairwells, graffitied bus stops, and Goodwill stores where many people bought clothes to wear without a hint of irony. In Troche and Turner's lesbian fantasyland, twentysomething women all wore biker jackets and baggy jeans and talismanic chrome dyke jewelry. To date a woman was to confess your desires over the telephone wires for hours on end. To go out was to frequent a lightless, airless, dive bar where half the fun was that the place was supposedly straight. *Go Fish* felt researched to the point of documentarian, thrillingly recognizable as real life in the big-city Midwest.

In the film's lesbo Wicker Park, there were house parties of all-women drinking games like I wished we'd played in college, where we generally just drank. "I never." As in: I never dreamed of bedding a pledge after gently gathering the soft curls of her hair while she barfed her grilled cheese all over my dorm room toilet seat. I look around, but nobody else is drinking.

One of the more experimental sections of *Go Fish* features a supposedly parodic group discussion of sexual identity that more closely resembles a police interrogation or a verbal firing squad. It's as if bisexuality, more than being distrusted or seen as the opposite of being a lesbian, is simply inconceivable. Alien. A mirage of sexuality. So many things were (framed as) binaries in those days.

Troche's decision to release the film in black and white gives it the low-rent, or should I say grungy, DIY ring of truth. Like live-action Walker Evans. The filmmakers' half-lit gestalt of the lesbian underground felt right because it caught so many of the little things. Troche was a brown butch who grew up in a big Puerto Rican family. Girly, doe-eyed Turner, in her backward ball cap, managed to muddy the femme waters, staking a claim for what would today be labeled "soft masc." The film's youthful awkwardness and lack of refinement, even its earnest activist stridency, is part of its lesbian charm. Those not-yet-great actors were good girls. Watching *Go Fish* now, decades later, and fact-checking myself, I see that Ely, the fair-haired, bespectacled dyke played by V. S. Brodie, is a double of my first adult girlfriend. Before Rachel and after Olga, there was Laura.

The ex I'll call Laura was tall and fit and manly, but also womanly to my inexperienced eye. Butch to the bone, she performed a type of lesbian gender to which I didn't even know I could be attracted at the time. She had short, originally dark, hair amateurly frosted blond. Downplayed under loose shirts and jeans, her full breasts and wide hips were still very noticeable. She paired faded Levi's ripped at the knee with sharp-yoked Western shirts and sometimes bolos. Her sun-bleached, size 10, rattlesnake boots were the color and texture of dry yellow onionskin spotted with black mold. They'd been through all kinds of shit and come out dangerously unpretty.

She was from Bexar (pronounced like "bear"), a county in the Texas Hill Country near San Antonio. An only child estranged from her small-minded, evangelical parents. By the time we met, she was already several years out and solidly in recovery. Not only from booze but, as I would later learn, from a near-fatal drug addiction. She was comedic and naughty and smart, and though she loved to watch me get drunk – the only condition in which I would let her go down on me – she didn't drink a drop.

Shortly after I moved to Chicago, we met at one of those popular Andersonville country nights with a dance on the second floor of a bookstore or restaurant. When I'd psyched myself into calling a cab to go to the bar alone, which took every cell of my being. If you could cancel a cab the way you can cancel an Uber, I never would have made it. One, maybe two songs had played, when Laura approached me from across the room and asked for a dance, chivalrously offering her hand. After a few practiced turns around the linoleum dance floor, I looked her in the eye and said, "You're shaking." And she *was* shaking. Quivering so much her toned arms vibrated under my featherlight grip. I had no idea why. Turned out that's how nervous the younger me made a former barrel racer from the Lone Star State who was built like a quarterback.

She thought me unbelievably mean for pointing it out and said as much later that night. Considering how long ago it was, my mind alights on that first encounter of ours quite a bit. I don't think I've ever again been aware of having that kind of impact on another woman. I'm still ashamed that, given the pleasure I took in her reaction, rather than putting Laura at ease, I mocked her for it. Though I hadn't meant to embarrass her or make her self-conscious, the disconnect between her tough shell and her soft center must have disappointed me.

Chicago wasn't Denver. And it certainly wasn't the recalcitrantly White North Shore. In those early days post-Olga, when I was recently out of college and living in my first-ever apartment and working at the auction house, I only wanted to be with someone tougher than me, both inside and out. I spent the day playing straight even when my coworkers knew better. When I left work, I wanted someone to remind me who I really was.

Where Laura was concerned, my dance-floor hauteur had a predictably Petrarchan effect, and we soon became an item. Dancing remained central to our incipient social life as a couple, but there was a steady stream of Mexican food, a handful of jointly attended AA meetings, and some movies too. I look back fondly on that extended adult coming out because inhabiting my dual identities in the '90s felt like — and was — a political act, an act of courage.

Merely walking down the street with a dyke as readable as Laura made me feel more authentic and radical; her butchness secured my femmeness, which ensured my gayness. My mother raised me to be feminine — as liberal as she is in some ways, to this day she speaks of "girl things" and "boy things" as if she believes there's really only one way to be, and to represent yourself as, a woman. Early on with Laura, I was learning the difference between feminine and femme. Being feminine was something I had failed at because, even if I wore skirts, I liked girls and didn't take shit from men. Femme felt like something I could exist as.

Once I learned to think of myself as Laura's opposite gender, my future as a lesbian seemed bright. I loved building our weekends around which club to go to when, and whether after one or two nights dancing for hours with many of the same couples, going to the afternoon tea dance would be overkill. Usually, after her Sunday morning meeting with the friends of Bill W. and the drive down to Pilsen for a breakfast of thick homemade tortillas and beef stew, we got back into bed and had sex for the rest of the day. When we weren't doing that, my three pairs of boots came in handy.

If widely popular "American" activities like partner dancing or golf or Little League baseball are how you spend your free time, you cut across a wide assortment of people. The only man I've ever loved to dance with frequented those country nights in Chicago, and there's little chance I would ever have met him anywhere else. Billy, as we'll call him, was a tall, pale White guy with a slight paunch, thinning red hair, fans of crow's feet around his kind eyes, and an enameled, foxlike smile. A mid-level manager at a small manufacturer somewhere outside the city, he had a nasal Chicago accent right out of a comedy sketch. None of these qualities was attractive to me. I liked Billy because, gentleman cowpoke, Sicilian by extraction, he raced us around anyone who got in our way with the heedless grace of a Formula One driver.

It is not in my nature to follow unless and until I fully respect the person in charge, at which point I become meek as a lamb. Though not petite, I am light on my feet, and I've always been responsive to a good lead. Billy took dance-floor risks, for which he needed to pull me in and hold me close. When he did, I could tell he was having as much fun as I was. Or maybe it was the inevitable encounter with my bosom, to which more than one gay man has annoyingly responded over the years. (I once had a gay male massage therapist ask me if I had names for my breasts after I rolled over on the table.) Whatever it was, when we weren't with crushes or loves, Billy and I rarely missed a chance to dance because we knew we were great together. He could move me fast enough to make the people watching us stream into a colorful blur, clapping when the music stopped and he spun me under his arm one last time.

After we'd seen him on a near weekly basis for probably six months, Laura invited Billy to join us for dinner before we headed to a country night, only to discover once our orders were in that, as a trio, we were incapable of finding conversational common ground. This was a little disturbing, since we'd amiably shot the shit between and during dances even while we were still relative strangers.

Absent the twang and shuffle, we spoke different languages. The xenophobic, working-class homogeneity of Top 40 country, its white-knuckle hold on patriotic, Christian, plainspoken, "just as I am" realness, was something Billy embraced both on and off the dance floor, as he could. Country was a lifestyle for him. I saw in an instant that once he was between the paneled walls of his shag-carpeted, fluorescent-lit HQ in Des Plaines or wherever the fuck he worked outside the city, Billy winkingly held doors for miniskirted secretaries and traded off-color jokes about butt surfers with the guys in purchasing. He was terrified of fags with AIDS. It didn't take much to imagine that there was a stack of *Hustler* magazines in Billy's desk drawer. Just for show. In his mind he was an Illinois ranch hand, a downstate dago, as he often referred to himself, who by chance liked to fuck other cowboys up the ass. After that dinner, Billy no longer inhabited the alter ego I'd assigned him as a haplessly dashing, humble homo hero in a summer straw Stetson or, when the seasons changed, a high-crowned black felt. What I had read as tongue-in-cheek role-play, as rodeo drag, was really just Billy leaving everything appealing about him, such as it was, on the dance floor.

One day around that period Laura called me at the auction house. She had the deep, melodious voice of a retro crooner, which she deployed to great telephonic effect. My drag king Bing. Anything Laura said over the phone sounded sexual, forcing me to constantly look over my shoulder when she was on the line, in case one of my coworkers overheard. I had been sitting at my white laminate desk in the fully surveillable corner cube I was given as a fledgling appraiser. There was no privacy. There was no texting yet. Not even personal emailing. There was a receptionist up front whose only job was to field calls from eight to five thirty and who almost certainly knew more about each and every one of us than we knew about even our closest friends at that place.

When a call came through the general number, the receptionist rang you at your desk to give some background before you took it. A call to your direct line was a wild card, as likely to be internal as external. Inevitably, when my phone simultaneously flashed and rang, signaling someone's desire to speak to me in particular, I picked up the receiver expecting the worst. I generally assumed, not wrongly, given the tenor of that workplace, that I must have done something to displease the woman with her name on the door, the former socialite in the corner office who monitored whatever scurried across her territory with the intensity of a treebound raptor. It is only later in life that I realize how much I learned from a woman who I believed at the time to have invented the expression "perception is reality."

Back then, I was probably about twenty-four, and my goal was to keep things professional at all times. I answered calls at the auction house with only my first and last name, in a crisp, descending enunciation. I'd wanted to sound as suave and authoritative as my grandfather. He still answered the phone this way even from his monastic cell of an apartment, when the likelihood that the caller would be a family member with whom he was on a first name basis was statistically very high. "Jim Lyon," he would intone in the same Don Draper voice he must have used prior to getting laid off from his PR job.

"Hello" was not my grandfather's style.

"Vanessa Lyon," I said gravely, relieved that the voice seeking my attention was only Laura's. "Hello gorgeous," she said in what had become her usual, efficacious greeting. I felt myself clench. Phone hard against my ear, I pretended to drop something and ducked my head under the desktop where I reasoned nobody could hear me.

"How 'bout a movie, missy," Laura said. "Bueno. Pick you up out front. Usual time."

When she did, of course it was in her red pickup. In those days, you didn't see a lot of executive directors of Chicago nonprofits driving red trucks in and out of the Loop and its underground warren of parking lots. My dad had taught me on a stick shift, so sometimes she even let me take the wheel.

I've always loved to drive. But tooling around the endless outskirts of Chicagoland with Laura was also educational. I couldn't believe that the many diagonal avenues and courtyard buildings and re-recurring downtowns of mom-and-pop shoe repairs and Elks lodges and diners were all part of the same city. In my final term of college, before I got the job at the auction house or the bookstore, I had taken a much-envied paid internship at a very posh interior design firm in River North. But even then I'd rarely ventured anywhere beyond the commercial neighborhood surrounding the Merchandise Mart – to which I was often sent to retrieve, and eventually try my hand at selecting, unconscionably expensive fabric samples of the metallic jacquard and chinoiserie varieties. Given my childhood artistic training at my mother's knee, I was well equipped to produce bespoke watercolors of a proposed window treatment in an imagined media room, or a settee upholstered in English striped silk to go at the foot of some Junior Leaguer's bed.

Those were the days when people read magazines; we spent money on subscriptions, tore things out. And really, I think I can speak for people of that decade when I say that nothing transported many of us more quickly than one of those shiny, deliciously inch-thick, perfect-bound catalogues of possibility. Whether your thing was *Vogue* or *House & Garden* or *Vanity Fair, Elle Décor* or any other glossy publication available at the grocery store checkout for roughly an hour of minimum wage, magazines showed life as you wanted to live it.

This was just before the *VF* cover that launched a thousand lesbians. That celebrated barbershop fantasy – with daring and darling Cindy Crawford providing a pillowy breast for hot butch k.d. lang to lie on as she gets fake shaved by the hottest model of the moment – hit the stands in 1993. Prior to that – queer-baiting ploy to raise circulation or no – mainstream media pandering to even vanilla dyke culture was not something you saw at the Safeway.

After I'd attended my share of authentic Chicago poetry slams at the Green Lantern, I knew the final project for my domestic abroad program would be a performance not in words but in images. How could I not make a lesbian pastiche of a design magazine? *Decorating with Dykes,* as I called it, was fastidiously assembled by cutting and pasting with real, live scissors and Mod Podge. Drawing from my prized hoard of shelter magazines, I superimposed a wife's head here on a husband's body there until the heterocapitalist rag I'd started with was twice its original size. After the weeks I spent snipping and gluing *Dykes,* only a magnifying glass revealed the pages I'd layered with women stuck on women and mock advertisements for old-guard purveyors like "Brunschwig & Filles."

I hadn't met Laura yet when I turned in my final project. But I was feeling more and more conflicted about my dual, if not exactly opposing, identities as corrosive sorority sister and/or big-city decorator-in-training. My college collage seemed like, and maybe was, the most militant art project I could think of. However proud I was of what I'd made – however clever and sophisticated I counted myself for subverting the establishment of which I was fast becoming a part – I was worried what might happen when I came out on paper to my peers and teachers. Coming out was not taken lightly back then. Coming out was irrevocable.

I think many of us who did come out in the '80s and '90s in college or after are floored by how early kids understand and declare their sexuality and gender/s these days – in middle school or earlier. I can't think of anyone at my very liberal and diverse urban high school – even in drama club – who was verbally, officially, out. Interestingly, in that time and place, "bi" was thrown around as a slightly more acceptable possibility – even before we knew about Sandra Bernhard. There would be rumors and occasional unkind gossip about catching someone exiting a gay bar (why were you there yourself, though?), or girls daring to dance together, that sort of thing. But I don't remember seeing public displays of affection between gays at school during high school or college. To come out amid the ignorant and sadistic frat boys on my supremely conservative campus would have been to put myself in actual, physical danger. Even if some of my closer "sisters" were tacitly accepting, disclosing my sexuality would have assured my social death.

In Chicago that term, we were asked to put together an opening for our group show of final projects (to which only my classmates and our faculty would be invited) in the Damen Street loft that served as homeroom. One fall evening, I laid out *Decorating with Dykes* on a small, skirted round table of the sort the design firm included in practically every room it touched. As props, I casually tossed around a few unadulterated copies of *Architectural Digest* and *The World of Interiors.* "My" magazine was shown open to the most seamlessly assembled centerfold spread, where two leggy aristocrats appeared to be going at it on a tufted leather Chesterton in a great room somewhere in the British countryside.

Fabricating lesbians out of White women who almost certainly were not queer was a prefiguration of my future dating life. Making and showing my fake magazine allowed me to come out in Chicago silently, through pictures, when I still hadn't found the best way to say it aloud. I wouldn't need to inform the overly eyeshadowed, Doc Marten–loving Goths that I was gay. The fact that I had made art out of a waking dream of lesbian domestic life was enough.

Plus, I truly believed I was on my way to becoming the next Elsie de Wolfe. Maybe I would have if, like the unashamed Sapphist regarded as the first professional interior decorator in America, I had found the backing of a sugar mama like Bessie Marbury. But as was becoming clear, full-on interior design is much more math based and client oriented than I'd bargained for. My taste might be impeccable, but my clients, those who could afford it, would likely be people whose generational wealth derived from some form or another of systemic racism or colonial extraction or just plain unsavory business practices. This was Chicago, baby.

After graduation, the now famous because indubitably talented Chanel-loving reactionary who headed the firm offered me an entry-level gig. With nothing else on the horizon, I found myself giving serious thought to living in the style to which I'd decided to become accustomed on $14,000 a year. Like everyone else on the payroll, I could always skirt my own tables and cover my thrifted chair seats in purloined Cowtan & Tout samples. But when I learned even the decorator I liked most (a gay British guy I had run into at the bars more than once) was married to a woman (he later came out!), I saw a repressed if well-dressed future before me and cut my losses. I had always felt myself in danger of being exposed by those designing women. Those Ella Fitzgerald–obsessed Republican matrons who repeatedly asked what my parents did and frowned on my boxy vintage purses sensed there was something "different" about me, though neither they nor I would say for sure what it was.

Think of me what they did, every one of those women was in love with my boyfriend. There was no boyfriend. But I had made sure to introduce them to "Mark," the former president of the fucked-up brother fraternity to my viper's nest of a sorority. Mark was a year ahead of me, but we had "dated" in college, which meant, to the delight of my prurient quadmates, that sometimes I didn't come home after parties because I had slept in his single. By all appearances: with him. Dating Mark meant we went to brunch together (just us) on Sundays. That when he was house-sitting for some local lady professional (and he was always house-sitting) I was off campus supposedly making him dinner to go with the movie rental. The time Mark and his actual lover rented *Silence of the Lambs* so that they would have each other and I would have Jody was probably the apex of this period. Though, me being a fraidy cat, it ended badly; back in our shared room on campus, I couldn't sleep for weeks until my three roommates were within arm's reach, tucked into their beds.

Mark and I hadn't known each other until my second semester junior year when, having met me at a party, he stopped by my room before dinner one night. I was just back from Italy and feeling out of my mind on that forested, claustrophobic campus. Some of Mark's frat brothers had once again made me their target—taunting me in public places with the cruelest, most graphic inside jokes. I was fat and my tits were too big, they decided, chanting from their phalanx in the dining hall. Again, though I was just barely single-digit in J.Crew ('90s J.Crew!), most of my generally anorexic, heavy-smoker sisters were in the 0 to 4 range. The way I dressed was cheap and disgusting, they said. Although what I wore was (in retrospect, embarrassingly) identical to that of every other Norwegian-sweatered coed in my wing. We were all of us devoted to pattern-patched 501s, Patagonia, and Tretorns. The end. The president of my sorority was a crude and garrulous White woman with a bigger ass than mine. Unkind, ill-read, and casually bigoted, she was a rather nasty piece of work. But while the frat boys made fun of her behind her back, they didn't do it to her face the way they did with me. At parties. In the library. On the single, unavoidable path home to our dorms. I hid from them sometimes, darting behind trees or out of library aisles.

Their viciousness was intersectional, of course; I was multiply wrong. Too curvaceous. Too brown. Too close to their women. Too good at school. And maybe, though they couldn't be sure, too poor. (Colorado's capital city used to lack rich suburbs with obvious class markers; we had no Darien or Farmington to put Stamford or Hartford to shame. "Denver" alone conveyed little about one's origins.) Yet the wolfish boys in Tevas and rainbow fleece assessed me as a threat the first time they saw me. Without my saying or doing anything other than outdrinking them at the parties or eliciting pleasurable cackles from my girls at "our" D-hall table, they seem to have grasped immediately that I would always be coming for them – and their pretty little girlfriends too.

My new friend Mark wanted, I think, to protect me from those cruel and proudly boorish Deadheads – now Trumpers, I would wager, to a man. But both relishing and wishing to protect his own secret, he was cowardly when it counted. He only admitted how terrible they were when we were alone, never getting between us while they were on the attack. The evening Mark came by my room, we played music at first, intermittently disturbing the smooth surface of our conversation with rippling innuendo about "people like that" and certain kinds of "feelings." Gradually we confessed to being attracted to some of our painfully attractive Panhellenic siblings. About an hour later, I smiled as I said something like "Which makes sense because I think I'm . . . you know." And he said, "Yeah. I am too." From that day forward we lived in our snow globe of a collegiate world as a couple.

Unless I'm wrong, Mark has dated men ever since. When we last met for dinner with his considerably younger partner of almost a decade in an understated Silver Lake restaurant, Mark was built and burly under tight coral cashmere with a flattering graying-blond beard and a big gold watch. I was his beard in college. Now he is a big-time entertainment executive who changes coasts like I change belts. Like Bret (also not his real name), Mark's first secret boyfriend in college, he seems always to have known he would someday be rich/er and famous.

Bret was two years my junior. Yet unlike Mark and me, he was conspicuously gay in spite of himself and thus, to our bastion of homophobes, ineluctably Out. Like me, he was a target from the start. Although I can't say how, since they made a point of "not knowing any gays," straight people at that school just knew. Could it have been because, with a shorn mane befitting Aslan, rainy-day blue eyes, and abs with more trenches than Ribera's saintly foreheads, Bret was simply too good-looking for a freshman?

Astute product choice since his youth might explain why Bret has aged so well, though he's what I'd call ruggedly handsome now. You've probably seen him. Now he's got the look of an exfoliating Scots Highlander, or that psychic guy from TV who wore three-piece suits to solve crimes in the late aughts. Twenty-something Bret was, however, simply flat-out cute. Not sugary-sweet cute but unanimously agreed-on cute, like the lead in a rom-com. Like the type of box-jawed, not very tall, prematurely mature, inevitably White and male, homosexual impresario who inspires confidence in (almost) everyone whose hand he firmly grips. Excluded from the category of "everyone" at our college, naturally, were straight cis White prep-schooled proud boys and the men they molted into. Guys who left college equipped with, in addition to their barely earned diplomas and expanded professional networks, a highly sensitive anti-gaydar, finely calibrated during the culture wars.

For the rest of us, Oprah apparently included, if it's not Bret's intrinsic taste in table toppers and properly folded throws, it's his ability to make grandmothers blush and little girls (and their mamas) squeal with joy. It's the topography of his chest beneath a V-neck sweater. It's the way he magpies the secrets you confide, retrieving them to dazzle you with years later when it's comforting to realize he really was listening. It's his knowing laugh at what you think are your cleverest jokes. (After my last DM to Bret, now that we are in touch again in our less competitive fifties – when last I checked he has 1.5 million followers – he wrote back immediately to say he is still in possession of one of the watercolors I made during our dueling decorator days, just after graduation.)

He is still cute. But that's not all he is. When they fell for each other, my gut also told me Mark and Bret would become incredibly successful at whatever they chose. Watching them get together was like studying a chemical reaction. In order to make the most of his affability, Mark needed Bret to teach him to live unashamedly and purposefully into his homosexuality. Bret needed Mark to introduce a nice Jewish boy from the Midwest to New England's unarticulated Protestant protocols, to teach him to fish in Cape Cod Bay.

Although – and maybe because – he has known tragedy, Bret seems to skate through life, sometimes projecting himself as above or without politics. Middle-aged Mark is equally equivocal, though his partner is brave and outspoken. He is a daddy like I am a daddy. We were born forty, with dry-cleaning tickets in our pockets and rocks glasses in our hands, prone to different types of excess, which we channel outward, full of the knowledge that an obsessive work ethic and dry but playful humor may be the only way through.

But whereas I was viewed as defensive, presumptuous, and conceited, Mark – at that time a not especially well-read or intellectually curious White guy in Stan Smiths, pressed khakis, and striped Brooks Brothers shirts – magnetized friends and supporters effortlessly. My mother still adores them both. So did my employers. Mark went on to work for the head of the design firm that hired me, easily assuming a well-paid position somewhere between butler and confidant. Is there such a thing as a WASP houseman? While I was working at the bookstore — having turned down the unlivable post-internship offer from the very rich designer — Mark was driving her nice car around, overseeing the renovation of her Gold Coast palazzo, perfecting the craft of passing as something if not exactly straight then medium-starched and lock-jawed enough to do in a pinch. In early '90s Chicago, a sun-burnished and gelled East Coast walker was always in high demand. For a while there, even after I left the design firm, Mark and I had the Bush lovers believing we were about to be engaged.

A year or so later, Bret had achieved more, and faster, leveraging his considerable charm but as yet inchoate talent into bankability. He started working at the auction house a few months after I did in an undefined position at the CEO's side. It wasn't the first time I'd looked on from the wings as straight White women in power made sure to have a younger gay man with them in the spotlight. A playmate, an accessory, a backboard, an advisor perhaps, but chiefly a fawning, good-looking audience who would lift her spirits and possibly be mistaken as a hot bf without outshining her. Bret could often be found in the chair next to our boss's desk, joking and smoking while the rest of us worked our asses off. By the time I left a year or so later, he had his own segment on an HGTV show set in an auction house.

We were still in our very early twenties when Bret left that business to start his own one-man design firm. At one point, I introduced him to my secret upholsterer — whom I'd been introduced to by (my) furniture dealer and consultant for the auction house. Another thing Bret and I joke about is his attempt to throw me some much-needed extra income with custom design work I promised him I could deliver, lacking, just as he often did, any real idea how I'd get it done.

All these years later, Bret and his photogenic younger partner and fellow dad, also a design professional, are now brands unto themselves. His handsome face, flecked with gray stubble and a bit less sculpted, pops up on IG constantly, an inexhaustible source of advice on reimagining an entryway or folding a blanket with military precision. Who doesn't love a vintage gilded mirror? You can never, ever go wrong with veinous marble. I see we both dress in the same sweatered and loafered camo we adopted as a means of disarming and defusing suspicion back when we were accustomed to tripping the outsider alarm; when Belgian shoes or bringing homemade brioche bread to brunch, while failing to convince anyone you shared the same origins, nonetheless put them on notice that you parlayed their patois as well, if not better, than they could.

As the purebred WASPs were models of comportment to me, I was a halfbred exemplar to my proudly hillbilly Texan girlfriend, Laura, with whom I shared my French scarves, diamond studs, or whatever else might occasionally soften her dykish edges for the work world downtown. She taught me how to be a pillow princess, and I gave as good as I got by teaching her what I was learning about modern furniture and Chicago style from the sexy consultant at the auction house. As a working-class Southern dyke breaking into the insular world of Chicago fundraising, Laura was an outsider herself. She was also one of those White women who find themselves most comfortable with people of color. For her it was Black men and brown women. In my eyes, unaccountably, it raised rather than lowered her status that she liked to flirt with the buxom, dark-eyed servers at the tiny Colombian place we often went to for arepas on Fridays. Ditto at our favorite Mexican restaurants. Always with the Tex-Mex Spanglish flirting with the pretty young waitresses in their plunging T-shirts and tight jeans.

Contrary to what was on the menu, the little round basket arrived stacked with both flour tortillas and corn tortillas. *Mitad y mitad.* She had to have both.

The afternoon Laura picked me up at the auction house for the movies, she drove us, slipping her hand between my legs after each shift of the gears, to a little art house theater on Chicago's West Side. You're gonna love it, she said. Just like when they opened, haven't changed a thing. She had decided on a movie I'd never heard of, one of Douglas Sirk's fifties melodramas, she said, as if that would mean something to me. The film was called *Imitation of Life.*

10

# IMITATION OF LIFE

> My memory is always under the control of the person I now want to and strive to be, and so rarely under the control of the facts.
>
> — ADRIAN PIPER, "Passing for White, Passing for Black," 1992

WHEN WE GOT back to Laura's Ravenswood apartment after seeing 1959's *Imitation of Life,* it was still early evening. We hadn't stopped for dinner. We'd come straight home and gotten into bed under her hideous purple brushed-cotton duvet. We had languorous, drawn-out sex, and now my last climax had segued into sobbing. I was crying uncontrollably.

"It's the movie, huh," she said.

How could I respond when I feared she had discovered who I was, not through the movie's story — the subplot revolves around an impudent "Black" woman who dreams of a life lived as White — but rather, through my reaction to it.

I was already yearning to mute the bloom of shame I'd experienced in the theater by means of the reckless abandon of never-done-*this*-before sexual release. Now Laura's reaction awkwardly coupled these desires. I was anything but ashamed to be having lesbian sex with an honest-to-God lesbian. But I knew I was vulnerable under the circumstances, simply for being so inexperienced and, for lack of a better word, needy.

I was just out of college. I was trying to figure out whether turning down indentured servitude at the design firm was the right move when the reward for my high-mindedness appeared to be a less interesting job that paid even less. In corporate retail. I knew Laura would be able to take care of me. To house me. She already fed me. In exchange, or gratitude, I'd just given myself to her in all the ways I knew how.

Why, now that we were back to ourselves, did I have to tell her more than she could learn from touching and tasting me? From hearing me yes, oh my God, yes her in the deliriously unleashed manner only a young person coming into her own sexuality can. Wasn't it enough to be living this urban outlaw kind of life together?

Laura held me tight and I let her, hoping if I kept crying she'd stop asking why I was so upset. She didn't. While I was wailing in her long, strong arms, she'd developed her own theory about my past. She also recognized, as I did, that the movie had made us think about being an interracial couple.

"Your mother was, uh, raped by your father, wasn't she?" Laura asked.

I don't remember the details of the sex we'd just had, but it was nearly always the same with her at that stage of our courtship. She was a traditional butch for the time. She gave and I received. A few months and several margaritas (for me) later, she would typically strap on a realistic (or so I imagined) silicone cock the peachy shade of a White man's skin. But on that afternoon, before we had moved in together, she did the fucking with her fingers, and I was the vocal bottom who pleaded for her not to let up. Sex with Laura wasn't aggressive or scary, and I loved it. Or maybe it would be more accurate to say the idea of having sex with a big, butch dyke like Laura was a huge part, as it were, of why I loved being with her. She was my first long-term sexual partner, and since pleasing me was what pleased her, everybody was happy. I liked the way she fucked me – lots of dirty talk, which was new to me – and I always felt safe. That Laura could put the notion of rape into my mind so soon after thrusting her fingers into me was somehow as upsetting at the question itself.

"Of course not!" I screamed, rolling away from her.

We were lying there in the curtain glow of her barren bedroom at sunset. Ironing board at the window, ceiling fan slowly circling overhead. I forced myself to think back to the film, from which I had started dissociating even while it was rolling. I imagined us still settled into our plush red seats at the theater, strangers on either side, the popcorn box in my lap full of empty mustard packets, because I love that tangy, messy combination.

This was the me I saw: A woman in her early twenties who hadn't yet confronted, never mind confessed, her racial identity. Not to myself, and certainly not to anyone else. This was me on a date with another woman, goaded by the director and the actors and the script to applaud the downfall of a narcissistic, uncaring girl who was meant to be a version of myself. But the woman on the screen wasn't me at all. One thing I knew: Had I been as small and pretty and feminine and obsessed with what men thought of me as *Imitation of Life*'s Sarah Jane, everything in my life would have been different. We were nothing alike, as I had just proved in bed. But, on the other side of my best orgasm yet, when I realized Laura now had a racial template to hold me up to, all I wanted was to throw back the sheet and run out of that apartment. I felt myself unraveling, and I wanted to escape before there was nothing left of the person I imagined I had been.

But where would I go? I'd just had sweaty, shuddering lesbian sex for maybe the eighth or ninth time in my life. I'd relied on the novelty of sex-induced atemporality to erase the ugliness and confusion from before. Only a few hours had passed since we left the theater, but I had forced myself to forget the parts of the movie I couldn't handle. Still, as far as I recalled, there were no rape scenes, no mentions of the saintly Black mother, Annie Johnson, having been sexually assaulted by what she calls the "practically White" Black father of her glossy-haired, brown-eyed, passable daughter, Sarah Jane. I remembered this description in the movie, yet I couldn't imagine what a man like that might look like. "Practically" White suggests not-quite-passably White, and that can encompass all sorts of appearances. I was no different than most people in imposing a personal and anachronistic understanding of what it meant to look White on whatever I saw or read about in the present. Historically, however, passing has been less about being perceived as ethnically "pure" Anglo-Saxon or (White) European, than about being not one single drop Black. Throughout the nineteenth and twentieth centuries people were considered to be passable as White even if they were "dark," so long as that darkness didn't derive from Black heritage. This leaves a wide berth for swarthy or dusky or "Mediterranean" olive-skinned types ostensibly not of African heritage.

Laura had gleaned that my biological father was not in my life. But we'd never discussed race. Born in semirural Texas in the early 1960s, she had grown up thinking about Black people and Mexican people in whatever way she had – I knew she wasn't "prejudiced" in the sense of ascribing lesser humanity or potential or value to people of color. I thought I knew, given that several young Black men worked with her on the inner-city youth-run program she oversaw, that she didn't believe Black men were predisposed to savagery or violence. So why was rape her first thought? Why did she assume my coming into the world in 1969 must be the result of my unmarried White mother being forced against her will to have sex with a Black man?

It strikes me now as a White Southerner's conclusion to have jumped to. Laura's was a Reconstructionist question born of a predilection, even a need, to regard my birth through a grimy Jim Crow lens. As historian Estelle Freedman, author of a study of some fifteen hundred rape narratives in American newspapers from 1870 to 1900, writes: "The gradual identification of the rapist as a violent black stranger who preyed on white women and children escalated soon after emancipation, when southern whites invoked the specter of 'social equality' – implying race mixing – to undermine African American claims to full citizenship." My then girlfriend's hair-trigger response felt White supremacist – that is, it seemed obvious to her that my WASP teenage mother had to have been an innocent whose purity was ravaged by a nameless Black assailant. Faced with a woman who looked to her like me, tragic and broken on the big screen, Laura assumed that confronting what she imagined to be my violent origins had induced a kind of psychic or emotional break for me.

She wasn't wrong about the break part. Watching *Imitation of Life,* I glimpsed myself clearly for the first time in a garish color film made a decade before I was born. I also saw immediately what the White-passing woman was for. As Hortense Spillers writes of Black women generally, "My country needs me, and if I were not here, I would have to be invented." In *Imitation of Life,* the maple-skinned Sarah Jane was crafted to impress the failings of the practically White woman firmly upon the minds of viewers of all races. When the young Sarah Jane's ugly secret was inadvertently revealed by her Black mother's sudden appearance at the White school she visits with her daughter's forgotten umbrella, my secret came out too. It's a shameful scene and I felt ashamed watching it. Was that why Laura had chosen the film?

It isn't fair. Neither of the actresses who play Sarah Jane in Douglas Sirk's *Imitation of Life* are Black and/or had a Black parent and a White one. Susan Kohner, cast as the older Sarah Jane, went on to play White roles in four more films, including *The Gene Krupa Story* (1960) and *Freud* (1962), before retiring from acting when she married in 1964. A promo on the Turner Classic Movies website describes Kohner as a "petite, dark-haired, exotic beauty." But of course, she easily passes for White in the film because she *is* White. Or, in any case, not Black. Kohner's mother, Lupita (Guadalupe) Tovar, was born in Matias Romero, a city in Oaxaca, Mexico, to Mexican and Irish parents. The actress's father was the Austro-Hungarian-Jewish producer Paul Kohner. Sirk's decision to cast Kohner was a cheaty approach that often earns the actor in question accolades for taking on such a challenging part (Charlize Theron in *Monster;* Jake Gyllenhaal and Heath Ledger in *Brokeback Mountain;* Brendan Fraser in *The Whale*). Awards are freely bestowed on White, heterosexual actors for "convincingly" embodying a character of a different race, ethnicity, size, or sexuality than their own. The question is, what kind of reverse alchemy needs to be performed on the White actor to transform him or her or them from a blank but exalted state into a lowlier (stereo)type easily recognized by the audience?

Kohner's skin was darkened for *Imitation of Life.* Then again, so was Lena Horne's for many of the roles she played. Movie studio makeup artists famously concocted a browner shade of foundation for Horne called "Little Egyptian," lest her romances with Black actors suggest miscegenation. Despite being the daughter of African American parents, it wouldn't do for her to *look* like a White woman who'd fallen for a Black man. Horne lost one of the "great" tragic Mulatta musical roles, *Show Boat*'s Julie, to Ava Gardner, only to see Gardner's skin darkened for the big screen so that it would more closely resemble what Horne's looked like absent makeup.

Like *Imitation of Life, Show Boat* exemplifies the Jazz Age craze for "passing" narratives written by and about women – in Edna Ferber's case, by a woman who was White. *Show Boat* was published in 1926, three years before Nella Larsen's *Passing* and Jessie Fauset's less known passing novel of the same year, *Plum Bun.* Twelve months after it appeared on shelves, Ferber's riverboat melodrama received its first production as a Broadway musical with music by Jerome Kern and book and lyrics by Oscar Hammerstein II. Hollywood film adaptations followed in 1929 (a quasi-silent film), 1936, and 1951 – the thirties version with *Gone with the Wind*'s Oscar-winning Hattie McDaniel starring as Queenie and the latter with screen goddess Gardner in the provocative role of White-passing Julie.

For the fifties adaptation of *Show Boat,* it was a double insult not to cast Lena Horne in one of musical theater's most memorable of-color roles. Not only did Horne naturally look the part, she had played Julie before. The star-studded *Till the Clouds Roll By,* a 1946 biopic based on Kern's life, opens with an extended sequence from *Show Boat.* In director Richard Whorf's ingeniously transhistorical frame-story, the first eighteen minutes of *Till the Clouds*

*Roll By* consist of a “Broadway” performance of *Show Boat* (distilled to a montage of the musical’s best songs). Four years before *Showboat*’s second movie adaptation, it was Whorf’s cutting and pasting skills that allowed the Black actress Horne to be cast as a White-passing Mulatta character in a musical set in the 1880s, supposedly being performed around 1927, in a film made in the 1940s. In *Till the Clouds Roll By,* Horne’s scene is strategically inserted between a very New Look “Life upon the Wicked Stage,” sung by the green-suited White actress Virginia O’Brien, and “Ol’ Man River,” musical theater’s most recognizable Negro anthem.

However — stay with me here — while in the onstage *Show Boat* segment of *Till the Clouds Roll By,* “Ol’ Man River” is performed by Black actor Caleb Peterson, the same song — written to be sung by a formerly enslaved Black man, is re-entrusted in the film’s bombastic grand finale, to a young and smarmy Frank Sinatra. Ol’ Blue Eyes performs “Ol’ Man River” in a white tuxedo (with matching white brogues) while an all-White orchestra, also dressed in white, and dozens of White women wearing all-white dresses swirl around him bearing cloudlike garlands of pristine “cotton.” According to *Collier’s,* as per Turner Classic Movies, in response to Sinatra’s rendition of the song previously made famous by Paul Robeson in 1936, Jerome Kern told the singer: “My idea with that song was to have a rabbity little fellow do it, somebody who made you believe he was tired of livin’ and scared of dyin’. That’s how you do it, Frankie.” Kern might have said “Brer Rabbity,” since the implication is that he had imagined a Black man singing this “Black” song, but, in fact, Sinatra performs Blackness even better. And indeed, when Robeson sang the song in the late thirties, he altered Kern’s lyrics, changing “Dere’s” and “Dat’s” to “There’s” and “That’s,” eliminating the N-word, and replacing Kern’s implied Negro docility with more empowering language.

Similarly to Ava Gardner, however, Sinatra was permitted to rewrite, or re-White, a racialized role so that Blackness, already appropriated by Kern and Hammerstein, disappears altogether. Like Ralph Ellison's chunk of coal coated in impenetrable Liberty white paint (*Invisible Man* would appear six years later, in 1952), it's no longer possible to see what lies beneath Sinatra's minstrelsy.

Somewhat differently, Horne performs her music in one of the film's nested scenes after she is rather suddenly abandoned by other actors (she can't kiss a White man if she doesn't appear with one). When movies featuring Black actors like Horne were shown in the Jim Crow South, it was common to edit out their compartmentalized scenes so that Whites wouldn't have to see Black people playing prominent roles. (The same rationale lies behind firing without cause, say, the first Black Librarian of Congress or deleting Black military and sports biographies from government websites.) At least Horne is the one singing her own song ("Can't Help Lovin' That [Dat] Man") in *Till the Clouds Roll By.* In the 1951 *Show Boat,* by contrast, the White vocalist Annette Warren (whose voice was dubbed for Ava Gardner's songs) gives them a flavor, from intonation to vowels to the swinging lilt, that plainly ventriloquizes – you might say vocally plagiarizes – Horne's singularly soulful vocal style. On the eve of the Civil Rights Movement, bourgeoise Lena Horne, with Black and White-European ancestry on both sides, was too Black to play "mixed."

Not until 1983, almost four decades after Horne's abridged film performance, would the multitalented Lonette McKee become the first Black woman to play Julie in a major American theatrical production of *Show Boat. 1983.* When Reagan was president, Sally Ride was the first woman in space, and unemployment was higher than it had been since 1941. I was in my freshman year of high school, auditioning for the chorus of *Pajama Game.* McKee received a Tony nomination for the part and *Show Boat* reopened on Broadway the following year. The actress-singer-dancer reprised Julie a decade later when a new production of *Show Boat* returned to the Great White Way in 1994.

Compared to all that's come before, McKee's curly-haired, sexy, upbeat, savvy, mature Julie marks nothing less than the complete evolution of the character (all the more so in the years between McKee's decade-apart interpretations of the role). It's a transformation that almost makes it possible to take pleasure in such a problematic story and show. McKee's rendition of "Can't Help Lovin' That (Dat) Man" is the most knowingly code-switching theatrical performance of Black female impassibility I have ever had the pleasure of witnessing. Even the blurry, abridged clip on YouTube *tears* me up and tears me up every time.

Though we've seen it before, there is something so right in the wrongness of McKee's Julie thrust by the director onto center stage. For most of the song's blocking, she changes places with characters who represent stereotyped Black and idealized White femininity. As the musical number opens, blond little Magnolia, the paragon of purity, rests her head in Julie's lap, something we watch the White mothers do with the foot-rubbing Black actresses who work for them in *Imitation of Life.*

In the '90s Broadway *Show Boat,* however, a mutual understanding between shades of Black women inflects Julie's interaction with Queenie, who is initially suspicious of the "racially ambiguous" actress. But then, when McKee's Julie wraps her arms around the skeptical (why not call her "butcher"?) Queenie, with cropped hair and a no-nonsense attitude, it's a way for Julie to endear herself to the "real" Black woman in the room. McKee's casually intimate femme embrace reads even today as deliciously homoerotic. It also communicates an intuitive level of racial solidarity between Black women of different complexions that I for one have only rarely seen. Or experienced.

According to the storyline, Julie has sung "Can't Help Lovin' That (Dat) Man" before for the younger White stage hopeful, Magnolia, her tacit protegée. But Queenie, the Black "Mammy" character, is shocked by the performance. She has never heard a "White" woman sing a "Black" song quite the way Julie sings this one. And McKee does indeed sing it "Black" — in a smoky, bluesy, growling mezzo — even as she parrots a cakewalk in the corset and bustle that were the fashionably racialized shapewear of postbellum White women. Queenie, of course, is presented as plain and unsophisticated for all her secret race knowledge.

Given the same threadbare material as her predecessors, McKee manages to transform a White-passing stereotype written by a Jewish woman in 1926 into a sympathetic, even modern, human being. It can't have been easy. Accepting the role meant McKee had to perform a tragically "mixed" figure for house after house of overwhelmingly White audiences. Yet rather than being constrained by the role's limitations, it's as if McKee's brave, beautiful, talented, devastated Julie turns the lens back on the viewer. If the perils of a White-passing Black woman subjected to the sexist, White supremacist laws of the Reconstruction-era South make for an enjoyable night of musical theater, that's the tragedy. Look what you're applauding, White audiences. What makes you love this, Black audiences? In order to play Julie night after night, McKee must have had to confront, and perhaps even make peace with, the symbolic charge of her own appearance. Night after night she was not a Mulatta but The Mulatta. We are not always her, but she is already us.

In a 1994 interview with Charisse Jones, then a *New York Times* staff writer, McKee expresses the frustratingly entwined emotions of pride and disappointment associated with being the first typecast Julie. In what was for the time a frank discussion of auditioning for parts as a woman with her features, McKee tells Jones, herself a Black woman, what it was like for her as an actress in the 1980s and '90s. The journalist summarizes McKee's words: " 'Certainly many of the roles that ended up being given to white actresses I've gone up for, and they said they didn't want to go with exotic,' she [McKee] said. 'And a lot of the black roles I've gone up for they said I wasn't black enough, though certainly I'm a black woman. So where does one fit in?' "

Where indeed? It is an interesting and, to me, troublingly common feature of the interview that while McKee continues to refer to herself and her characters as "Black," the interviewer twice categorizes the roles she has played as "mixed race."

There is no mention in the interview of the word "Mulatta." But the intimation is there. At one point, the reporter, Jones, designates what she calls the "dilemma" of being biracial as "the subtext" of much of Ms. McKee's work on stage and screen. But "subtext" is putting it mildly. Cultural unbelonging and the temptation of race disavowal are inextricable from the parts McKee has played; her characters are inevitably women of color whose racial unreadability is a source of strife, even when it doesn't result in their cultural exile or undoing. The problem of people of mixed blood. Whose dilemma? Your dilemma.

Just as inevitable in the interview is the invocation of McKee's biography. To this day, artists of color are rarely reported on or reviewed without some mention of their parentage and heritage and racial, ethnic, and socioeconomic backstory. In the *Times* piece, Jones writes: "The daughter of a white mother and black father, Ms. McKee has often played mixed-race characters who are struggling with their identity." You see how easily McKee's "dilemma" – projected onto her by the interviewer – is linked to the racial identity crises experienced by the characters she has played. Aside from the reporter's imposition of an existential quandary, McKee's actual parentage is presumably intended to clarify for the reader how "Black" she *really* is. And how confused. A little later in the interview, discussion of *Show Boat*'s Julie as a "mixed race" character again surfaces the semantics of racial authenticity or purity: "Ms. McKee knows Julie's struggles, not her ambivalence," Jones writes. "She herself never considered passing for white. 'I was always too proud of my heritage,' she said. Still, 'I see that she [Julie] was a black woman trying to survive in a very racist society. And I'm the same. Not all that much has changed.'"

On paper, anyway, Detroit-born Lonette McKee's parentage accords with mine. While as far as I know she is not queer, McKee has deftly played gay (*The Women of Brewster Place*). But even before she transformed *Show Boat*'s Julie into a palatable and believable character, McKee held a special place in my heart for her sublime version of "Ill Wind" in *The Cotton Club* (1984). Resigned as it felt to a lifetime of misrecognition and sorrow, that on-screen performance began to make a place in me for myself. If this is what it is to be a tragic Mulatta, I can live with that.

I need a stronger word than "irony" to sum all this up. In the course of putting the particulars on paper, I have to stop. Over and over, I've paused to work it out in my head: An actress considered legally Black in the United States was not permitted to play the part of legally Black Julie in those first film adaptations of *Show Boat* in 1936 and 1951. Given the race-hypocrisy of studios and casting directors, it is a marvel that Fredi Washington, the daughter of African American parents and future sister-in-law of Adam Clayton Powell Jr., was cast as Peola alongside Louise Beavers and Claudette Colbert in the 1934 version of *Imitation of Life.* Washington, viewed with suspicion by many as an exemplar of passability, was a vocal civil rights activist who never attempted to pass as White. I don't think it's a coincidence that Hollywood deemed it permissible to cast a woman with Washington's looks in a black-and white film, where the racial ruse was more easily achieved than it would have been in Technicolor. Washington's astounding performance was also feasible because the first film adheres more closely to Fannie Hurst's abhorrent novel. In the original story, Peola's romantic life takes place later and off the page, in Seattle, where she has been passing for White and intends to marry a White man who is none the wiser about her heritage. Of the many disarming passages of dialogue in Hurst's *Imitation of Life,* the following scene between the Black mother, Delilah, and her demonized daughter, Peola, stands out:

> "You ain't lovin' nobody but yourself in dis here passin'. Your man will live to curse de day when your lie comes out in your chillun . . ."
>
> "I've taken care of that!"
>
> "Peola!"
>
> "I'm not ashamed. There are millions to populate the world besides me. There is no shame in being sterilized in the name of the happiness of another."

The novelist makes a conspicuous appeal here to eugenics at precisely the time pseudoscientific ideologies concerned with bettering the White race were showing up in "progressive" American politics and higher education. The speech is especially vile when given by a woman about to “commit” the same miscegenation that eugenics policies were engineered to blot out, only to ensure that, voluntarily sterile and mule-like, she will never reproduce damning “half-blood” offspring. What must it have been like for Washington to play a role based on this novel? According to the Amistad Research Center in New Orleans, home of the Fredi Washington papers, the actress received innumerable letters in response to her appearance in the film, many of them pointedly inquiring about her own racial background, as for example, a missive from a woman named Mary Flecknoe:

> I wonder just how much white or dark blood you have. I should say you are a quadroon, or perhaps an octoroon. Would you mind telling me? Please don’t think me impertinent, but I truly am interested in this problem of people of mixed blood.

Letters like these may well have been the reason Washington railed hard against a proposed 1944 film adaptation of *Uncle Tom’s Cabin.* For a column that year in *The People’s Voice,* Washington wrote:

> For white America to see parade across the silver screen Negroes as they would like to see them—in their so-called places—would tend to bring to the surface many of those inhibitions which have been laying dormant in their breasts.

Director Douglas Sirk heightened the “romantic” and sexual stakes for the Peola character he rechristened with the more racially neutral name, Sarah Jane, in the 1950s film. But Sirk’s supposedly radical politics cannot excuse the exploitation and violence he enacts on the White-passing woman. Fredi Washington's assessment was jarringly prescient. Perhaps Sarah Jane's graphic suffering and punishment emerge from just the sort of dormant inhibitions Washington wished not to see surfaced at the movies. Or be asked to act out. In the event, she retired from acting in the early fifties, shifting her energies to lobbying for equity in the entertainment industry as cofounder of the Negro Actors Guild.

We aren't nearly suspicious enough of or attentive enough to the prevailing cinematic assumptions normalized by Jim Crow segregation. If the black-and-white version of *Imitation of Life* is, like the novel, essentially neo-abolitionist (i.e., anti-miscegenation propaganda), surely the tragedy of *Show Boat* in Technicolor is White Ava Gardner playing a Black character – a stereotypical "performer," no less – who shamefully passes as White both onstage and off. The film's emphasis on Julie's deceitful race is so great that the casting itself had to be a lie.

*Show Boat* first floated into the periphery of my Broadway-musical-loving self when I started getting parts in high school shows. Chosen by my voice teacher, "Life Upon a Wicked Stage" was a song I used for auditions – but then again, "Bali Ha'i" was also foisted on me. My grown-up encounter with the 1959 version of *Imitation of Life* came at an even more critical juncture of self-making. In those early nineties years when AIDS was very much with us and bodily death and mainstream judgment were all too often followed by silence, it seemed most necessary and most urgent to craft a way of being in the world as a homosexual. As a lesbian. As a dyke. As "gay" in the flawed, constraining, and ill-considered way I hear many White people talk about queerness today – as if it is a separable but universal quality transcending all the other cross-cutting particulars that make us who we are. At that stage of my life, I had known very few Black people, even fewer Black lesbians. *Their Eyes Were Watching God,* contrasted with Faulkner's work by a good lit professor, is the only book by a Black author I recall being assigned in those four undergraduate years. Sadly, Black and brown writers and poets and visual artists were even less a part of my day-to-day existence in segregated Chicagoland than they had been in Denver. Black people were no more my people to me than I was to them. And although I wasn't the only person from the margins to feel she needed to choose one aspect of a complex identity to put ahead of the others, to choose one battle to fight in the sometimes fatal skirmishes of the culture wars, I wish I had known better. I wish I had understood that the fear and shame and exclusion I was feeling became a part of my backstory as soon as I was born in America.

In the most famous passing novel we have, Nella Larsen's aptly named Clare claims that Whites are less savvy than Blacks at identifying people of African ancestry. Having had little or no experience with variations in African American hair or skin tones or eye colors or breasts or legs or asses, many White people simply don't know what to look for—or, in some cases, simply see what they want to see anyway. (If you don't believe me, gird your loins and drop into any archived Reddit discussion of Meghan Markle when she became engaged to Harry or since. The hatefulness and bigotry voiced by some of her White [former] fans when they learn she isn't "White" is horrifying, though no more than continued and apposite claims by other Black [and White] people that it's impossible for her to face racial discrimination because "nobody" sees her as Black.)

For my part, I knew the duchess was one of *us* seconds after she walked onto the small screen in USA Network's urbane, fast-talking legal series *Suits.* The indeterminately brown, obviously dyed, and silken texture of Markle's locks was one tell, especially where they broke ranks ever so slightly at the racial Rubicon of her hairline. The perkiness of Meghan's nose threw me, I'll admit. But here was the funnily typical dusting of brown freckles and that sometimes golden, sometimes ivory, not exactly suntanned but not exactly bronzed-off-the-shelf hue of her skin. The fulsome arches over her dark eyes cinched it. Women like us are often blessed with good brows.

I also clocked Markle's ultrapetiteness. Much on display in the show is the compact, flat-chested, gymnast's physique that has surely insulated the actress from any accusation of Black hoochie massiveness, though the same body might invite suspicion if she put on weight in the expected places, growing suddenly thick around the middle or hippy and voluptuous of buttocks. From some combination of these attributes—and not from her character Rachel's on-screen delivery, which, like mine, is restrained, soprano, "articulate," and uninflected by dialect or regional accent—I simply had a feeling about her. With Susan Kohner's Sarah Jane, by contrast, there was not a whiff of recognition. No trace of the rare but immediate *I know you* sensation that has surprised me during a face-to-face encounter with other real-life impassable Black women—even if such encounters have been relatively few in my life.

But no. The Sarah Jane character in *Imitation* is unrecognizable to me as "White passing" simply because she is so artificial. Unrecognizable, because I can perceive her only as I perceived Ava Gardner. As an actor made up to look and, we imagine, act darker than a White woman and Whiter than a Black one. In that the film's viewers will carry the notions of race Sirk gives us into the world beyond the theater, there's something obscene about his decision to groom the White gaze even as he undermines it. While Hurst's officious novel shapes the reader's concept of Blackness and Whiteness through relentless, grossly contrasting descriptions of the four women's appearances and demeanors, the film had the option of showing rather than telling. Given that the book is peppered with freighted ekphrases of Delilah's enormous and grotesque Black body, Peola's unnatural coloring, and the two White women's downy skin and high, perfect breasts, Sirk could at the very least have cast a "passable" Black woman as Sarah Jane. He did not. And as a result, his cowardice immeasurably affected civil rights–era perceptions of negritude. It still affects our perceptions today.

Instead of challenging racial mythologies based on physical traits and behaviors, Sirk's adaptation tells us that no Black woman could ever truly be mistaken for a White woman. His art fails to imitate life by casting a woman who shared Peola/Sarah Jane's heritage. In theory, "we" believe in the phenomenon of Black women passing. But ironically, for someone working behind a lens, Sirk fails to force us to see or not see the dual nature of passing, what it requires of the viewer as much as the viewed. Sirk's moviegoers are not forced to adopt the taxonomizing Jim Crow gaze on which passing depends, even though interrogating noses, skin, lips, breasts, hips, legs, hair, voice, comportment, and dress for racial "truth" comes as second nature to many Americans, especially those "of color."

And besides, as Sirk seems to suggest, maybe who we White-passing women truly are is as much about our inevitable internal "dilemma" as it is about our external appearance to other people.

Maybe it's not how the world looks at us, but how we look back at the world with an eviscerating sidelong glance. Through a glass not only darkly, but acidly. Left to our own devices, maybe all impassable Black women exhibit the same intrinsically broken and disconsolate psychologies, that is, pathologies. Perhaps we make ourselves known through ironic or derivative turns of phrase, general deceitfulness, and uncontrolled shows of emotion – in the absence of our race's more conspicuous perfidies and outwardly visible signs. Maybe the essential admixture of Black realness and White innocence comes across in the way we captivating, though selfish and ungrateful, women are genetically predestined to act. If Sirk disagrees with such an assertion, you'd never know it. For beneath the delicate features and careful diction of his revisionist fraud of a Peola – what Hurst labels a "white nigger" just like her father – lurks an angry, vain, and morally sterile little savage who can't stop looking in the mirror. Hot-tempered and greedy as she is unfeeling, the White-passing woman is *Imitation of Life*'s only true villain.

Like me, filmmaker Douglas Sirk was a student of art history. And not just any student. In his 2021 monograph on Sirk, critic and philosopher Robert B. Pippin describes the director as the "star" pupil of the foundational German Jewish art historian Erwin Panofsky, for whom he wrote a thesis about medieval paintings and plays. As did Panofsky, Sirk emigrated to the United States in the thirties in order to escape the rising tide of Nazism. Although he was not Jewish, his second wife was. The strident cultural, even political, critiques said to characterize Sirk's mid-century, immediately post-McCarthy-era films are often attributed to his life-threatening brush with German fascism. He is praised as progressive for shedding light on hypocritical aspects of middle-class values, especially where living with "others" was concerned. Sirk's films are applauded for giving the lie to, or showing the rotten core of, the American dream.

Panofsky's "iconographical" and "iconological" approach to reading images is a still widely taught and practiced (by me for one) method of art historical code-breaking. Scholars aware of Panofsky's personal and political context have pointed out that as a Jew fleeing the Holocaust, finding logic and meaning where there appear to be none seems to have taken on an extreme importance to the German art historian. Both during and after World War II, Panofsky's concept of "disguised symbolism" demonstrates the interpretive significance, the deeper meaning, of the preponderance of everyday objects – mirrors, vases, shoes, pots and pans – we see represented in some genres of art, especially paintings dating from the early Northern "Renaissance" in the Netherlands and Germany.

The best-known example of Panofsky's method is his 1934 study of the fifteenth-century painting by Jan van Eyck famous to many as the *Arnolfini Wedding Portrait.* The fact that, to this day, an oddball Flemish portrayal of a patrician Italian merchant and a woman with a penchant for fur-lined green velvet is a virtual shoo-in for Western art history survey exams in classrooms throughout the world, we owe to analysis conducted by Panofsky almost exactly five hundred years after the panel was made.

Northern European oil painting was especially indebted to sumptuous miniatures found in medieval illuminated manuscripts of the thirteenth and fourteenth centuries. Noble and wealthy patrons commissioned Bibles and breviaries as well as secular literature accompanied by enamel-like images painted in vivid colors on the smoothest leaves of parchment. For more than a millennium, as Panofsky knew, art lovers had associated

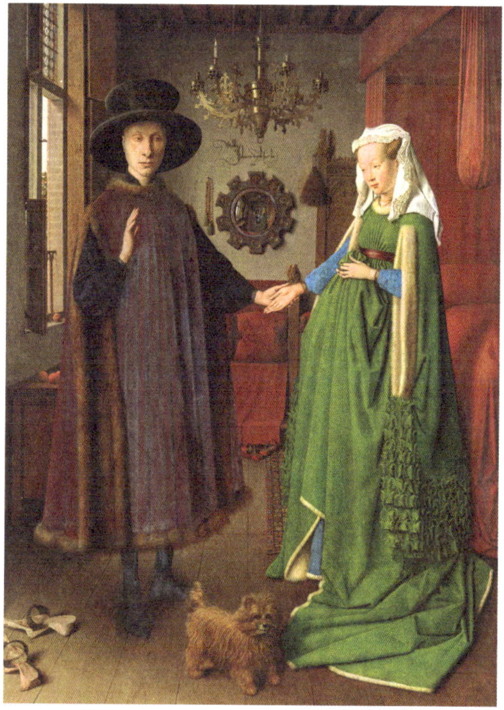

Jan van Eyck, *The Arnolfini Portrait*, 1434

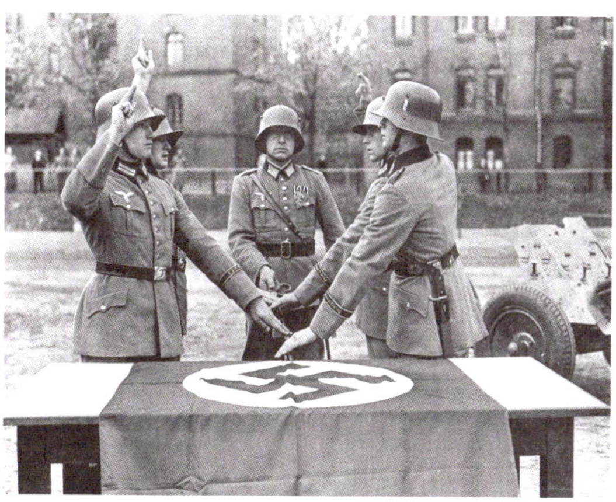

German soldiers pledging allegiance to Hitler, ca. 1934

any image whose sole subject is a male and female couple with the sacrament of marriage. And not just any marriage, but the one implied in all those illuminated Bibles, that of the first parents, Adam and Eve. Just so, Van Eyck's cozily chromatic oil painting on oak shows a man and woman alone together in the comfort of their home. Relationality and materiality are the point of this double portrait. Although the pair are shown indoors, the richness of the setting – the glittering metallic surfaces and costly, fashionable textiles we expect from Northern artists – might even suggest a newly bourgeois kind of Eden, the divinely sanctioned marriage of Italian business acumen and Netherlandish perspicacity. Though I'm not the first to impose a slightly Marxian, that is, economically attuned, vibe on the painting, an interpretation of this sort would never be possible without Panofsky's exhortation to look both at and beyond the surfaces of things; to part the curtains of literal representation in order to reveal figurative and spiritual meanings initially hidden from our view.

Ready, set, go: Look at what you're seeing. Catalogue the objects on display. Be precise. Describe what is before you in all its imponderable madeness. Figure out the narrative. Let the hunt for its visual and textual sources begin. And remember: Nothing in Renaissance art is an accident. There are no happy photographic mistakes of light and shadow, no paranormal overexposures or strays wandering onto the set. No random acts of any kind.

When looking at art, Panofsky urges us, do not settle for the superficial. In obviously religious works based on biblical stories, an iconographical reading interprets, for example, a clear glass vase or a burbling fountain as an allegory (a speaking-otherwise) of the Virgin Mary's immaculate and transparent purity. A latticed fire screen or a metal sieve invokes her physical virginity. Fido the dog embodies fidelity, though not necessarily to religious "faith."

Within his magisterial analysis, Panofsky productively fixates on several pregnant details in Van Eyck's painting: the chandelier's one unextinguished candle as the "all-seeing wisdom" of God; the tiny wooden finial of St. Margaret, patron saint of childbearing, as proper to the couple's expectations of married life, etc. But above all Panofsky focuses on the meaning of the man's raised and open palm in relation to his "handclasp" with the woman facing him. This apparently rare gesture he links to a fourteenth-century illustration of an Old Testament marriage scene in a French Psalter. The raised hand is for him "fides levata," the oath-taking posture of a husband (or a wife) in the absence of a priest, as described in legal texts from the previous century. Formally, the sedate, full-length composition itself reminds him of couples sculpted in relief on Gothic tombs in Germany. The inscription famously painted in the mirror, "Johannes de Eyck fuit hic" (Jan van Eyck was here), is interpreted by Panofsky as an "affidavit" of the presence of an invisible witness to the betrothal we see portrayed.

And so it goes. Panofsky's reader/beholder is likewise a witness to the deployment of a rigorously researched if no less peculiarly personal train of associations made by a German Jewish emigrant for whom oaths and their witnesses were presumably of even greater importance given current and recent events in his life. Keep in mind: On August 2, 1934, all German military personnel were ordered to raise their hands in a new oath of allegiance not to the office of chancellor but to Hitler himself. A year later, when Panofsky and his wife, Dora, were safely ensconced in New Jersey, taking an oath to the Führer would become law for all German officials. By the end of the Holocaust, the new professor hired by New York University and Princeton would lose some thirty-five family members to the genocidal Nazis.

Douglas Sirk, as I mentioned, had studied the history of art under Panofsky in Hamburg in the early thirties. For this reason, it is easier to understand – if not the logics of race and gender the director seems to follow, then at the very least his obsession with performance and surfaces. With an apparent first level of meaning. With looks. With makeup and dress. With American ways of disguising skin and identities and family and heritage as more, or less, than meets the eye.

Beyond adolescence I had never allowed anyone who really knew me to think I was interested in boys or men. But with race, with *my* race, it was different. I did not understand my race as a young person. Even though I'd been shown how I was Black when my mother drew it for me as a child. And much later, since I'd heard her pronounce me into Black being at a barbecue. I'd known on those mornings before school in the downstairs bathroom where I detested the curliness and frizz, the readable Blackness, of my hair as I ironed and moussed and gelled it. I'd known when it hadn't even helped to sleep with my kinky ponytail wrapped around an empty frozen orange juice can as my mother said some girls did in the sixties. I'd known when my fourth-grade teacher confused me with a Blacker girl at our school named Michelle, who wore her bushier hair in two Laura Ingalls braids as thick as ropes, just as I did. I'd known when, unlike the White girls, I secretly liked singing Negro spirituals in grade school or running sprints between the lines on Field Day. I'd known I was Black when men whistled and sucked their teeth at me as I walked home from high school in form-fitting Lacoste. Or when they hooted at my shape from the ski lift as I meandered down the slopes below. I'd known it every summer I avoided swimming lest my skinny blue-eyed friends and their pale families see my too-large-to-be-White breasts. I'd known it at the house parties where I was never, ever, one of the girls the beer-soused boys in their polos and 501s wanted to make out with or corner in an empty upstairs bedroom to cop a feel. No matter how well I imitated the White women in my midst, the gaze I was perpetually caught in released me and threw me back.

Does this dress make me look Black?

There is a not insignificant canon of literature centering White-passing women. Some of these novels, short stories, and plays have been written by authors who identify as White, some have been written by authors who identify as Black. Relatively little has been published by women who consider themselves to have a footing in both racial and cultural identities. Even less has been written by women who, not always having a say in the matter, are considered by others not ourselves to have passed.

---

FURTHER READING

Freedman, Estelle B. "'Crimes Which Startle and Horrify': Gender, Age, and the Racialization of Sexual Violence in White American Newspapers, 1870–1900." *Journal of the History of Sexuality* 20, no. 3 (2011): 465–97.

Spillers, Hortense J. "Mama's Baby, Papa's Maybe: An American Grammar Book." *Diacritics* 17, no. 2 (Summer 1987): 64–81.

## 11

# ON LIKING TO PRESUME

> She was herself unconscious of that faint hint of offishness which hung about her and repelled advances, an arrogance that stirred in people a peculiar irritation. They noticed her, admired her clothes, but that was all, for the self-sufficient uninterested manner adopted instinctively as a protective measure for her acute sensitiveness, in her child days, still clung to her.
>
> — NELLA LARSEN, *Quicksand,* 1928

ON THE LAST morning of a recent trip to Los Angeles, I found myself at the Huntington Library and Gardens with the promise of a full day of sun before I returned to cold, dreary Vermont. Although my Airbnb host had left a place for my luggage on the back deck, he'd kicked me out promptly at 11:00. I had ten more hours in California, and even my favorite Cuban café on Sunset wouldn't take kindly to me camping out for that long, no matter how many eight-dollar coffees I ordered. Several years before, during my first tenure-track teaching gig in Iowa, I'd been awarded two blissful, nose-to-the-grindstone, every-day, all-day, summer research fellowships at the Huntington, which in spite of its rigid archival protocols felt welcoming and comfortable to me. I love a conventually silent reading room. And I love a garden that's big enough to make getting lost a real possibility. There was no better place to while away my final February day in California.

I used the first few hours to retrace some of my favorite paths, the parts of the gardens to which research fellows had full access when we needed a break from the sepulchral reading room, whose air seemed climate controlled for scholarly competition. I started with a slow wind through the undulating Desert Garden. Then, with no archive to return to, I parked myself on a shaded cement bench and spent at least half an hour watching a school of giant black-speckled orange and white koi as they bobbed and weaved in a murky lily pond. Next, I headed to the café.

At my table on the crowded patio, I sat with a glass of white wine, lingering over an overdressed salad and recalling the summer days I'd done exactly this with my last girlfriend, Paige, a vastly read, quietly hilarious, and high-strung scholar of Caribbean slavery who happened to be White. The hours we'd spent among the toweringly phallic *Fouquieria columnaris* caused my ex to speculate that Massachusetts-born Theodor Geisel might have based some of his world-building on fantastical cacti like the ones we both loved. (We later learned specimens of *Fouquieria* reminded a famous Edwardian botanist of a Lewis Carroll character when he first saw them, thus the succulent's English designation as the "Boojum Tree.") Where language and imagery are concerned, Paige is something of a savant. Fifteen years my junior, she helped me pack up my small house in the Midwest when I accepted my current job in New England.

For my first six years at the college where I currently teach, I was the only self-identified Black woman, and certainly the only queer Black woman, on the faculty. I hadn't realized this would be the case when I took the position, eager to move several states closer to my smart young girlfriend, who was, at the time, finishing her doctorate in African American Studies at an Ivy. She was the advisee of three foundational scholars of AfAm, all Black, though one was on the English faculty at Columbia. Paige's dissertation, a revisionist analysis of one of the most notorious and comprehensive archives of Jamaican slavery, even won a prestigious Black Studies prize at her home institution, not the most typical outcome for a White scholar. I often said when we were together, and I still think it's right, that I learned more about Blackness in theory, if not in practice, from a thirtysomething Southern White girl than I had anywhere or from anyone else at that time.

Paige opened my eyes to radical methodologies and bodies of knowledge by diasporic authors and artists of color invested in upending the White European canon. Both Harvard's and Yale's AfAm departments were founded in 1969, the year I was born. By 1971 more than five hundred Black Studies programs and departments had been established in US institutions. In my seminary days, beginning around 2000, I'd initially read Black feminism as a subset of women's studies. But so much had developed in Paige's field since then. She introduced me to work by Saidiya Hartman, Hortense Spillers, Sylvia Wynter, Hazel Carby, and Kobena Mercer, a wide-ranging Black British art historian (with a PhD in sociology) I'd never learned about at Berkeley. Paradoxically, Paige couldn't seem to see me as part of the histories she studied and the cultures she admired; to be sure, she was *down* in ways I simply wasn't. Her dazingly self-centered, too-cool-for-grad-school yet astoundingly immature Black friends never gave me—an established academic with similar interests—any grace; and truth be told, with one exception, I disrespected them right back.

What could have been an opportunity to find community where I had none proved to be business as usual – my White partner was accepted as a scholar of Blackness by her clique of early millennials; I was not. Could it be that they just didn't like you? one might reasonably ask. I assure you they did not. Twenty years older than the youngest of them, I was published, tenure-track, eager to help with interviews, job applications, networking, and whatever else – and definitely willing to go out drinking. But nobody could tell those young women – it's tempting to call them "race women" – anything: they already knew it all.

A handful of cis-het Black men taught at my new college when I arrived, though none of them made any effort to welcome me. There were, and are, more Asian and Asian American women on the faculty than any other non-White group. Many if not most full-time BIPOC faculty hail from outside the United States. In 1951, according to the Ohio State University, where she received joint PhDs, the artist, future curator, and publisher Samella Lewis was the first Black woman in the US to receive a doctorate in art history. She was the first tenured African American faculty member at Scripps College, where she taught from 1970 to 1984. At the time I'm writing, I remain (they don't seem to know for sure) the first Black woman with a PhD on the full-time faculty at my school. I await the day my critical race theory–grounded pedagogy counts as Black Studies where I work.

The way I approach art history has been informed by histories and theories of gender and race since I started solo teaching for extra cash as a grad student at Berkeley around 2006. At the prestigious college in Iowa where, until my first sabbatical, I was a member of a small art history department, my students were almost entirely White, as were my two fellow art historians. This changed when the one I still call a mentor and a friend retired, and together with the one who was left, I hired a woman who happened to be of Asian American heritage to replace her. An Upper West Sider down to her scuffed ballerina flats, the new hire had, apparently, not thought or written much about race broadly or her race in particular during her Ivy League education. I think she was truly surprised when it became clear that students who identified as Asian American and/or Pacific Islanders were more or less flocking to her demanding classes. She didn't seem to understand that that's how representation works in the undiversified academy. For many BIPOC entering essentially White spaces, all that talk about "seeing someone who looks like you" running the classroom, etc., is actually very real.

My fellow assistant professor was not Chinese, but Chinese students were no less eager to work with her. Not because she bore any resemblance to them, but because she was a bracingly smart, sophisticated, and prolific scholar who was Asian American. I don't know that any of my younger colleague's advanced courses examined or included Japanese woodblock prints or Chinese scrolls, never mind contemporary Asian art—never mind critical race theory or Black feminism. Regardless, I began to grasp that just because she didn't resemble her students in demographic terms didn't mean she and they didn't experience our small town and the larger world in similar ways.

As word of my own methods and interests spread at the Midwestern college, I began to attract the occasional, usually queer, BIPOC student. Yet White queers were even more likely to come my way. Excepting HBCUs, liberal arts colleges have been historically and continue to be overwhelmingly White. Although I attended one and have exclusively taught at them, I haven't had Black women, let alone queer Black women, as teachers, or colleagues in my field, or friends at these schools until the last couple of years. This may have something to do with my reluctantly owning the role foisted upon me as that unelectable, histrionic, preachy, and it goes without saying, *angry* Lesbian of Color who is always waffling on about diversity. (However loudly my wheel squeaks, the faculty at my own institution has grown less rather than more diverse over the years.) Nor, throughout most of my career, have I had more than a handful of Black students as advisees or art history majors, though this is finally changing, thanks be to God.

The history of art is typically even more stubbornly socioeconomically elite and White than the colleges and universities that house it. Despite its mid-nineteenth-century, largely Germanic origins as a male-dominated discipline, today's art history is a feminized academic field. There are a number of gay White men in the discipline, some of whom, in my experience, have been less than outspoken allies in anti-racism, choosing instead to align themselves with the field's comparatively few but powerful straight White men. As I write, around 85 percent of all holders of undergraduate degrees in art history are "female." This hasn't necessarily translated into prestigious curatorial and directorship positions for women, and especially women of color. A 2020 study (from Data USA) claims that around 60 percent of undergraduate degrees in "art history, criticism and conservation" conferred by select American colleges and universities were awarded to White people. Fewer than 3 percent of the undergraduate degree recipients in art history that year were Black women. At the doctoral level, the meager percentage of Black female degree holders in the study of art plummets to 0.513 percent. Half of a percentage point. (If you're thinking "mixed" women weren't counted as Black, note that art history, criticism, and conservation PhDs awarded to *all* people identifying as "two or more races" in that sample amounted to a mere 1.54 percent. So much for DEI taking away all those fellowships that would have gone to White grad students.)

In view of the numbers, it's not surprising how few brown and Black women I have studied with or have studied art history with me at these schools. And yet. I remember very clearly, since it was a long overdue wake-up call for me, something one of those few Black women once expressed during a seminar class I was teaching.

It was one of the surreal early spring afternoons when my country campus takes on an incandescent fairy glow — birds singing, peeper frogs chirping, mountains looking like purple velvet against a panorama of wide blue sky. We had been discussing the evils of American twentieth-century progressivism. This has been a recurring theme in my courses since I arrived at an academic institution that fetishizes its birth in the New Deal era — but refuses to interrogate racist beliefs that were part and parcel of that political and cultural moment (when proponents of eugenics, among other horrors, dovetailed with many institutional histories, including ours). But anyway, on that hard-won spring day we were discussing how not every founding trustee of what was initially an avant-garde women's college was as unbiased as some of my magically thinking, self-avowed liberal White colleagues would have it — when someone brought up the diversity of the college's current faculty.

"We straight-up need more BIPOC teachers," someone said, smiling in my direction. This received a general round of yeses and finger-snapping from the other students.

"And we need to talk about the college's history," said someone else. "Why don't they teach us this in orientation?"

At which point the artist raised her hand. The same artist whose paintings I had defended against the all-too-frequent art-school dog whistle that her color-blocked *abstraction* was more interesting, and better, than her portraiture. The same student for whom, based on our discussions in office hours, I had included a reading that term about Frantz Fanon on the French colonization of Algeria, where she was born before being adopted by a White Parisian couple.

The same young woman I had known for three years and who often wore her dark curls natural, in a soft aureole around her face. She was browner than me and tended to imaginatively vary her look — one day she was giving downtown hip-hop backup singer in giant jeans and a tank; the next, '70s *Cosmo* model in a tight dress and silk bandanna. That day she wore a turban made of red-and-bright-blue-printed cotton wrapped tight and high on her head.

Once the students settled down, I gave the artist the your-turn nod.

"I just wish," the young woman said, looking me dead in the eye, "that we had someone Black in this department."

---

In 1985, Adrian Piper, the contemporary artist, analytical philosopher, and, of late, advanced yoga practitioner, created a work entitled: *A Tale of Avarice and Poverty.* It's a wall installation, perhaps more recognizable as Piper's for the framed pages of single-spaced Times Roman than the black-and-white photograph flanked by six blocks of text. Here again, it's difficult not to read this work as a gesture to the early Netherlandish tradition. Structurally, like Kerry James Marshall's photo-based art, it resembles a triptych, albeit an unhinged one. In a Renaissance three-panel winged altarpiece, a saint or religious narrative is given pride of place in the middle. Typically smaller, adjacent panels represent deeds or people that help us understand the significance of the main character.

In addition to its tripartite form and old-fashioned-sounding title, *A Tale of Avarice and Poverty* suggests its devotional quality by way of the icon-like image at its center, a serene, somewhat wistful-looking woman with large, dark eyes, thick, sculpted brows, and a shapely peaked mouth. Her averted gaze and serious expression make the woman's age difficult to guess. Late twenties? Early forties? The photograph's date is less uncertain, since the woman's hair and clothing suggest the Jazz Age. Close to 1930 would be my guess. We can discern the texture of the woman's bob but not the contours of her face. The photographer has overexposed the bridge of her nose and the jut of her cheekbones into a flat plane of flawless, masklike white. Even the sfumato shadow cast by a softly square chin reads as modernist geometry rather than a descriptor of volume. A prominent, stylized signature and New York City studio location float on the photograph's surface, a reminder that the face on view is a work of art.

On either side of the portrait, texts reading from top to bottom prove to be a mordant fairy tale in the tradition of the Brothers Grimm — nor would I be surprised if the artist is wryly invoking the bi-colored figure of the "pied piper." From the first line, the viewer is introduced to a complex familial history of "Avarice and Poverty" distilled (by Piper?) into a counternarrative of Apathy and Disloyalty, venal behaviors that are in fact the polar opposites of devotion.

Understood as an act of truth-telling and demystification, Piper's assemblage invokes an unofficial deadly sin, that of Vanity. Specifically, the vanity of a stylish and privileged Black woman who, according to the texts surrounding her, callously valued her looks and reputation above all else. One learns from elsewhere in

Piper's writings that the portrait is of the artist's grandmother, Beatrix (also the name of her paternal aunt), a resident of Harlem. While some reviewers have wrongly speculated that this might not be Piper's actual relative, the woman's full name appears to be handwritten in the photograph's bottom right corner, and she is mentioned in the artist's chronology. It seems intended to come as a shock that the painstakingly refined sitter who gives herself to be seen was, in life, cruel and withholding to Piper's father. In *A Tale of Avarice and Poverty,* Piper pillories her own grandmother for estranging herself from the son who refused to pass as White the way some of their female relatives did.

At top left we read: "Once long ago there was a woman who was very beautiful, intelligent, and strong willed. . . . Her mother was a local beauty, temperamental and imperious. The woman's family was a very important one where they lived, very proud and well to do. They were not quite white. But they were all very fair skinned, pale and pink, with visible blue veins in their hands and wrists, amber eyes, and wavy auburn hair."

"But your Peola is so exceptionally light, Delilah," exclaims White Miss Bea Pullman, the Lana Turner/Lora Meredith character in the book version of *Imitation of Life.*

To which Delilah, the Black Juanita Moore/Annie Johnson character, responds,

"Accident, honey. And style. Her pap jes had style mixed in, I guess, wid a teaspoonful of white blood back somewhere, an' it got him through life an' three wives widout ever turnin' them lily pink palms of his. Style, but not a half-moon to his finger nails, an doan' you forgit it."

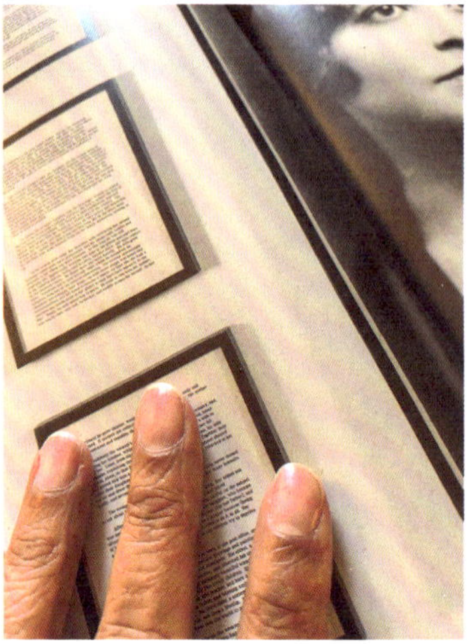

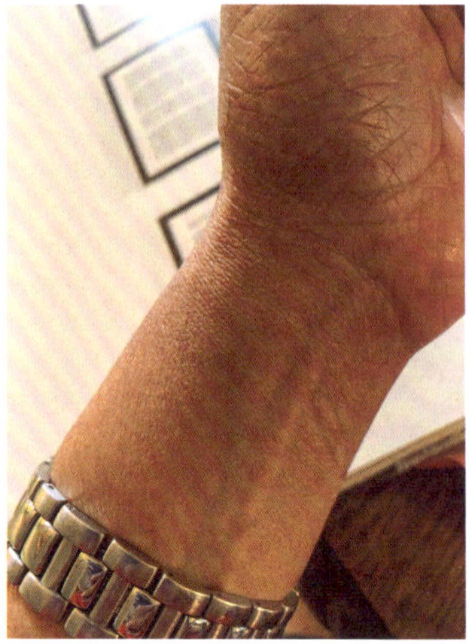

Adrian Piper's painful *Tale* is a genealogical troubling of conceptual art that reaches back beyond her ever-growing personal archive and philosophical work. The piece feels like a blunt explanation of why things are as they are. For her and maybe for me too. According to the summation of 1985 in Piper's unexpectedly playful and idiosyncratic personal chronology, she created *A Tale of Avarice and Poverty* the same year her ostracized father died of cancer. The same year she was denied tenure at the University of Michigan. (In 1981, Piper had received a PhD in philosophy from Harvard followed by several highly competitive postdoctoral fellowships.) The same year Piper evidently viewed "every episode of *Dynasty* made up to that point," an accomplishment we share. (*Dynasty* is, after all, set in "Denver.")

Consistent with the hermeticism of much of Piper's art and performance, *A Tale* gestures at various understandings of Blackness and Whiteness peculiar to her own family. The artist has explored the phenomenon of passing and notions of "racial ambiguity" in other works. Or, one could say, these are the themes and experiences she explores in all of them.

My introduction to Piper was not in a museum or a gallery but in the copy room of the school that gave me my first tenure-track teaching job. The printer was shared by about fifteen of us faculty in the Fine and Performing Arts Building. One day when I went down to retrieve an article I had assigned for my Rubens seminar, the bold, all-caps title of the previous print job immediately caught my eye: "Passing for White, Passing for Black." I remember looking around. As far as I knew nobody in that building taught anything vaguely to do with this kind of subject. Though I realized I was being paranoid, I felt called out and convicted — as if the printer, and its operator, were sending me, and anyone else who might see the article, a message. I had recently started attending Faculty of Color Caucus meetings. But aside from that, I hadn't tried to align myself with the small number of other, mostly senior, Black faculty at the college.

Where (my) race was concerned, however, the circumstances of my hiring should have been a red flag. I was a visiting assistant professor in Portland at the time. I can see myself, BlackBerry against my ear, pacing excited circles around my cute Sunnyside one-bedroom for the duration of the telephone conversation with the lady in Iowa. It was the last stage of negotiations — there was an offer from another institution — but I had given an inwardly delirious verbal acceptance mere seconds earlier. The woman finished the call by weirdly effusing about how she couldn't wait to tell the students an African American woman would be joining the department. My heart rocketed through my chest.

In the first place, I had intentionally described myself as a "woman of color" in my application materials. I reminded her of this. Second, this was the outcome I'd spent my entire graduate education, perhaps my whole life, trying to thwart, namely being marked first and most decisively by the race ascribed to me. My White future colleague recognized the most obvious aspect of her misstep immediately. "Oh, I'm sorry. It's just that that's how one of your recommenders identified you," she explained. I knew immediately which one.

It stung. From the moment I started applying to PhD programs I had made the choice again and again not to seek funding or awards contingent on choosing *between* Black and White – such as, for example, the fellowships offered at the time by the Ford Foundation. Even once I got into Berkeley, I remember this time when I went to pick up a stipend check in the business office and the woman doling out the envelopes, who was Black, informed me that I'd have to disclose my race in order for her to release my rent money to me. When I refused to do so, she rolled her eyes in a belittling and unforgettable expression and said: "All right. I'll just guess, then." I couldn't understand why she was so nasty.

For someone closing in on an advanced degree, I sure was naïve.

When my mother had revealed my race to a curious stranger a few years earlier, I realized that some people, including my girlfriend Rachel, would see me as Black from that day forward. Didn't mean I saw myself that way. And that was the crux of it. Seeing isn't always believing, especially when you see yourself being seen and disbelieved. Not passing for White. Not passing for Black.

I say again, I have never claimed to be White. I have longed to be thin and *Flashdance* beautiful. But I have never wanted to be straight. And I have never wanted to be White. Not only because it seemed to be simply not possible given what made me "me," but also because from the time I started holding up what I saw in the mirror against what seemed to me better examples of womanhood and femininity, I have yearned to inhabit a composite identity that feels truly mine. To which I have an authentic claim. Whiteness has never felt true to me. But in the absence of role models and friends who were Black or brown – of fellow art history students, especially queer ones (the other Black student in my PhD cohort, a woman in her twenties, left the program shortly after the first year) – I certainly didn't feel I could claim to be Black either. Despite being legally Black, I was raised by Whites, inundated and inculcated by Whiteness. What could I know about seeming, or being, legitimately Black?

Shall I admit to cowardice? Shall I concede to making what might seem like a choice not to be "out" about being Black in those years? I can do that. I fully admit to being terrified of being seen for what I was, given who was doing the looking. But really, what did it matter when the choice was made by others all along? To some, at least, I must have resembled that genus of obviously, pathetically, homosexual homosexual who honestly imagines she is keeping her secret to herself. Impossibly White. Impassably Black.

While evading the question, I let myself believe people weren't already answering it for themselves. With my race undeclared, I let myself believe I had earned what I achieved regardless of my race. But now, suddenly aware that the Iowa woman on the telephone had been thinking of me as African American based on someone else's description, my open secret no longer was. As soon as her words hit my ear, I was forced to acknowledge how many rec letters written by someone I considered a mentor (but who was not, happily, my advisor) had endorsed me in terms of my desirability as a diversity hire, that rarest of dean-pleasing quarry, the Black woman art historian.

While I stood in the college office waiting for the printer to catch up with the file I'd sent, I grabbed the Piper article and read the first few pages. The department administrative person suddenly reappeared at her desk and asked me if everything was okay, so I folded the article in half and pretended to be checking the grid of wooden boxes opposite the copier. In fact, I did have mail. I reached in my cubby and retrieved what appeared to be some type of article on the need for diversity in higher ed. There was a short note on the Post-it attached. Someone was trying to school me on race.

If I were Adrian Piper reading this book, I would probably say to myself: *The parts about the canonical art are okay, I suppose. Besides that, there is nothing here I didn't describe and unsurpassably break down in that article I published in 1992.*

The less things change.

Indeed, the uncanniest thing about speed-reading "Passing for White, Passing for Black" as a newly minted diversity hire almost twenty years later was the way the article starts. Piper begins by recounting an event from her earliest graduate study at Harvard. There, at a 1974 gathering of the philosophy faculty and their incoming grad students, she describes how her Blackness was openly challenged by a White man – "an eminent professor" – as never before. The only other person to do this to her face, she writes a few pages later, was a White woman junior professor who grilled her on exactly how mathematically Black she was. The "implicit accusation," Piper observes, was that "I had fraudulently posed as black in order to take advantage of the department's commitment to affirmative action." Whereas in Iowa, I had been blatantly asked if I was against affirmative action, "like Clarence Thomas." One simply cannot win.

Born into the civil rights era, Piper is almost exactly a generation older than me. Yet there is devastatingly little in her devastating thirty-page recollection published the year I graduated from college that doesn't resonate with, if not replicate, my experiences in the three decades since. Much of the essay consists of anecdotes not unlike the ones I've been relating—racial incidents and other insults, slights, and challenges to her very existence. Comments made in passing. On passing.

Piper's essay is a memoir in microcosm. But it fits just as well into cultural or American studies. She includes, for example, a predictively Gatesian section about genetics and what happens when White people learn that, according to the traditional US legal definition that is the one-drop rule, they are Black. Along these lines, there is quite a bit about colorism and outright racism in Piper's family, and especially the unjust and unkind treatment of her brave, forthright, and principled father. Closer to home for me, she writes a good deal about the enduring difficulty of finding acceptance or good will from Blacks, no less than Whites. Given some of her prior art and performance, the authorial Piper is far more forgiving of people who pass for White (thereby jettisoning a "doubly alienated and alienating social identity") than most Black and any White writers I can think of—though she is saddened by the inevitable loss of familial connection and history for those who do. Piper's "light-skinned" parents both identified as Black; the words "bi-racial" and "mulatta" do not appear in her discussion of passing.

Written the same year as Toni Morrison's *Playing in the Dark* and bell hooks's *Black Looks: Race and Representation,* Piper's acerbic and unsettlingly candid essay is a tour de force. Nearly every sentence is worth quoting for its ability both to offer as evidence the distressingly similar lived experiences of women like us, and to provide cultural and historical contexts for those experiences. She writes of the "groundless shame of the inadvertent impostor" and the ridicule that marks us "not as having *done* wrong but as *being* wrong." She describes the demoralizing "Suffering Test of blackness" that requires the passable Black person to match racism for racism with more readably Black people in a quest for legitimation that often ends in distrust and alienation for both parties.

I think of posthumous social media attacks on the incomparable late poet Nikki Giovanni, for having a "colonizer" (read, White, and in this case, female) partner. I think of how much writing by younger, self-described "mixed" American authors these days includes an apology for their parentage or ancestry or appearance and how the accompanying "privilege" they feel makes them (feel) less worthy to be seen and fully respected as Black Americans and Black creators. I want to say: Look, you are and probably always will be considered legally and racially Black by the country of which you are a citizen. Octoroon, quadroon, Oreo, zebra; whatever way you do the math, a lil' dab will do them. Yet while indubitably, unimpeachably groundless, I want to tell them/us, y/our shame for being who and how you were born is (still) palpable. You can blame your White mothers for not knowing how to teach you to be Black, but systemic racism is bigger than her. Enough. I have no use for this triple, or quadruple, consciousness. Though I may live at a cultural and racial impasse, I am not the one playing in the dark; being seen by myself will have to suffice.

That said, I am under no illusion that I move through the world or am received or rejected by it in a manner akin to that of a Black woman with a broader nose or fuller lips than mine, with an Afro or hair that curls more tightly, and a complexion of a far deeper, or blacker, brown – regardless of her age, socioeconomic background, or education. Nor will my experience likely resemble that of a queer White woman with long legs and a cute ass. Or a trans Asian woman with green eyes. Or a tall, passable, straight Black man with a Caribbean accent. Or a slender Black woman with B-cup breasts. Or a bisexual *Vogue* model of any race or ethnicity. This is one competition I am happy to lose. I want no part of it.

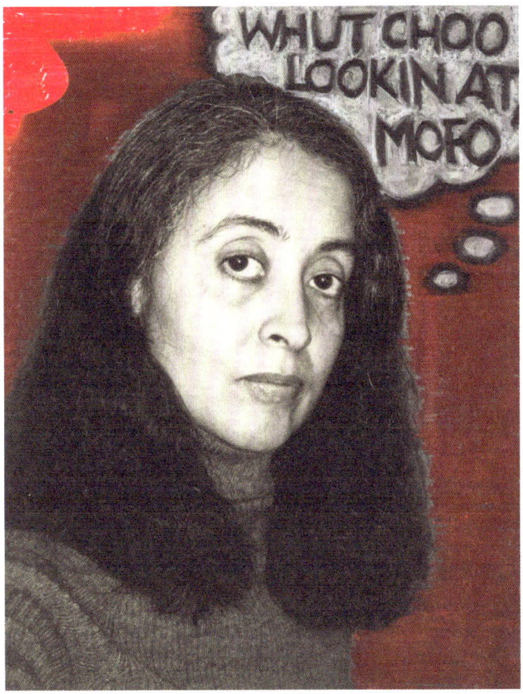


Adrian Piper, *Self-Portrait as a Nice White Lady*, 1995

Except, I sort of do. Remember how at the age of fifty-three I decided to request a copy of my birth certificate? How in the process of doing so, I discovered that the state still upholds the patriarchy? It was that fall in New Hampshire that I finally found the courage to go online and fill out the forms requesting the documentation that would, I halfway hoped, reveal the name of my biological father. My Black father who, for all I knew, was still living in Denver. There is, however, a point in this bureaucratic rigamarole where you are asked to provide the names of your mother *and* your father before proceeding to the cart. At first I tried filling in my mother's name alone and hitting submit. Red asterisk! Red asterisk! Please correct your errors. No go. I was crestfallen.

Arriving at this decision was a big deal. It had taken me over half a century. To have come so far emotionally and psychologically only to be rebuffed by THE MAN was intensely dispiriting. If I hadn't had the mental space afforded by the picture windows and cheerfully upholstered womb chairs in the library where I'd chosen to spend most mornings of my writing residency, I'm not sure what I would have done.

As I had recently learned, I couldn't ask my mother.

After dinner at our favorite Mexican place, she and my stepfather parked us at the marble kitchen island to eat cookies and have a nightcap. My dad poured a smidgin of tequila in some seltzer and pineapple juice. My mom poured one finger and I poured three of fragrant double-matured whisky, a Father's Day gift, before we proceeded to head in a conversational direction we really shouldn't have.

My sparkly-eyed, beekeeping "Poppo," meaningfully in my life since I was eleven, had never officially adopted me. We had, however, discussed the idea at length about a year after he married my mother. We'd even met with an attorney in an office across from the capitol. But as I clearly remember, there was a point in that meeting when the lawyer took my mother aside to explain something to her, and she had returned upset and unwilling to go ahead with what we were there to do.

At the time, I spent weeks doodling my new monogram in a cool, continuous cursive circle. But after that day in the law office, we never talked about why the adoption hadn't happened. That was never explained to me. And it wasn't, in fact, a big deal. I loved my stepfather, and I knew he loved me and my mother. "Mr. Wonderful," my grandmother always called him.

It had seemed fun for a while to imagine myself with a last name that means "harsh, rough, or difficult" in Latin. But I also liked the name that belonged to all the other family members in my life. Lyon was my maternal grandfather's name. I'm Scotch-Irish on that side. My grandfather's parents, I've recently learned, were Okies who fled to Southern California in the Dust Bowl exodus. Unlike many migrants, they hadn't become farmworkers but had settled more comfortably in a town called Monrovia near the Santa Anita racetrack, for which my grandfather always displayed an inexplicable, or unexplained, affection. Little did I know, when I was cast as Aunt Eller in high school, that I had Oklahoma roots myself. My grandfather was born in Tulsa the same year as that city's race massacre.

Anyway. As they sat and I stood in the kitchen, sipping and eating shortbread, I made what was probably a passive-aggressive mention of the fact that Pop had informed me earlier that day that it was my mother who stopped the adoption from going forward back in 1980. This is how information is often exchanged in my tiny family, via the smallest game of telephone in the world.

Whatever I said caused my mother to tear up. She is like me. Or I am like her. We don't get sad, we become immediately irate—

externally, internally. She yells, I shut down. Seeing her about to cry was very disturbing.

"What he told me," she said, "was that in order to move ahead with the adoption they were required by law to place an announcement in the newspaper. All I could think about was that he would see it. I know it was irrational. But that's how I felt."

I had never heard her refer to "him" as if he were a living, breathing person with eyes to read a newspaper. I also realized that back when we had gone to see the lawyer, he had almost certainly been living in Denver. For whatever reason, the thought that this man would know he had a daughter (did he not?) and that she was about to be adopted (would he care?) was too much for my mother. Even more than a decade after I was born.

Finding this out so late in the game incensed me. If we'd had the conversation while I was still in elementary school many things might be different today. Why? Because at the age of eleven, ill-equipped and completely unable to confront my racial identity, a Black man appearing out of nowhere to make a parental claim would have provided incontrovertible evidence that I had a reason to feel not quite White, that there was a flesh-and-blood explanation for the way I looked. The way I felt. Depending on who he was, it might have helped a lot. Or not.

I'll never know.

My mother was deeply sorry and I have no idea what happened with this man whose genes I share. But that hasn't stopped me from having a father figure for most of my life. Now, maybe two years after learning why I wasn't legally adopted as a child, I can't say that decision has had much of an impact on me.

Is that possible? Could it actually not matter? Can an American reader contemplate the possibility that I do not need to find out more than the race of my biological father? That I do not need to know his name? Or anything other than that, as my mother says, he was a good-looking young man who she never spoke to again. Is such reluctance on my part to find and meet the man, if he still walks the earth, a sign of race evasion or disavowal? Or does the need that some readers might feel to know precisely the name and background of a particular Black father say more about them, about you, than it does about his ambivalent child? I'm not claiming that knowledge wouldn't give me something. But what would it give you?

All families have an operating system. Ours is: Do not ask, do not tell. Ours is: If you wanted to know, we assume you would have said so. Their line is: Why didn't you just ask?

My line is: Why couldn't you just tell?

Although for most of my life I believed myself to be the sum only of the parts I knew about, I don't believe that now. No more than I believe I can't continue to learn good things and let go of bad ones and find joy and make contributions based on new experiences and new information. For anyone whose true vocation is teaching, it cannot be otherwise.

In the end, while logged into the birth certificate portal, I successfully hack the apparatus of the state by making up a biological father. After all, it isn't the first time. Off the top of my head, I append a common saint's name to the last name of one of the founding fathers and boldly type the letters into the form. I'm hoping the people doing the detective work will "correct" my error by providing the right full name on the form they return.

It seems to work.

Six weeks later, back in New England, an envelope from the Denver County Court arrives.

Standing in my kitchen, I'm not the least bit tempted to rip it open. I know I can't discover the contents of this envelope in any place where I regularly spend my time. The name on the certificate has the potential to alter my life. Or the way I feel about my life. I don't want to be in the same location where I found out who my father is the next time I fry an egg or curl up to watch Netflix or fall asleep. I know myself well enough to plan around a lifelong sensitivity to settings. I decide to wait to open the envelope until I am somewhere both aesthetically pleasing and geographically separate from my everyday life. Somewhere I could choose never to return to if that's what I want. I tell myself I'll know it when I see it.

---

NOTE

If I'd had my druthers, this chapter would have included two additional revelatory, self-representational works (*Self- Portrait,* 1968; *Self-Portrait Exaggerating My Negroid Features,* 1981), which, while not made available to me, can be seen in the MoMA catalogue accompanying Piper's 2018 retrospective: *Adrian Piper: A Synthesis of Intuitions, 1965–2016.*

FURTHER READING

Piper, Adrian. "Passing for White, Passing for Black." *Transition,* no. 58 (1992): 4–32.

12

# IT'S SO HARD TO KEEP UP, WITH TROUBLES THAT CREEP UP

It was from her mother that Angela had learned the possibilities for joy and freedom which seemed to her inherent in mere whiteness. No one would have been more amazed than that same mother if she could have guessed how her daughter interpreted her actions.

—JESSIE FAUSET, *Plum Bun,* 1929

AT ONE POINT in grad school, I imagined writing a Mulatta dissertation. Not about drawings or paintings or prints of "mixed race" or "biracial" or "Colored" or "high yellow" women. No. I wanted to study the Mulattas so designated in the visual archive. "Blond Negresses" would be considered on a case-by-case basis.

The idea came to me, as many have, when I realized that a White person who perceived me as uppity was hell-bent on putting me (back) in my place. When had that started? Could have been with Mr. Potter, the gym teacher, when eleven-year-old me put together a Title IX petition against his chauvinistic free-throw rules. I'd had help from our downstairs neighbor, a feminist lawyer from Jersey with whom I ate Special K most mornings. We argued in an accompanying letter that girls shouldn't be forced to shoot hoops with silly, smaller, nonregulation basketballs on the presumption that we couldn't handle the real thing. I did not prevail. But it may have been my first realization that just because you're fighting for what you know to be right and reasonable doesn't mean you'll win. Or even get taken seriously. Except perhaps as a troublemaker. A loudmouth. Or someone to steer clear of. "Life is not fair" was a favorite response of my harried young mother when I complained about having to refold the bathroom towels or go to bed. She may have intended the riposte more humorously than I perceived it at the time, but she wasn't wrong.

The reason I didn't end up doing a PhD on Mulattas like me was my sense that a straight White male art historian, a widely respected lion in my field, a man still celebrated by feminists who don't know any better, a big name in the doctoral program regarded by many as number one, didn't care for me or my work. In fact, I don't think he thought I deserved to be there at all. Who was I, a brown lesbian of a certain heft and demeanor, to ask him to join the committee of three who would read my master's thesis concerning a tapestry series by Peter Paul Rubens? The possibility that he might be willing had occurred to me when, during my first year at Cal, a group of us students were invited to the man of the people's massive house in the hills for a meet-and-greet cocktail party.

Once there, we did what grad students hosted by the faculties of supremely competitive programs, first- and second-years eager to be seen for the like-minded geniuses we thought ourselves to be, do. While the grown-ups drank in the kitchen, we snuck around the house looking for evidence of the great man's inner desires and unspoken preferences, so that when the time was right, we might unassumingly drop a mutually admired artist's name or an obscure literary obsession, hoping for a show of recognition, or at a minimum, a gray-eyed wink of mutuality that might culminate in a coveted admission to his cherry-picked seminars. Basking in his glow might even, as I witnessed happen to a White male friend, result in introductions to other (White male) eminences from Harvard or Paris or Princeton, inclusion in standing-room-only conference sessions, and invitations to contribute to edited volumes. In other words, he could, if he wished, award career-making golden apples. He could, if he wished, take them away.

I was at Berkeley to become an early modernist, to become a specialist in Northern and Spanish Baroque painting of the seventeenth century. He, by contrast, was famous for his searing studies of art generally from a time much closer to our own. He was a firebrand. A provocateur. The Dean Martin of my institution's Rat Pack.

That night, a few of us peevishly gathered at the threshold of the professor's library, unwilling to go cross over until one of his advisees, a thick-haired "doctoral candidate" this close to graduating, pushed open the door and strode in before us as if he'd unlocked the gate to Shangri-la. Our little number instantly fanned out to memorize the contents of the room's colorful and heaving floor-to-ceiling bookshelves, each on a quest for something relevant and revealing. It was then that I realized the great man liked Rubens too. Or so, at least, his multiple shelves of monographs and catalogues seemed to suggest.

Not everyone likes Rubens. And so, when the time came, I sent an email asking if the professor would consider joining my MA committee. He agreed to do so.

Like most theses, mine began as a research paper. In this case, one I'd submitted for a seminar on Baroque art that was co-taught by some of the leading international scholars in the field, visitors to the university that term. To those outside, the notion of a celebrity art historian is something of an oxymoron, I realize. But trust me, these were the hottest seventeenth-centuryists of the early aughts, people whose work I revered. It was incredibly exhilarating just to be in a room with them. Anyhow, the paper that became my first thesis emerged from those circumstances. I had presented a version of it entitled "Lesbian Baroque" at the graduate symposium. It was deemed a success, and my advisor did not foresee a problem. Admittedly, the process was still quite anxiety inducing, with all members of the department ultimately reading your work and weighing in. But, said my advisor – a prolific scholar who had published on Rubens and was herself a tenured associate – it was also very rare for any student not to pass when their project had already been vetted.

I was a teaching assistant that term. I will never forget what it was like to come out of class minutes after the lecture and see my advisor rushing toward me. There might even have been tears in her eyes. It still astounds me. One imagined that one's dissertation advisor was made of stuffs so rarified as to be patented. To us they were sheathed in chain mail and titanium armor that rendered them impervious to assaults of any kind. We backed our jousters in the face of all comers.

My advisor was and is an actual genius. She is a woman with an encyclopedic mind for all things painted and Netherlandish. Fluent in multiple languages. A crafter of illuminating, witty, and elegant prose. Each lecture was a master class, like something you'd see in a movie. Her feminist scholarship is so subtly subversive and pleasurable to read, I knew, even before I knew, that she was queer.

And here she was. My White lady hero and academic exemplar. Telling me I'd failed. I would not receive my master's degree for this thesis. With their vote of no confidence, the gossip was I might even be dismissed from the program altogether.

My advisor was speechless. But I was furious. I had begun to believe I was meant to be there. That I would make what we students referred to with admiration and longing as an "intervention" in the field. I had made discoveries. I was a straight A and occasional A+ student, which means something a bit different at that level of play. Most of all, I was fucking thirty-five. A decade ahead of most of my peers and too old for hazing or pretty-girl deference to men. I'd worked in the corporate world. I'd fundraised for nonprofits. I had an MA and successful PhD coursework from my previous program. I might get fired, but I didn't fail. "How??" I practically screamed over the din between classes in the basement of Doe Library.

Days passed, phone calls and meetings took place, and I came to understand that one committee member in particular had shut me down. I met with the Chair, who privately expressed their own surprise not only at my rejection but at their colleague's mean-spiritedness. It was an outcome that, as I recall, this person could only remember having happened to other women of color students in the department. I wasn't to receive feedback from the famous professor in person – he wouldn't even speak to me. But a female colleague of his had deigned to explain where I had fallen short in his view. It was something to do with the writing, she implied as we sat in her office. Or was it the methodology? With assistance from her and perhaps others in the department, she was tepidly sure I could revise my failed project into something more acceptable.

Finding the situation untenably vague, I told her I was confused as to why he wouldn't meet with me. I also refused to accept what I viewed as an insincere offer of help from someone not a specialist in early modern art. I met again and again with the frustrated Chair, who finally confessed apologetically: "Professor X finds you presumptuous. He didn't like the tone of your emails." It was the only explanation that made sense.

After that, my advisor suggested I scrap the first thesis entirely, change committees, submit a strong submission from another class, and hope to turn the page. This I did. That thesis, an unrevised paper on medieval illuminated manuscripts and exegetical theology, sailed through with flying colors. It's useful to observe to whom (the desire for) vengeance is permitted. One of the few times it's been mine, this same graduate thesis was published with no substantive editorial changes in a prestigious peer-reviewed journal the next year. (For reasons known only to her, one of the members of the department, a White woman junior faculty member, strongly discouraged me from submitting the piece to the journal that accepted it. But that gratuitous unkindness, as we like to say, is beyond the scope of this essay.)

I spent the remaining four years trying, with great difficulty, to avoid the great man, who refused to countenance me, unless, as when we found ourselves in line for coffee at the Free Speech Café, it was truly impossible not to look me in the eye. In retrospect, I can only believe that these circumstances and their handling were fueled by a potent admixture of personal animosity (it certainly seemed to exceed indifference) toward me and intersectional bigotry at the institutional level.

Anyone's success in academia comes down to connections and luck. Not only is it not a meritocracy, but the anointing of the chosen is too often subjective, arbitrary, implicitly and explicitly biased, and from what I've seen, deeply political. It's only upon revising the manuscript you're reading now during some of the most rabid attacks on justice and equity and truth and mercy and civil rights this country has ever seen that I allow myself to acknowledge that I would never be sitting in the sun in Santa Fe doing what I'm doing today if someone else's exalted advisor had had his say. I was *this* close to not having a chance to get hired by three respected liberal arts colleges to do what I love and what I am called to do. To follow and excel in the vocation that is me at my best. There may be an explanation other than my identity or their prejudice for my near miss in California. But it wasn't the quality of my scholarship.

Since entering the academy twenty-five years ago, I have resigned myself to becoming less liked by the majority of my colleagues with each passing year. I used to be respectful. But even back then, I didn't try to please all the people all the time, although that is the unspoken requirement of women and women of color in these places. What galls me still is that the relatively conservative art history I produced in my early years was praised and supported most by those who had never met or seen me — via "blind review." When my readers and teachers learned who I was, things had a way of changing.

---

There was to be no Mulatta dissertation. But of equal importance to me as a grad student and as a human being, there was a Mulatta seminar paper. A seminar paper in which my authorial consciousness as a queer Black woman first pierced the soil's rocky surface, even if it had gone to seed by the next term. That paper, written in 2006, was entitled “Look, a Negress!”

I had meant to do something on Adorno. Or maybe Kafka, both of whom we read. But once the old White men in my department failed my thesis, those other old White men felt newly alien and dangerous to approach, even if only through their writing. But we’d also read Frantz Fanon for that seminar, far less common then than it is to read him now.

First published in French in 1952, *Black Skin, White Masks* is the best-known work by Fanon, a Martinican-born psychiatrist, member of the Algerian Revolutionary Front, and foundational transdisciplinary postcolonial theorist. After what happened with my committee, I suddenly felt a connection to the famous chapter in the book where Fanon performs the experience of being un/seen and dis/regarded by White people only to find that he is an “object in the midst of other objects.” “Look, a Negro!” exclaims a little White girl once, then twice, when she encounters an unassuming Fanon on a train. But her seemingly benign reaction, which first amuses Fanon, is soon transformed into something more malicious and violent. “Mama, see the Negro! I’m frightened!” she cries, forcing Fanon to consider what his appearance, his very existence, represents to the White colonizing gaze. “I was responsible at the same time for my body, for my race, for my ancestors,” he writes. Doctor or not, educated or not, kind, generous, altruistic, or not, he becomes swiftly and inalterably conscious of being at once invisible, “epidermally” savage, and threatening, regardless – or because – of the perfection of his diction and the refinement of his mien.

> When my restless hands caress those white breasts, they grasp white civilization and dignity and make them mine.
>
> — FRANTZ FANON, *Black Skin, White Masks*

All these years later I vividly remember the excitement of reading Fanon with Judith Butler and Shannon Jackson in an ahead-of-its-time course on performance taught out of the Rhetoric Department at UC Berkeley. We had to audition to get in.

Once we did, sitting around a table each week with Butler filled me with a kind of intellectual giddiness I can only equate to . . . well, better not to say. But I lived for those mornings. And I certainly dressed for them. Butler's swoopy hair was completely enthralling. They were soft-spoken and monotone, thoughtful and about as reactive as a Buddhist monk. When they considered a response or a comment, you could smell the wood burning, as my mother would say.

People tried to make Butler laugh, to flirt with them, to wow them with their preparedness and undoubtedly rehearsed off-the-cuff literary analysis. At most, Butler would half smile. Or maybe slowly nod. Catching them after class was like trying to hold a moonbeam in your hand. Butler's office had no number and was not listed on any college web page. (While I was there, it happened to be hidden among the balconied art history offices in a building half a block from their home department.) This I learned when I was granted a single, terrifying audience that temporarily levitated me above the existential mire in which I found myself. Shannon Jackson, not a lot older than me, was especially kind at that very public moment of academic failure.

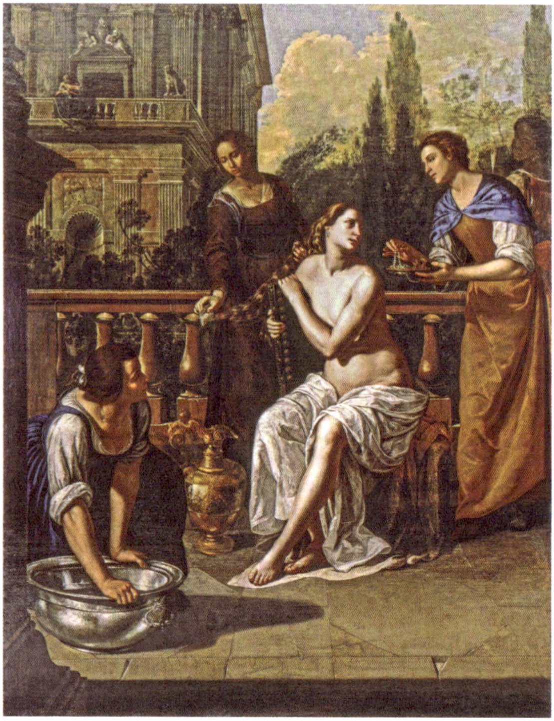

Artemisia Gentileschi, *Bathsheba,* ca. 1636–37

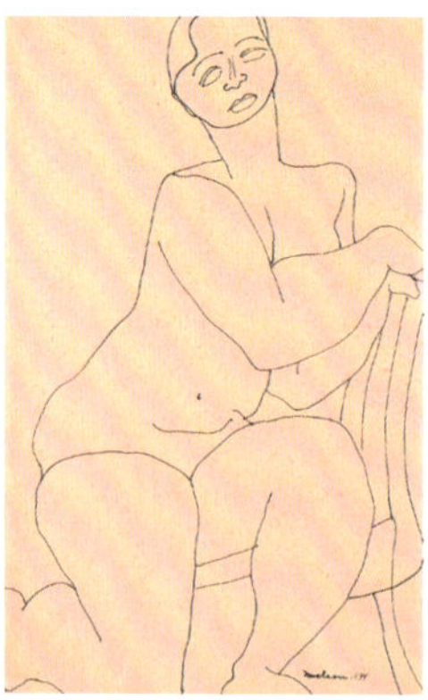

Louise Nevelson, *Seated Nude,* 1934

But Bush was still president. And I am a lesbian. And Judy, as they were known by their familiars, was my god. They had been spotted lifting weights at the local Y. They favored T-shirts and their biceps were as legendary as *Gender Trouble.* After my department failed my thesis, my intellectual production had come as close to shutting down as it had when my grandmother died during my last term at seminary. I was unmoored and hopeless, but I couldn't not write a paper for Judith Butler.

One thing about Fanon — Black for him means Black man. He may analyze the neuroses of the Negress and the Woman of Color through the Francophone literature he dissects, but the plight of the colonized Black man is his true concern. With Butler in mind, my heavy-handed essayistic performance transformed "Look, a Negro!" into "Look, a Negress!" as I read a lesser-known work by the Baroque painter Artemisia Gentileschi through a Fanonian magnifying glass.

Likely painted around 1636, *Bathsheba at Her Bath,* like so many voyeuristic scenes of women and water, is at once a visual meditation on and a reenactment of the power of the gaze to possess the female body, for which the image-as-object becomes a substitute. In the story from the second book of Samuel on which the pictorial narrative is based, King David spies the beautiful Bathsheba from afar. He is moved to "seduce" the married woman and later, once her soldier husband is dispensed with, to become the father of their son. Gentileschi, a painter as focused on the female sex as Fanon was on the male, takes the opportunity to represent an enigmatic play of scopic exchanges between different types of women. What initially attracted me to the scene, naturally, was the prominent and central presence, rarely mentioned in art histories of the painting, of a brown-skinned woman among the White ones.

Returning to the canvas these years later, I remain taken—perhaps moved is more accurate—by the scene's erotic charge, what reads to me as the artist's knowing suggestion of transgressive desires performed across race and within gender. Thus, the White woman seen at Bathsheba's left, classical in profile and fashionably attired in silks of gold and blue, offers her mistress costly jewels appropriately echoed by her own fanciness. This maid's solicitous gesture leads the eye to Bathsheba, whose lunar effulgence—pale, naked arm and shapely leg—continue the line of a pleasing diagonal that concludes on the ground. Gentileschi has constructed a chain of feminine being. What begins clothed in refinement becomes nakedly sexualized, and finally, mannishly crude—devolving to a butch baseness suggested by the burnished Caravaggesque forearms of the presumably lower-born servant, who crouches, unladylike, over a cistern on the floor.

These are the bodies that have mattered to art historians, though not in the impertinent way I've queered them. If the shadowy brown-skinned woman is mentioned at all, an iconographic, meaning-making, purpose for her race has not been explored. Yet she is clearly, if unoriginally, employed by the artist as a darker foil for both the glowing white statuesque body of Bathsheba, who turns away from her—and also for the decorative, jewelry-bearing maid. The angle of the brown woman's head aligns her with the lowlier, water-bearing servant, whose gaze redirects ours to the immaculate seminude. It is the job of the darker woman—let's call her the Mulatta—to bolster her mistress's beauty by attending to her gleaming long hair. Look closely and you will see that she is in the process of passing a large comb through Bathsheba's unruly auburn locks. My absolute favorite detail here is the brown maid's tight grip near this White lady's delicate roots. While ostensibly this is to avoid a painful pull from a tangle, I find something delightfully menacing in her fisting grasp, to which Bathsheba's hold on the chairback seems to respond. (Does Louise Nevelson impose Gentileschi's torqued "white" im/modesty onto the seated Black woman in her drawing made three centuries later? Have I?) The artist's unusually intimate hairstyling bit is an interesting compositional move in that, of all the servants, only the woman of color makes physical contact with the eroticized White purity on display.

Which brings us back to Rubens, as so much in painting does. Isn't Gentileschi's central female dyad a subtle improvisation on Rubens's *Venus with a Black Woman and Cupid Holding a Mirror,* ca. 1614–15? Caravaggio was not the only artist with whom Artemisia placed herself in competitive artistic dialogue. A well-traveled painter in high demand, she shared patrons and admirers, such as Britain's King Charles I, with the cosmopolitan Rubens. It seems to me entirely possible that Gentileschi's *Bathsheba* thus takes up a Rubensian conceit where the beholder's access to White female beauty is vicariously engendered through the intimacy, if not the touch, of a Black woman. When Manet performs his version of feminized chiaroscuro in 1863, the first year Juneteenth was celebrated in Texas, Black Laure with her wrapped bouquet has replaced the White servant and her string of pearls. (A more recent reinversion of these roles – and a reminder of how unthinkingly race and color are conflated with servitude – appears to occur in a 2014 "reenactment" of Gentileschi's *Bathsheba* by "teen interns" then working at the Columbus Museum, where the painting is housed. If clothing and props are any indication, the website photograph shows a Black young woman cast *not* as the "Mulatta," but as the maid on the ground, the lowest of the servants, silver bowl in hand. The bedazzled blond intern and a presumed staff member play the roles of Bathsheba and her blue-and-yellow-clad attendant, respectively.)

Indeed, Gentileschi, like Rubens, provides a Baroque model for Manet's famous play of contrasts. But only if we see what is right there on the canvas. Namely, the fifth, perpetually ignored, figure in Gentileschi's composition. Rebound. Allow the gaze to follow the diagonal back up from the reflective surface of the maid's silver vessel to its logical conclusion at top right and your eye will land on a less easily discernable though tastefully dressed Black woman presumably outside the barrier. See how Gentileschi has craftily inserted an architectural obstruction that appears to separate, or should I say, segregate, this other Black woman from the central performance of upholding White female purity – in which "even" the Mulatta plays a necessary role. With its full-bellied balusters, Gentileschi's stone parapet is also a color line. Eclipsed and side-lined, the darkest-skinned woman is twice marginalized. Poised perhaps to escape this tired scenario – her back to Bathsheba as well as the beholder – the other Black woman looks over her shoulder and directly at us (the only figure to do so!), clocking it all with a knowing glance.

It took me until my mid-thirties to seek out Mulatta role models. In the beginning, I thought I could align myself, using a food metaphor if I felt like it, with any café-au-lait woman of African ancestry. I've since realized that while many people seem to think all "light-skinned" Black women can be called Mulattas, history and culture haven't viewed it that way.

Race is a construct. But as I'm always the first to contend, the experience or phenomenology of racialization and prejudice are very, very real. Race is not solely about appearances – think how often people are said not/to "sound" or "talk" Black. But perception of racial "difference," that is, any divergence from stereotypically White "European" looks or ways of knowing or eating or dressing or joking or dancing or loving or running or making, is often what has sounded the alarm when they not-so-innocently ask: "What are you?"

Light-skinned women from Black families – that is, women with two Black-identified parents – are not viewed and characterized the same way in the historical, political, and literary record as women with one Black and one White parent. And inside the latter racial rubric, Mulattas are viewed differently depending on the sex of our Black parent. Within a supremacist American racial imaginary, Mulattas with White fathers evoke and invoke the legacy of slavery, wherein it was common practice for White slave owners and overseers to rape the enslaved women who were considered their concubines or possessions – at times with economic increase as the goal. Within this same American racial imaginary, Mulattas with Black fathers and White mothers summon up White supremacist notions of Black men as hypersexual savages out to taint the purity of the White race by violating the "White men's" women. In America, a Mulatta's Black father might also be tacitly presumed foreign, a cultured (colonized) man from elsewhere who is therefore (more) acceptable to the White grandparents: he is African, Caribbean, British – from outside the US, he is Black but not African American.

Given these categorizations, the pool of possible passable Black, Mulatta role models, women who look somewhat like me and *are* like me grows smaller. I cannot, for example, claim Jeanne Duval, the "biracial" mistress of Baudelaire painted in

1862 by Manet; she is disqualified by her White father and heterosexuality. Edmonia Lewis, the nineteenth-century lady-loving American sculptor, was the proud daughter of a Black father and an Indigenous Ojibwe mother, so no to her as well. Complexion-wise, there's gorgeous Fredi Washington (whose sister Isabel, as noted, married Adam Clayton Powell Jr.). Having two (light-skinned) Black parents, however, Washington was not technically typecast for the Mulatta role in the 1936 version of *Imitation of Life.* No White parentage for Fredi, so no role model for me. Billie Holiday? At least she was bisexual. The singer's Black-Irish-American mother is said to have passed for White, though Holiday herself was not so passable. Lena Horne: both parents Black of/with White ancestry, so nope. Josephine Baker's mother and father were Black and Indigenous and Black and Spanish, respectively. I do love the fact that, while living in Europe in the twenties, Baker had a notoriously modernist zebra-striped house designed (but never built) for her by the famous Viennese architect Adolph Loos.

And then there's Bette Porter. Bette, the connoisseurial, suit-wearing, power femme/lesbian domme. Bette the art history major at Yale. Bette the dean of the made-up Los Angeles art school. Bette the gallerist. Bette the cheater. Bette the hot-tempered high-yellow nonsense to Kit's in-recovery real, real. Bette the racial flip-flopper where her revolving female partners are concerned. (For the record, I'm team Plumber.) The degree to which I wish not to write about Bette's impact on me as a thirty-something lesbian with near-identical parentage is surely Freudian. I don't want to talk about her because, though I'd never risk it with a Saab, on paper we're practically the same person. Practically. If only for her "coloring," Jennifer Beals, like Vanessa Williams, was a secret, I might even say unconscious, role model for the younger me. *Flashdance* came out while I was a freshman in high school. *The L Word* ended the year I turned forty.

Jennifer Beals, who is straight and an ally, seems like a perfectly nice woman – I'm simply no longer settling for imaginary people as exemplars these days. I hope it's enough to remind y'all that beautiful, slenderly buff, perpetually miffed, aesthetics-before-ethics, Stendhal-syndromed, womanizing mannequin of a hot mess Bette does not exist – though, notably, her moral ambivalence, vanity, snobbishness, and questionable decision-making track well with her fictive (tragic) Mulatta predecessors. I'm grateful to creator Ilene Chaiken – as well as writers Rose Troche and Guinevere Turner of *Go Fish* fame – for putting BIPOC lesbians on the lily-White, cis-het radar of 2000s mainstream media, which too often still evades the impact of intersectionality (and size and class and ability) on living queerly. In this country's art world and academy, however, you'd *better* look – and dress – like Bette if you want to get ahead. Icky and reductive memes comparing Bette (not Beals) to Kamala were hot off the sapphic internet as soon as the VP announced. Suits may perform power, but they don't win elections if you're as unreadable as Porter and Harris.

Were I not a queer Black Episcopalian, I might never have learned about the Rev. Dr. Pauli Murray. Happily, in recent years Murray has become a queer and trans icon, whose pronouns remain controversial among scholars and devotees (here I defer to the Pauli Murray Center, which suggests he/him/they/them for Murray's early life and she/hers for the Rev. Dr. Murray's later years, per Murray's own identification/s). For a lifetime of freedom fighting, Murray was designated a saint by the Episcopal Church in 2012. Murray's ancestry was both Black and White on both sides, in part the result, in earlier generations, of rape by a White slaveholding great-grandfather of an enslaved woman who would become Murray's great-grandmother.

The Reverend Dr. Murray's achievements are too numerous to list in full. They coined the term "Jane Crow." They fought ceaselessly for desegregation as an attorney, author, teacher, and mentor. They received an LLM from UC Berkeley Law School (formerly Boalt School of Law) and a JSD from Yale School of Law. In 1951, they published the book *States' Laws on Race and Color,* described by Supreme Court Justice Thurgood Marshall, according to the Pauli Murray Center, as the civil rights "Bible" for litigators. In 1977, when I was eight years old, she became the first African American person perceived as a woman to be ordained by the Episcopal Church. In 1956, they published *Proud Shoes: The Story of an American Family*. Murray wrote most if not all of this genealogical history of her family's race in the fifties during their tenure in a one-room shingled cabin at MacDowell.

Though Murray's heritage and (trans)gender expression do not align in some respects with my own, their queerness, attraction to women, and liberational Episcopalianism certainly do. When I found myself writing and living in a studio called Schelling as a MacDowell Fellow nearly seventy-five years after Murray had, I chose to accept as a sign what some people might have brushed off as coincidence. That I landed where Pauli Murray had already been was the best possible indication, or so I continue to hope, that I was writing what I was meant to write when and where I was meant to write it. I believe those who paved the way embolden us across time in the only ways they can, through signs translated into a language we understand. Call it a spiritual semiotics. By means of the uncanny, the familiar, and the serendipitous, there's a hopeful futurity in the queer past. What, after all, are the chances that two middle-aged, passably Black Episcopalians like us would sit in front of the same New Hampshire window to write queer life stories with miscegenation at their core?

---

FURTHER READING

Murray, Pauli. *Proud Shoes.* 1956. Reprint, Beacon Press, 1999.

Pabst, Naomi. "Blackness/Mixedness: Contestations over Crossing Signs." *Cultural Critique,* no. 54 (Spring 2003): 178–212.

13

# READ SOMETIME WHEN U FEEL LIKE IT

HAPPY 21ST BIRTHDAY, BEAN!" reads the first line of my mother's almost-calligraphic handwriting. It's in fine black ink as ever, this time on a lined sheet of businesslike paper with a blank gutter along one margin for "Action Items." We've both always liked loose-leaf notebooks. I turned twenty-one in 1990 and would have been in college at the time.

Recently, I found this roughly thirty-year-old birthday letter while rooting around in some boxes in the basement of my Vermont house. I'd been looking for a drawing my mother made of me when I was little. I could see it in my mind's eye. When I'd finally unearthed the '70s plastic box frame, tucked away carefully, I instantly remembered how annoyed I had been that she wanted to draw me doing something as boring as watching reruns on TV, a partial explanation for my sullen, but also somewhat forlorn, expression. I'd always admired this two-color pencil drawing from a technical standpoint – the foreshortened arm beneath my favorite ribbon-trimmed "peasant dress," the softness of my features. It's virtuosic for an artist of any age, but when I calculate that my mother wasn't yet twenty-five when she made it, I'm

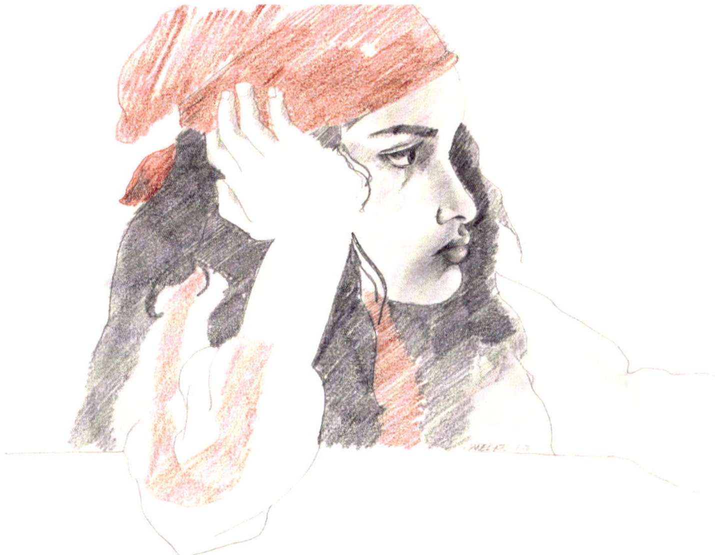

Jane Lyon Asper, *Vanessa*, 1976

astounded by the sureness of hand, the confidence. I wonder if I've ever been more known by her than in this drawing.

In a classroom lecture I might point out the iconography of my red bandanna. Regardless of the artist's intention, my head covering could be interpreted as a soft-peaked Phrygian cap (see Delacroix). As such, it evokes the classical emblem of the freed slave, which helps us recognize me as a woman of color. (I reveled in sculptor Martin Puryear's variations on the cap's floppy shape as a symbolic form of Black liberation at his astounding and political American pavilion for the Venice Biennale in 2019.) Only now do I realize, or let myself acknowledge, that I'd never had my mother's drawing professionally framed or hung on a wall in my first apartment or anywhere else because I was embarrassed that

I looked (so) Black in it. It's difficult to admit I ever felt that way. I was vain in that how I was seen by others meant everything to me. And I was fearful and cowardly and ignorant too. Full of a despicable kind of self-hatred, living in a state of determined evasiveness. Perpetually worried something I said or did would reveal who I truly was. I'm ashamed to have lived that way for so long. But I also remember how things were and what it might have been like for me to claim an identity as a Black woman with absolutely no sense of what that meant. With no role models but the ones to whom I feared being compared.

As I was grabbing another box in the basement, a thick paper rectangle had slipped out of a flaking album of black-and-white photographs of my grandparents' wedding in the forties. When I went to unfold this discovery, I saw the words "READ SOMETIME WHEN U FEEL LIKE IT" written between the blue, ledger-like lines. I don't remember anything about this letter, which was obviously from my mother. But I can imagine myself stashing it with something I knew I'd never throw away so as not to lose it.

My college days were self-involved and dissolute in the extreme. Chances are, I tossed this folded sheet aside to look for the accompanying birthday check I'd been counting on to keep me in gin and cardigans. Neither do I remember the "Bean" nickname, which would be uncommon in my family, though I've since often bestowed such endearments on girlfriends and others I'm attached to.

I haven't received many letters from my mother, which is a little odd in that we are a family of readers and writers and valuers of language and words. My stepdad wrote dark and beautiful poetry as a grad student, and may still do so. My mother, though an artist all her life, also studied English lit in grad school, where she met my dad. Her love of Virginia Woolf and my grandmother's love of Jane Austen and my dad's love of Wallace Stevens all figure in my formation. Every apartment and house I grew up in featured homemade or built-in bookshelves loaded with Norton anthologies and Shakespeare and Matthew Arnold and Melville and Metaphysical poetry and Anaïs Nin and Hemingway and the Eliots – on and on. The books and their obvious dominion over my parents' workaday and intellectual lives felt special and significant. When my grandmother came over and we sat on the front porch drinking Sunday margaritas, ours were so unlike the kinds of conversations I overheard in the houses of my rich White friends, who didn't even watch *Brideshead Revisited,* unanimously our favorite show. Whereas for me, the Western canon of art and literature was an entrancing material presence; the fabric, and fabrication, of my youth. I considered that those mysterious titles at the top of the stairs might be an inheritance of antique weapons that I, too, would be permitted to take down and brandish when I was ready.

Ready or not, when the time came, English lit was barely on my undergrad radar. Art history, the preferred subject of hot straight girls, ultimately made the most sense to me. And just as my mother the artist went inexplicably out of her way not to professionally practice what I have always thought was her true calling, I, too, once I graduated from college, ran as far and as fast as I could from an academic life.

"In years to come your memories of this day and mine will be completely different," the letter from my mother begins. She continues with cheerful birthday greetings and a spate of adoring adjectives describing the daughter I have become – too embarrassing to reproduce here.

And then: ". . . you and I had a lot of years together before [my stepdad] and despite the fact that I wouldn't have picked the order of these events or lots of things about the first ten years of your life, those years were very happy for me. I would have chosen those years to be different for your sake more than mine, because I know they were hard ones for you in many ways. Part of the reason I'm so proud of you is because I think I understand some of the difficulties you faced more than you think I do. Keep honest with yourself and the rest is easy."

Outside the Huntington Library, on either side of the wide, dusty path leading to the gardens, there are two rows of anterooms. They aren't actually rooms in the interior sense. But each dirt-floored square, walled off by tall hedges and set widely apart, feels private and chamberlike. The spaces are differently furnished. Some have an enormous umbrella, some a couple of hefty bleached teak benches. Some a circle of chairs facing small trees.

Both times I was in residence at the Huntington, I began every day in one of these pleasant green rooms. Starting al fresco with coffee and biscotti and maybe a draft printout in hand, I prepared to enter a silent but sometimes enervating atmosphere that will be familiar to any funded researcher who has feared for what she might not dig up before the sand, and the dollars, run out.

I've been fortunate at the Huntington, however. In addition to getting to spend contemplative mornings outside the reading room, I eventually published what I found, and took pleasure in the paintings, roses, myriad camellias, and the discounted Caesar salads and prosecco that should be the rewards of all good scholarship.

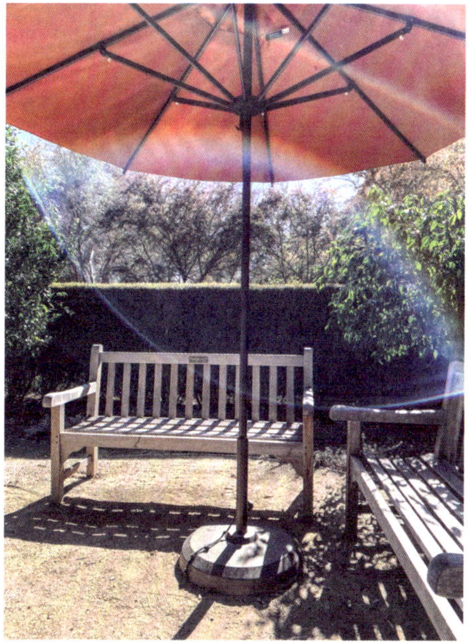

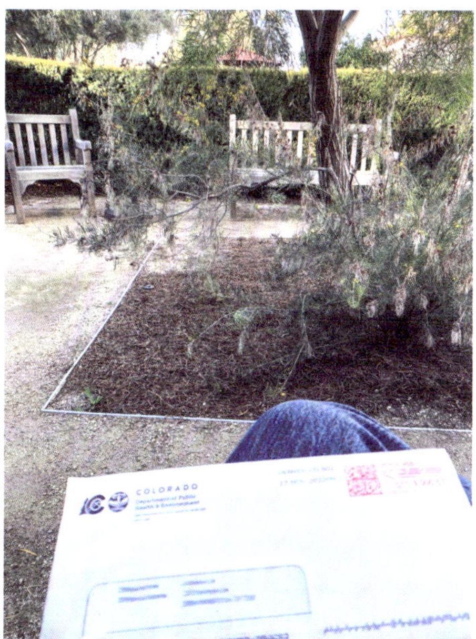
COLORADO
Department of Public
Health & Environment

But for today's brief return as a non-Fellow, the pressure is off. That is to say, it's entirely self-inflicted. I am already in possession of the archival document I need. All that remains is to give it its due.

I can't say I've waited for this moment all my life because that's simply not true. I haven't wanted to know the name or the identity of this always absent man who was my Black father. And I don't want to know it now. But I've become a diligent historian in the course of the last two decades. I know very well that new evidence is bound to change the way you're spinning the story — since spinning stories is what historians do.

I take a deep breath, say a short prayer, and slide my thumb under the envelope's flap. The watermarked paper is as stiff as a new dollar bill. It even smells minted. I quasi-eagerly scan the page. My eyes flit past my mother's name, and age, and the time I was born (which is indeed within the cocktail hour, as my grandmother contended). But there, to the right, where I can only imagine a father's name should appear, the space is completely blank.

The fabulously talented Eartha Kitt was born destitute in North Carolina to a Black teenage mother from whom she was separated at the age of four. As her daughter recounts it, Kitt spent most of her adult life attempting to obtain her birth certificate, only learning, at the age of seventy-one, the date she was born. According to a 2013 story in *The Guardian,* Eartha Kitt finally received her official birth certificate in 1998, "only to find her father's name had been blacked out," presumably to save face with his White Southern family.

---

I came across another letter from my mother while I was digging around in those dusty basement boxes. This one is dated 2000, a little over ten years after my twenty-first birthday. It's postmarked Denver with a heart stamp and addressed to the little bungalow across town in Cherry Creek where I lived at the time with Rachel, my emotionally inaccessible, morally compassed older girlfriend.

While I don't remember the contents of this rediscovered letter, I remember the occasion. It arrived in my mailbox nearly a year after that fateful summer barbecue with the nosy French lesbian. After the summer night when, as I have come to think of it, my mother spoke me into Blackness. Although she could see how upset I was, we certainly hadn't talked about it at the time. We're not the kind of people to disrupt a social gathering with what is now called drama, or even a momentary retreat to the kitchen to put a pin in it. I'd arrived at the barbecue as a woman of color – a thirty-one-year-old who evidently resembled the French Algerians our friend had known – and I'd left the party as Black.

I brought the second letter upstairs with me and let it sit. I

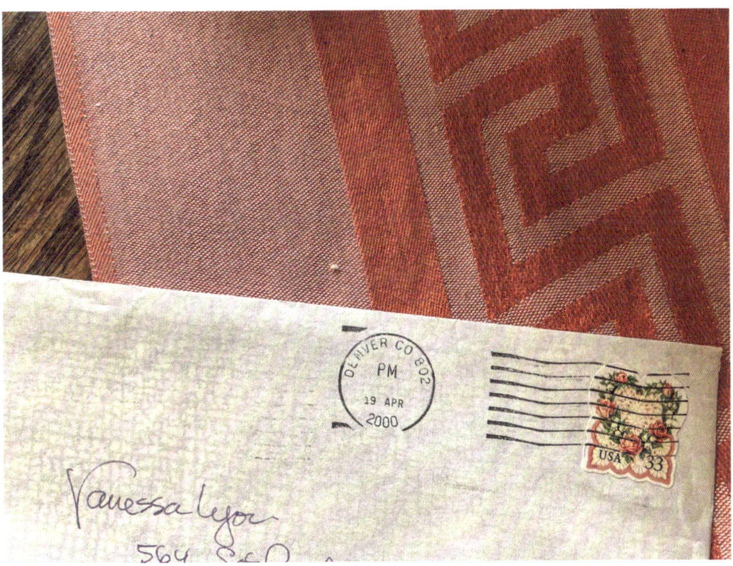

knew I wouldn't be back at the Huntington, or at a residency, anytime soon. And yet I also knew I'd need to read what was inside that envelope to bring my story to a close.

Tomorrow will be the day, I kept telling myself.

I admire my funny, endlessly creative mother, and I love her beyond words. But for years now, I've also been angry about the way I was brought into the world. Not because of my Blackness but because of the estrangement from my Blackness, which I feel was enabled or encouraged. At the very least allowed. While I was still very young, scared, ashamed, and obstinate, as I know myself to have been, my family alone might have gotten me to think differently. I knew I was loved. But identity politics—theories and accounts of how the lived experience of marginalized and (multiply) oppressed people shapes and is shaped by dominant societies—was growing up alongside me (e.g., where Black/queer/feminism is concerned, the Combahee River Collective's foundational statement dates from 1977). I had little in the way of guidance on how to become my true lesbian-of-color self. Few "tools," as people like to say. More importantly, the last time my mother bestowed optimistic advice about how to live, I had stubbornly failed to heed it.

I was not honest with myself. And the rest has certainly not been easy.

---

"I read your letter the night you gave it to me and I haven't re-read it since. I will, but it was very hard for me to read and I'm not ready to read it again."

So her second letter to me begins. I sit down, shocked. Some twenty years later, I have no recollection of writing whatever my mother was not ready to read again. I have no doubt it was the first time I had given the uncensored version of what it was like growing up passably Black in our house and at my school and in our city, my college, etc. She repeats that it was very hard for her to think how much pain I felt and, as she puts it, still feel.

This one is more defensive than the birthday letter, and that makes sense, given that it is a response to what was likely an attack on my younger years by her then unempathetic, newly adult only child. Knowing my mother as I do, I see that her tone on the page is restrained.

I am struck by two passages in particular. In the first she asserts what I've long realized for myself: As a child, I was not open to talking about being Black or "bi-racial." And even less so as a young adult. As my mother puts it: "you were extremely unresponsive to the topic." A few paragraphs later she expresses how sorry she is about the shame and sadness I have felt over the years. "I am very glad you are trying to let it go," she writes. "It may be easier than you think."

Nor can I believe I actually claimed, or thought, I was attempting to "let it go" back then. I was very active in my Episcopal church in those years and had recently enrolled in a school of theology to undertake religious studies, so I must have been making an attempt at forgiveness, not only of myself. But all these years later, I'm still T-boned by a then hopeful notion that my coming to terms with White supremacy and Black suspicion in the times and places I've lived could be in any way easy. Or that once squarely faced, the dis-ease and self-loathing of living with myself, absent a secure racial identity, might just lift away.

I think about the technically complicated and much-loved socks my mother knits me. And the fearlessly colorful, intelligent paintings she paints. How when I was maybe eight or nine she taught me to separate eggs using their broken shells, and how to make choux paste. When she showed me how to sew a backstitch or spiral a needle with a French knot. I see her full-throttle encouragement and belief in me at so many crucial stages of my progress into personhood and professional life. The cheering me on that continues to this day, when I am well into middle age. I imagine her reading these words and feeling angry or hurt, which is the last thing I want. This is about me not you, I have said preemptively. Knowing it is about both of us. But also knowing it is quite a bit about a confused and self-hating former self that I no longer am, in very large part because she has taken such good care of me all these years.

In another passage of her letter to a thirtysomething daughter, my mother writes of love. Her belief, shared by her new baby's grandparents, was that love was the answer. It was the late '60s. Communes were a thing. In the golden age of *Free to Be . . . You and Me,* there was, she explains, a feeling that if a kid was surrounded by care and support and deeply felt and expressed affection, nothing else mattered. With their concerted adoration of the Mulatta who was my mother's fatherless daughter, race, my White family thought, wouldn't need to be an issue.

*Was* love enough?

This much I know: Love was enough to convince me that I could do anything. Regardless of—though not because of—what I looked like and came from. Regardless of how my friends' parents treated me. "Keep shooting out the arrows!" (As I now find myself advising my students.) My mother's love, the love of my grandparents, and, once he entered my life, the love of my dad has steeled me and launched me and carried me through.

Love was surely enough within our tiny familial bubble of *New Yorker* articles and Swiss fondue and *The Nutcracker* and

Head Start centers (where the teachers spoke to me in Spanish) and ski lessons and swing dancing and Botanic Gardens concerts and Annie Dillardiana and PBS. But it was not enough to stop a budding Black lesbian from being prematurely yanked up by the roots. It was not enough for her to flourish the way she might have had she been made aware early on of the worlds and the wonders and the sustenance that exist outside of Whiteness.

Concerning the end that is our earthly end, I do believe love is everything. It wasn't always easy, and today I would not contain the parts of me without it. But neither love nor my Whiteness were enough to help me secure a true sense of self when I needed it most. That would have required the presence in my life of kindly disposed women and girls whose looks and experience were at least somewhat recognizably like mine. And not only Black women, but Mulattas. It would have required some hard conversations. And much more music and art and many more books and movies by and about people who are not White. And Black lesbian feminisms. And queer Black priests. And charitable, open-minded Black and brown colleagues. And peers. And beloveds. And friends.

# AFTERWORD

I AM STILL SINGLE. Other than that, lots has changed. At the microcosmic level, it feels important to end this part of the story with the news of my legal adoption. Shortly after our kitchen island revelation about his first attempt to officially make me his daughter, my sweet Poppo put the bureaucratic wheels in motion with my blessing. A few weeks later, I stood in my own Vermont kitchen with another envelope from the secretary of state – this time with the blanks filled in. It all happened long after this memoir was sold and – for me psychologically and emotionally – put to bed. There is, however, no doubt in my mind that the hard conversation that started us back down the path to legal recognition of my stepfather's support over the course of some forty-five years would never have occurred if I hadn't first written this book. If we hadn't returned as a family to my wish, really my need, to be seen in the eyes of the law as the daughter of the mother *and father* who raised me. If there is more to learn about the man who played no role in my care and development but who is inescapably part of who I am, so be it. That door is finally open.

At the macrocosmic, or at least the political, level, this memoir is a product of the early post-COVID years, when many people believed the next US president would surely be Kamala Harris. Although I am a gambler, I was never one of those believers, as those in my classes at the time will tell you. Like many Black and brown women who have lived our lives in this country, I knew someone like Kamala would not be running the United States anytime soon.

And unlike my White women friends and colleagues and family, some of whom seemed to feel we were all in the same bullet-riddled boat post-election – I was not "shocked" that a nation built on and by transatlantic slavery chose a White supremacist dictator over a Black woman who was California's former attorney general (albeit a fairly ruthless top cop) before becoming our vice president. For the whole of the election season, I watched with interest as commentators and cultural critics struggled to figure out how to talk about Kamala's race. With the usual irritation, I listened to Black pundits, mostly women and mostly cis het (as far as I am aware) – many of whom I usually respect – effuse over the prospect of our first "Black woman" president. But weren't these the same rhetoricians to virtually ignore the existence of the White anthropologist mother who raised President Obama – to ding him in editorials and book chapters for his White parentage, or worse, for his implicitly compromising and cowardly "White" qualities? Weren't these the same talking heads to come at women like us for not being Black enough?

In fact, as we all know, Kamala Harris is the daughter of a Black Jamaican father and a South Asian mother – she has family in the southern Indian state of Chennai. Harris's parents met at UC Berkeley, and she was born in 1964, a few years after President Obama and ahead of me. Smack dab in the outcome of the era of American civil rights. What continues to irk me most about discussions or avoidance of the cultural constructedness of Harris's race was largely the same issue during the Obama years. Many Black people are eager to criticize other Black people in "interracial" relationships with White partners. They are also fine dismissing and demeaning Black people with a non-Black parent – especially a White one – if they decide we are intentionally trading on our racially "ambiguous" appearance and (indisputable) social capital and privilege. But as soon as the eyes of the world are watching, we half-breeds and posers are admitted to the club. Adding a Black *anything* to the historical record is important. Especially now. If nothing else, our kind are good for the numbers.

Cynical, strategic, or both, there's nothing novel about playing the race card. Inconvenient though it may be, however, some of the most written-about and respected Black Americans and Black intellectuals had a White parent. It has not been my intention to give anything like a comprehensive analysis of that complicated truth in this memoir, but it's worth noting that Sally Hemings, Frederick Douglass, and Nella Larsen are on that list. If you go back in their families a generation or so, W. E. B. Du Bois, Jean Toomer, Paul Robeson, Carol Channing, and opera diva Maria Ewing are among many who have been perceived as White when also Black or the other way around. bell hooks had Indigenous ancestors. Hazel Carby's mother was a White Welshwoman. Appearance outfoxes genealogy. Black families don't always get consistently "Whiter" over time after "White blood" is introduced; within a single generation, skin color and physiognomy can vary tremendously. You can't "tell" how much miscegenation has occurred in a family – or an individual – by sight. It's ignorant to try. More's the pity to those who hate themselves or others for color of skin or straightness of hair or sharpness of nose – permutations that may have been dictated decades before we were born. Sometimes owing to violent colonizers and/or rape, it's true. But what have such horrendous histories to do with our personal value/s and authenticity or the multifaceted individuals we have become?

And anyway, none of this should be news given the history of the United States. As the Reverend Dr. Pauli Murray writes in the 1978 introduction to *Proud Shoes,* the biography of his family's racial origins first published in 1956: "Over more than two centuries, enough criss-crossing of racial lines and recirculation of genes within designated races has occurred to make the notion of racial purity a highly questionable biological concept for many future Americans. Multi-racial origins of both blacks and whites are realities; they may be ignored but not wholly discounted." Where Kamala Harris is concerned, I am of the opinion that it wasn't her Blackness as such that lost her the voters she needed. Rather, it was her im/passability as a woman of color who identifies and was identified as Black but "could" be mistaken for something "else." In this respect, Harris was confronted with the more nuanced and pernicious second-order Mulatta stereotypes that I've suggested are reserved for Black women who are perceived by Black people and White people in particular as racially unreadable, ergo invalidly Black. Those distrusted owing to their/our inborn deceitfulness and apparently neither/nor nature and loyalties. Women resented for their/our presumptions to agency and autonomy, inclusion and power sometimes on behalf of no racial identity other than ourselves. That said, I freely and hopelessly acknowledge that misogynoir was chiefly to blame for Harris's loss. Compare the minuscule number of Black women presidents in film and television to their Black male counterparts. Or consider the tired, ultimately negative, characterization—and typecasting—of the self-disclosed female "octoroon" character in *Sinners* (2025). Like Peola and Julie before her, unvirginal, go-between "Mary" is not only a "light-skinneded" woman but also the first human in the film who turns on her Black kind. Slender and pretty and pale and passing, she is the hypersexualized and seductively miscegenated feminine gateway to White-supremacist, Klan-embracing, colonizer-adjacent, monstrously vampiric *blood mixing*—long the ultimate sin in America. When the Blackest film around remorselessly relies on stereotypes of Mulatta treachery, I despair. Representation deserves interpretation. Had Stacey Abrams run in 2024, I believe we'd have seen a very different type of race.

But that's just me.

# ACKNOWLEDGMENTS

To Deborah Garrison, my incomparable editor at Pantheon, gratitude beyond words for your grace, generosity, discernment—and empathy—at every stage of this project. Much appreciation to Marisa Nakasone, Zuleima Ugalde, and the whole Pantheon team.

The brilliant Lisa Lucas, thank you for being there for me and for us. To my agent Madison Smartt Bell at Ayesha Pande Literary—everything changed when you believed in me, ever grateful for your sage guidance and astrological forbearance.

The memory part of memoir is all. Recollection by definition. In writing this story of my unreadable self I've *remembered* in the sense of putting pieces back together. The result is true to what I recall of my experiences and deeply researched where art and its histories are concerned. Even so, some of the people who have mattered most to me in life are not in this book. I am continually grateful for my old friends Shannon Good, Laura Brown, Meryl F. Bailey, the Reverend Sally K. Brown, and Susan and

Ira Strauber. More recently, for good conversation and support, Annette Lawrence, Rage Hezekiah, and Anina Major—plus Ben Anastas, Mariam Rahmani, and Sawyer London, who kept writer-me relatively sane in VT. Thank you, Caro Fowler, for your intellect and kinship. Emily Hinojosa, keep doing what you're doing!

In countless ways, this is a MacDowell book, and I am grateful for the transformative experience of writing in an unforgettable community that included Mat Diafos Sweeney, Xavi Marrades, Ruby Hansen Murray, Jessica Gandolf, Marti Epstein, and the bewitching Sydney Acosta, Summer Hart, and Laura Marris. To Jennifer Tseng, infinite love and gratitude. Thanks, too, to my dear talented and encouraging Bread Loaf people: Christina Berke, Sarah Cadorette, Kyanna Sutton, Leah De Forest, Augustine Blaisdell—and Melissa Febos, whose work inspired me to undertake this kind of writing. Lorelei Goulding, what a gift you are.

A portion of Chapter 2 appeared in Book Post as "All the Better to See You With," and I am grateful to editor Ann J. Kjelberg for her enthusiasm for this material in an early form. Often, the only good and sustaining thing about collegiate teaching has been my smart, compassionate students, deeply appreciated daily. Of the many wondrous ones who have changed my art and life, I owe a special debt to the stellar Venice crew of '22, Tinashe, Dorian, Eve, Lily, and Alexa.

Thank you chefs and baristas of Iconik Coffee, Lupe and Lena, for your, sometimes daily, hospitality.

And finally, thank you, Poppo, for talking with the younger me about poems and writing and antique silver and for being my excellent dad.

# ILLUSTRATION CREDITS

22 Rijksmuseum, Amsterdam
29 H. O. Havemeyer Collection, Bequest of Mrs. H. O. Havemeyer, 1929, Metropolitan Museum of Art
33 Private Collection Christie's Images/Bridgeman Images
43 Photo courtesy of the author
50 Manuel de Arellano (attributed to), *Rendering of a Mulatta (Diceño de Mulata),* 1711. Gift of Frederick and Jan Mayer, 2024.425. Photograph courtesy of the Denver Art Museum
65 Paul Marriott/Shutterstock
72 Yale Center for British Art, Paul Mellon Collection
85 British Library, London, UK. From the British Library archive/ Bridgeman Images
94 Gallerie degli Uffizi, Florence, Tuscany, Italy. Luisa Ricciarini/ Bridgeman Images
96 National Gallery of Art, Washington, DC, USA/ Bridgeman Images
98 Sammlungen des Fuersten v. Liechtenstein, Vaduz, Liechtenstein © Erich Lessing/Bridgeman Images
101 487000:1073, The Huntington Library, San Marino, California
107 Musee d'Orsay, Paris, France/Bridgeman Images
108 Gallerie degli Uffizi, Florence, Tuscany, Italy © Raffaello Bencini/ Bridgeman Images
112 Philadelphia Museum of Art, Pennsylvania, PA, USA, Philadel-

phia Museum of Art/John G. Johnson Collection, 1917/Bridgeman Images
124 Photo courtesy of the author
127 Photo courtesy of the author
128 Photo courtesy of the author
129 Photo courtesy of the author
136 Sterling and Francine Clark Art Institute, Williamstown, Massachusetts, SA/Bridgeman Images
138 Illustration from *Brer Fox and Brer Rabbit* by Beatrix Potter. Image reproduced courtesy of Frederick Warne & Co., Ltd.
158 Louise Nevelson, *Seated Nude,* 1934, collection of the author, image courtesy of Swann Auction Galleries
162 Kerry James Marshall, *Heirlooms & Accessories (triptych),* 2002, Ink-jets on paper in wooden artist's frames with rhinestones, Image (Each): 51 × 46 in., Edition of 2, Studio Museum in Harlem, Museum purchase made possible by a gift from an anonymous donor, 2005.7a-c, Photo: John Berens
176 Louise Nevelson, *Self-Portrait,* ca. 1935
229 National Gallery, London, UK/Bridgeman Images
229 Sueddeutsche Zeitung Photo/Alamy
244 Photo courtesy of the author
244 Photo courtesy of the author
251 Adrian Piper, *Self-Portrait as a Nice White Lady,* 1995, Black-and-white autophoto with oil-crayon drawing, 18¼ × 14¼ in. AP/L-75, Studio Museum in Harlem, Museum purchase made possible by a gift from Barbara Karp Shuster, New York, 2004 2.5 Photo: Marc Bernier
266 Columbus Museum of Art, Ohio: Museum Purchase, Schumacher Fund
277 Drawing by Jane Lyon Asper, courtesy of the author
281 Photo courtesy of the author
281 Photo courtesy of the author
283 Photo courtesy of the author

## A NOTE ABOUT THE AUTHOR

J. VANESSA LYON is the author of *Figuring Faith and Female Power in the Art of Rubens* as well as *The Groves,* an Audible Original, and *Lush Lives,* an inaugural title from Roxane Gay Books/Grove Atlantic and an NBC News Best LGBTQ Book of the Year. A James Baldwin Fellow at MacDowell and a Fulbright Scholar, Lyon holds a PhD in the history of art from UC Berkeley. She is the recipient of fellowships from the Yale Center for British Art, the Lewis Walpole Library, and the Huntington Library and Art Museum, among others. Her essays have appeared in or are forthcoming from *Art History, Huntington Library Quarterly, Word & Image, Representations,* and elsewhere. Lyon is professor of art history at Bennington College, where she has directed the Visual Arts Lecture Series since 2017. She and her cat divide their time between southern Vermont and Santa Fe, New Mexico.

## A NOTE ON THE TYPE

This book was set in Agmena, which was designed by Jovica Veljović for Linotype in 2012. Inspired by the forms and proportions of Renaissance fonts, Veljović created Agmena with the intent of making the perfect text face for books. Agmena was awarded a Certificate of Typographic Excellence by the Type Directors Club in 2013.

Typeset by North Market Street Graphics,
Lancaster, Pennsylvania

Designed by Marisa Nakasone